Istanbul

Istanbul

Between the Global and the Local

edited by
Çağlar Keyder

ROWMAN & LITTLEFIELD PUBLISHERS, INC.
Lanham • Boulder • New York • Oxford

ROWMAN & LITTLEFIELD PUBLISHERS, INC.

Published in the United States of America
by Rowman & Littlefield Publishers, Inc.
4720 Boston Way, Lanham, Maryland 20706

12 Hid's Copse Road
Cumnor Hill, Oxford OX2 9JJ, England

British Library Cataloguing in Publication Information Available

Library of Congress Cataloging-in-Publication Data

Keyder, Çağlar.
    Istanbul : between the global and the local / Çağlar Keyder.
       p.   cm.
    Includes bibliographical references (p.   ) and index.
    ISBN 0-8476-9494-1 (cl. : alk. paper). — ISBN 0-8476-9495-X
(pa. : alk. paper)
      1. Istanbul (Turkey)   I. Title.
DR719.K49   1999
949.61'8—dc21   99-20624
                                 CIP

Printed in the United States of America

♾ ™The paper used in this publication meets the minimum requirements of
American National Standard for Information Sciences—Permanence
of Paper for Printed Library Materials, ANSI Z39.48-1984.

Contents

Acknowledgment

I would like to thank Mark Selden for his encouragement and support and the authors of these articles for their patience.

Part I

Introduction

1

The Setting

Çağlar Keyder

HERITAGE

Unlike other global cities, Istanbul has always been a *world* city: an imperial capital for more than fifteen hundred years, its splendors were the stuff of legends, attracting the jealous gaze first of Europe then of the Balkans and the Middle East. Not only its riches but also its sheer size dwarfed every other urban conglomeration in the West until into the modern age (Girouard 1985). At first its size was something of a marvel, reflecting the might of the empire it commanded. Then this scale was seen to be monstrous, defying the economic logic that was fast being normalized in European discourse. Istanbul's riches were regarded as pathology—the result of anachronistic despotism. This despotism, plunder of its own subjects, allowed the survival of an overgrown body supported on weak legs (Valensi 1993). Thus, Istanbul (*the city* to the Greeks, *der Saadet*—the seat of bliss—to the Muslims, *tzarigrad* or the "emperor's city" to the Balkan peoples) was reduced to its consumption dimension, a vampire writ large.

In fact, Istanbul had always been more than the seat of agrarian empires, Byzantine and Ottoman. Of course, it collected taxes and provided the palace and the bureaucrats with splendor; it attracted the artisans, the scholars, and the entertainers; it housed vast populations of soldiers guaranteeing the survival of the empire and armies of bureaucrats administering the land. But it also commanded a unique geographic position. Even before Constantine moved his capital east it was recognized as a crucial location for commercial passage: the Bosphorus held the key to Black Sea trade, the Golden Horn was a splendid natural harbor. Any long-distance travel between the Middle East and Europe, between the Balkans and western Asia, perforce passed through the city. And its urban economy always reflected its privileged location: the axes of the old city were drawn along

3

its docks and warehouses and the gates in the land walls through which overland traders entered and exited (Mantran 1962). It was not only a consumer of imports, it also served as the biggest mart in the region. Merchants and travelers arrived from all over to buy and sell: everything could be found in its markets, brought from China, India, Persia, Caucasus, Russia, Egypt, and Syria, and then from the Balkans, Genoa, and Venice, and points to the west. For most of its imperial history, its location made it the largest permanent market place in the area between India and western Europe.

These two logics, the imperial and the commercial, constantly intertwined, with the first at times stifling the other. Agrarian empires only tolerate and fervently wish to regulate trade; merchants are not easy to control, and their activities lead to economic practice not readily imagined within the confines of imperial logic. Besides, the accumulation of wealth by merchants and bankers may come to rival that of the imperial ruling class. For this reason, unless the empire itself relinquishes its own logic, trade only escapes its shackles when empires weaken—as in the end of the Byzantine (Necipoglu 1995) and Ottoman Empires. This, however, is only an escape; it remains a temporary liberty unless legal and institutional underpinnings follow. Istanbul has been burdened, in all the three states that ruled it, with political designs to control the parameters of mercantile activity. The result has been various forms of informality; a pattern of accumulation that reflects the attempt to avoid or bypass political control.

GLOBALIZATION IN THE NINETEENTH CENTURY

During the second half of the nineteenth century, Istanbul did acquire all the accoutrements of a port city evolving without the support of its imperial polity (Keyder, Ozveren, and Quataert 1993). It became a teeming metropolis of a million inhabitants just before World War I, with 130,000 foreign subjects attracted by economic opportunity (Toprak 1982, 65). The Genoese and the Venetians had been the prominent foreign merchants of the final years of Byzantine rule; at the end of Ottoman rule, Levantines of all origins from around the Mediterranean and western Europe, but also Turkic, Tatar, and other ethnic groups from the Russian empire, crowded the city. They had come primarily because of the unprecedented increase in the volume of trade and foreign investment; but, also, Istanbul was the political, cultural, and educational capital of a multiethnic empire where various Balkan, Arab, Anatolian, and Caucasian groups organized, intrigued, attended schools, and published broadsheets. Even before the new influx of population so overcame the city it was always a collection of religious and linguistic groupings where traditions survived without mixing, and coexistence was mostly cordial. Muslims, Greeks, Jews, and Armenians lived side by side, almost never intermarrying; their religious and cultural lives compartmental-ized into corporate entities in a collusion between the community elites and Ottoman authorities. This is how the eleventh edition of the *Encyclopaedia Britannica* (1910) describes Istanbul's population:

> The inhabitants present a remarkable conglomeration of different races, var-ious nationalities, divers languages, distinctive costumes and conflicting faiths, giving, it is true, a singular interest to what may be termed the human scenery of the city, but rendering impossible any close social cohesion, or the development of a common social life. (van Millingen 1910, 8)

Ottoman administration had generally been successful in devising ways to keep ethnic groups separate, internally hierarchical, and accountable to the palace. This *millet* system worked well within the more static balances of the empire, but in the much more globalized world of the late nineteenth century, with a weakened central authority, Ottomans found it difficult to continue with their high-handed ethnic corporatism. A new understand-ing of citizenship inscribed in legal reforms and framed within state mod-ernization had already disrupted the traditional balances. Another mod-ern ideology, that of nationalism fueled by uneven incorporation of ethnic groups into the European system, led to a new type of urban conflict. In addition, there was intense imperial rivalry played out among the British, French, Russians, and Germans with their various strategies and designs, setting favorite client groups against each other and imposing administra-tive constraints on the Porte. Long-established imperial habits of bureau-crats and intransigence of Great Power competition collaborated to make legal and institutional accommodation of an expanding and market-determined world-economy dynamic difficult. But most important, imperial rivalry could find fertile ground precisely because the population of the city was so divided and unlikely to act together in any semblance of civil soci-ety. Istanbul was, both geographically and demographically, a disunited city. Even if the authorities were willing, it would have been difficult to de-volve power to a sufficient degree in order to establish the matrix of au-tonomously operating markets. Successfully established "civil" organiza-tions such as municipalities, chambers of commerce, commercial exchanges, masonic lodges, and cultural associations could potentially off-set the threat of arbitrary intervention; however, not only were these com-pelled to operate within an uncertain legal and political framework, but they also became identified with the factional interests of particular ethnic or religious groups. Even projects aiming at no more than rudimentary municipal autonomy for the arrondissements of the city floundered in the face of divisions fueled by imperial rivalry and its jealously maintained balances (Rosenthal 1980).

Uncertain foundations and shifting grounds made Istanbul less of a world city than it could have been: it was rich in accommodating multiple cultures, but the economy that supported this apparent exuberance was built on shaky grounds. Compared to Egypt, for example, the level of direct foreign investment or financial incorporation remained puny (Pamuk 1987). The physical infrastructure of trade in the form of port facilities was never brought up to the standards of the day. Railways were late in coming: the Sofia-Vienna line opened in 1888, and it was not until after 1892 that the eastern line reached Ankara, connecting the imperial capital to Anatolia. Despite the undeniable expansion of its commercial role vis-à-vis the region, Istanbul never acquired the solidness of the built environment created by bourgeois accumulation in other nineteenth-century urban centers. To be sure, there were a few bank buildings in the international nineteenth-century style, solid and dark; there were embassies reflecting "national" heritages in monumental scale; and, of course, the Parisian and Italianate *art nouveau* architecture preferred by the global bourgeoisie of the period (Barillari 1996). Istanbul's bankers, merchants, visitors, and refugees of various hues built for themselves mansions, apartment buildings, hotels, clubs, restaurants, and cafés, as well as less reputable locales for entertainment; but this was all confined within the narrow dark streets and dusty and mud-ridden roads of Pera (Beyoglu), historically the "other side" from the old city, where foreign styles were permitted to penetrate, where all the foreigners and most of the upwardly mobile non-Muslims came to live (Cezar 1994). The larger part of the city, the older quarters, remained predominantly residential. A vernacular architectural style did develop during the period, and the contours of the modal "Ottoman house" came to reflect more of the influence of European currents. Prosperity was not sufficiently widespread, however, to allow a remaking of the old city's visible aspect.

Plans to impose an overall or even partial logic to the new developments, through rudimentary urban planning or renewal, were confined to the new city and limited in success (Çelik 1986). In fact, the improvement of the urban infrastructure in the form of paved roads and sidewalks, city gas and electric trolleys, was haphazard and spotty: it was the most willing who could suspend their disbelief to talk about yet another Paris of the East. While a seat of empire such as St. Petersburg was constructed from scratch, Bombay acquired a monumental (albeit colonial) grandeur, Alexandria permitted settler accumulation to be reflected in its bourgeois buildings, Istanbul's transformation was uneven and incomplete. There was very little continuity in the urban fabric: newly erected modern buildings existed alongside hovels; parquet roads ended in dusty squares. The political logic of the empire had certainly been undermined and subverted but could not be supplanted. The imperial polity was not potent or determined enough to impose a project of its own on the developments, nor was it willing to relinquish its prerogatives. What resulted was an uneasy coexistence of a sphere of autonomy in the port-city mode, evolving as an extension of the nineteenth-century world economy but constrained to exist within the uncertain parameters of an old empire. Without the blessing or at least the benign neglect of the political authority, the port-city potential was difficult to realize.

Within a world-historical scheme where the great cities of the world attain some autonomy in certain periods only to subsequently yield to the political logic of territorial states, the end of the nineteenth century, especially in the peripheries, witnessed an increase in urban potential to self-rule. In fact, this period corresponded to the ideal of the mode of diffusion of the capitalist world economy where cities outside the core would become the outposts of a certain economic order, would represent new habits of consumption and production, and would in time civilize the rest of the territory (Basu 1985). For such transmission to occur, these cities had to be isolated from their political context—as in the treaty-ports model (Murphey 1970). In a sense, this nineteenth-century development represented a swing back to the late medieval independence of European cities that had emerged as the seats of a new economic and legal order within the feudal environment. Yet, as with the formation of territorial states in the early modern period, World War I, the subsequent dismantlement of the world market, and the eventual emergence of stronger nation-states out of weak empires once again signaled the end of urban autonomy.

Istanbul had only in the palest manner approximated to the blueprint of urban autonomy mostly because it was not a simple port city (as were Izmir, Beirut, or Alexandria in the empire) that collected goods from its hinterland and conveyed them to distant markets; in fact, its exports were never of much significance. On the contrary, it was an importing and consuming city like all imperial capitals. Because it was the *imperial* capital, it also suffered disproportionately in the evolution of the nation-state after World War I. Not only was there the global impact of the erosion of the constituent coordinates of a world economy based on free trade, but also adverse regional developments; and, finally, the advent of the new Turkish republic whose founders actively isolated the city. Istanbul was under occupation by the British, French, and the Italians through the duration of the Turkish-Greek war until 1922. There was, however, no attempt to establish a lasting administration. A project to internationalize the city on a long-term basis was entertained only half-heartedly. An additional factor that favored short-term management was the influx of White Russian refugees escaping the civil war in the Soviet Union: administrative measures were focused on the accommodation and safe conduct of about one million Russians, most of whom had departed by the end of 1922 (Johnson et al. 1922; Criss 1993). The civil war and the formation of the Soviet

Union also signaled the effective closure of the Black Sea and an end to the lucrative transit trade from which Istanbul's business had benefited.

In other directions, the war and the partitioning of the empire meant that Istanbul would no longer play the metropolitan role toward the territories in the Balkans, Palestine, Syria, and Iraq that it earlier had. The Ottoman sultan who had also served as a symbolic caliph for the world's Muslims, especially when anticolonial sentiments began to stir toward the end of the period, was no longer sovereign. With the abolition of the caliphate, Istanbul ceased to hold any particular interest for the Muslims of the world; Islamic intellectuals would no longer look at the city as a site of cultural and political pilgrimage.

An important dimension of Istanbul's global role had derived from its location at the intersection of two civilizations: Western travelers saw it as the door to the East, whereas Muslims regarded it as an occupied but not fully conquered outpost of the West. In the well-known cliché, Istanbul was said to be the bridge between two continents and two civilizations. Yet, often in its history, this privileged location was experienced negatively, as a fracture rather than an articulation. Ambiguity and tension had been endemic ever since Constantine moved his capital east and his descendants embraced the Greek over the Latin tradition. In time, the rivalry between Rome and Constantinople came to represent much more than an internecine conflict: civilizational lines were thought to follow the contours of the Catholic-Orthodox split. If the Ottomans did originate in Asia, their kingdom (which effortlessly took over the lands and the administrative structure of the Byzantines) nevertheless focused on the Balkans and represented a new incarnation of Orthodox power within Europe. Istanbul thus became the center of two religions: the Greek Orthodox patriarch domiciled in the city, who was *primum inter pares* among Orthodox patriarchs, was a loyal and well-accommodated subject of the empire. Mehmet the Conqueror, the Ottoman Sultan who granted perpetual rights to the patriarchate to remain in the city, learned Greek, entertained notions of conversion to Orthodoxy, and apocryphally declared himself as the avenger of the Trojans—against an undefined Europe. Throughout the Ottoman centuries, Istanbul was the largest Greek Orthodox city. After the independence of Greece in the nineteenth century, the wealthier and more sophisticated Greeks of Istanbul, reluctant to capitulate to an irredentist policy orchestrated by Athens, even attempted to redefine the Empire as a binational one (Augustinos 1977).

Additionally, of course, the Ottoman Empire had been unrivaled among Islamic states of the era. Although symbolic in nature, the sultan officially appropriated the title of the caliph after the conquest of Cairo in the early sixteenth century, and the palace gradually become a reliquary of Islamic holy items. When, in the eighteenth century, European expansion universalized a pattern of thought based on civilizational difference, Istanbul acquired a new significance; the caliphate was taken more seriously as conflict intensified and Muslims of the world sought to find new symbols of resistance. Before World War I, Islamic movements of various orientation, seeking a purchase on anti-imperialist mobilization, had congregated in the city. In their civilizational opposition to the West, they avoided most of the ambiguity and dilemma that beset secular, modernizing (yet anti-imperialist) movements such as third world nationalism.

Ottoman Istanbul was no less cosmopolitan than Byzantine Constantinople, but perhaps ethnic divisions remained more clearly defined and were brought under corporate categories. While this state corporatism operated successfully until nationalist ideologies were imported into the empire during the nineteenth century, it was far more difficult to contain localist reactions against attempts at modernization. These often originated from within the palace and the ruling circles but were effectively countered by "the street." During the seventeenth and the eighteenth centuries, localist reaction in the name of tradition, which came to define itself as Islamic, had constituted an unbroachable barrier against various attempts to emulate the rapidly encroaching West. When the state adopted a stance of modernization-from-above during the nineteenth century, resistance in the name of the local quickly came to define itself in the form of a politicized Islam. Istanbul became the arena where essentialized oppositions—East versus West, Islam versus Christianity, and local versus global—were played out. The denizens of the city separated themselves into camps with mutual suspicion and resentment. Had Istanbul not been the symbolic presence on the ideological map that it was, accommodation and synthesis might have been thinkable; but it was a global city at the cultural level precisely because of its symbolic location, and it was this symbolism that exacerbated the divisions.

REPUBLICAN DILEMMAS

The formation of the nation-state might have been expected to draw new protective boundaries and recuperate Istanbul's fracture in the name of nation building. A nation, after all, is an attempt to accommodate the global within what is considered the local. However, this was not to be because of two reasons, both due to the peculiarity of the nationalist vision championed by the republican elite. One, the kind of modernization represented by the actual experience of the Ottoman empire, and especially of Istanbul, was considered to be inauthentic because it was compromised by the nature of its adherents. In other words, since the westernized population was mostly non-Muslim, they could be dismissed as an excrescence, and even a

parasite over the "real" nation; thus, they fell outside the purview of the local. This drawing of lines also meant that the Muslim fellow travelers could
be dismissed as compradors, not only inauthentic but also in bad faith. Second, according to the modernist republican cosmology, the local itself was
also suspect because it was compromised by its adherence to Islam and,
therefore, obscurantism. In the ideal version, the local had to be fiercely ir-
religious, embodying all the virtues of tradition without its vices: ready and
willing to be injected with positivism and progress.

The two dimensions of this vision served to marginalize Istanbul's experience with westernization, on the one hand, and with the high culture
of Islam, on the other. By prescribing a national ideal to be constructed on
the basis of the exclusion of these very real histories, republicans idealized
their project to a point of unreality and irrealizability—with Istanbul embodying all the imagined impediments that had to be expurgated. This
need felt by the nationalists to exclude Istanbul's past from the construction of the national imaginary constituted the cultural dimension of the
Ankara-Istanbul dynamic during the heyday of republicanism. Yet, the
logic of Istanbul's location and its economic status soon required them to
dilute the ideal: by the 1970s Istanbul's economic primacy was reluctantly
accepted. From then on the gradual dilution of nationalist modernism
yielded to the familiar dialectic that had dominantly characterized Istanbul's cultural heritage—namely, its status as a global city that ostenta-
tiously accommodated the East-West dilemma and thus belied republican
hopes for pure westernization.

The high Republican period of 1923–1950 imposed on Istanbul the nationalist project of the Ankara elites. The most important dimension of this
imposition was the translation of anticolonial sentiments to ethnic purifi-
cation (unmixing of the peoples of the old multiethnic empire) that accompanied the establishment of the new republic. The composition of Istanbul's
population had changed during the latter part of the nineteenth century,
both because of migration from outside the empire and through the movement, in response to economic opportunity, of Christian and especially
Greek Ottomans from the provinces to the capital city. By the 1890s, the
non-Muslim population constituted the majority; in 1914, after refugees
from the Balkan Wars arrived, Muslims increased to 55 percent (Toprak
1982, 65). Although interethnic hostility generally spared Istanbul's population (with one notable exception in 1896 against Armenians), in 1923
Greece and Turkey agreed on an exchange of their Muslim and Orthodox
populations (Pentzopoulos 1962). Istanbul Greeks were exempted from this
forced movement, but much of the recent immigrants found it difficult to
prove that they had been *établis* in the city prior to the war. Christian population declined from about 450,000 in 1914 to 240,000 in 1927; total population had declined from one million to 700,000. Subsequent decades wit-

nessed an undeclared policy to drive the non-Muslim population out. The Republican state was nationalist, but it was ambiguous in defining the constituent coordinates of nationhood. Mostly it veered toward an ethnic definition rather than a constitutional one, and when ideological propping was required, religion was brought in as a defining element despite the state's avowed secularism. Thus, wartime measures led to the departure of non-Muslims after 1945; in 1955 there was a government-instigated riot destroying Greek property; in 1964 there were demonstrations against Istanbul Greeks and a legislation requiring those with Greek citizenship to leave the city. By the 1980s the Greek population had dwindled to less than two thousand, Armenians to fifty thousand, and Jews to twenty-five thousand. Istanbul came to reflect the ethnic balances of Turkey as a whole, where the population is said to be more than 99 percent Muslim.

During the first two decades of the Republic, the loss and the change in the composition of population deprived the city of a large number of its merchants, businessmen, artisans, and shopkeepers. The subsequent move of the seat of government to an undistinguished market town in the Anatolian steppes meant that the larger portion of the new republic's physical and cultural investment would be made in Ankara, to the detriment of Istanbul. The headquarters of the national radio network was established in the new capital; and the semiofficial print media were also moved there (although the bulk of the newspaper circulation and the nationally diffused printed matter still originated in Istanbul). The founders of the new republic in the new and culturally uncontaminated capital were hostile to any urban autonomy based on the institutionalization of market operations, and they were anxious to bring the economy under their control. These were projects they shared with interwar antiliberalism and anticolonial nationalism. Additionally, however, the new rulers in Ankara (although they were natives of Istanbul in overwhelming majority) pretended to regard Istanbul with suspicion, as a den of corruption and intrigue with ambivalent allegiance to the nationalist project. The city seemed to represent a temptation they tried very hard to keep away from: Mustafa Kemal did not visit it for five years in an attempt to resist the siren's call. Gradually, however, as nationalist *assabiyyah* eroded, Istanbul regained the favor of the Ankara political elite. Perhaps it was an exaggeration to speak about *"la mort d'Istanbul"* as one French journalist did (see, however, Eldem 1993), but by this time the city had lost most of its cosmopolitan character; it had become simply the primate city of a rather poor and isolated nation-state.

Major changes began to occur in the final years of World War II. First, in a xenophobic move, the government sought to punish and oust the remaining non-Muslim businessmen of the city, imposing on them a wealth levy supposed to tax wartime profits. This measure succeeded in destroying confidence in the government, and a large number of Jewish and Greek businessmen left immediately after the war. More important, shortages during the war and black market profits had created a new group of wealthy provincials who arrived in Istanbul seeking gentility (see chap. 6). They became the vanguard of an immigration that continued without stop, although in time immigrants drew from the poorer segments of the rural population, and they sought employment rather than civility. Their penetration of the complacent social life of the city proud of its past glamour signaled an irreversible momentum of nationalization of the metropolis.

During the postwar period of national development, heavily regulated by political decision making and reliant on strict control over imports, foreign investment, and international exchange, Istanbul remained resolutely provincial. Imported consumer goods were few and sold at a high premium. The currency was not convertible; possessing dollars was considered a punishable crime. Cultural interaction with the rest of the world was in the monopoly of an elite. During the entire decade of the 1950s, the biggest "cultural" event of world significance that occurred in Istanbul (aside from official visits of foreign dignitaries) was the opening of a Hilton, which was attended by a few international celebrities. Not until the early 1970s was another five-star hotel opened. In the absence of television, which did not start until the 1970s, and then in the form of state channels full of official news, there was no access to foreign media and independent information. The enthusiasm for developing the newly emerging national community marginalized the cosmopolitan heritage of the city; populism ruled the day.

Under developmentalist policies, Istanbul became the privileged location of a new generation of large-scale, private manufacturing enterprises, encouraged through financial incentives and protected from world competition. Thus by 1973, 44 percent of all private manufacturing establishments employing more than ten workers were located in Istanbul, accounting for 51 percent of total employment in Turkish private industry (Ozmucur 1976). This growth was accompanied by a much larger number of labor-intensive, small-scale manufacturing and commercial enterprises in and around the city core. Needless to say, the largest concentration of middle-class demand for the products of import-substituting industry was also located in the city. Throughout these decades of rapid economic expansion and chaotic growth, Istanbul's progressively deteriorating physical infrastructure and declining financial resources failed to generate action on the part of national governments in Ankara (Danielson and Keleş 1985). In the national political arena, the overriding theme was the incorporation of peasantry into electoral politics; thus, scarce resources were destined to agricultural subsidies of various sorts. Such subsidies accelerated the rural transformation, one of whose consequences was rapid urbanization and the growth of shantytowns—especially in Istanbul.

POSTNATIONAL DEVELOPMENTS

The year 1980 was a turning point, not only because the global underpinnings of national development were withdrawn by then, and it was obvious that the project could not be extended any longer no matter how much mortgaging of the future were permitted, but also because under a cynical military government that took over in Turkey, all lofty sentiments of the earlier period crumbled. Structural adjustment, liberalization, and privatizations signaled that internationalization of capital was now an inescapable reality. It was gradually admitted by all that national regulation was compromised; that there would be no real challenge to the global logic of capital; and that the contours of the material world, ranging from the sites of investment to the patterns of consumption, from land development to building practices, were increasingly being determined by choices made by private capital that was rapidly being inserted into the accelerated flows of globalization. Political authorities had to be aware of this and do their best to attract capital and to accommodate it.

The Turkish experiment with economic liberalization and structural adjustment in the period following the military coup of 1980 was relatively successful (Öniş 1993). The coup ushered in a regime that became identified with orthodox policies counseled by the International Monetary Fund and applied in the hope of restructuring the economy toward greater openness and liberalization. It entailed attempts both to dramatically reduce the scope of the state sector and to situate the Turkish economy within the unitary logic of global capitalism. This project contained few explicit attempts to position Istanbul as a global city to attract foreign capital. One such (unsuccessful) project was the formation of a Black Sea economic cooperation area with Istanbul as the center. The application for customs union and eventually full membership in the European Community envisaged an international but subordinate role for Istanbul and its business community.

Projects to establish a regional position for Istanbul were not necessarily misguided, although politics did not allow their realization. The city was and had always been the largest market in the Balkans, the Black Sea, and the Middle East. During the nineteenth century, its role in transit trade increased in tandem with the growth of world commerce; and it acquired a new commanding position in the world economy with respect to financing of trade, banks, and insurance. Foreign businessmen lived there and organized in chambers of commerce; commodity exchanges were established as well as futures markets; regional centers of foreign banks were also located there. Especially during the two decades prior to World War I, German attempts to rival Britain and France in the Middle East were launched from Istanbul, as German policy regarding the empire seemed to favor its preservation as a pliant informal colony rather than its dismantlement.

Coinciding with Turkey's *apertura* in the 1980s, Istanbul seemed poised to recapture its regional role which had been largely forgotten during the heyday of national development. The oil boom brought merchants and contractors much business. Istanbul also emerged as a tourism center for Middle Easterners. Arab banks opened offices to benefit from the interface with Western finance. The long war between Iran and Iraq provided many opportunities to merchants and businessmen who acted as conduits between the war zone and Europe. In addition, Beirut as the traditional capital of Middle East finance and high-level services was torn by a civil war. In this conjuncture Istanbul could emerge as a regional service capital, but developments in this direction were stymied by political and cultural suspicion between the Arab world and Turkey. Rival international alliances and diverging aspirations of the political elites did not allow the realization of what technology and geography permitted. A second chance was offered in the form of the dismantlement of the Soviet Union. Once again the immediate response was euphoric and highly optimistic. Real and imagined linguistic and religious ties with the Turkic republics, as well as the shared heritage of the empire in the case of Transcaucasia, were brought to the fore. In fact, during the initial years of confusion when Europeans and Americans were too timid to enter the fray and Russia was yet unsettled to reassert dominance, Turkey seemed a plausible contender for influence and business primacy in both the Caucasus and the Central Asian republics. Istanbul became a meeting place for the elite of the Turkic and the Caucasian republics, where they met with Westerners seeking to obtain concessions. The government convened conferences in an attempt to attain a diplomatic role of mediation between the West and Central Asia. The more permanent legacy of this initial period of optimism was in the economic field: Turkish businessmen invested in undertakings ranging from small bakeries to large shopping complexes in a geographic area reaching from Romania to Kazakhstan, including Russia and Ukraine. Most of the larger investors originated in Istanbul, and producer's services derived from the city's financial and professional sectors.

The accompanying economic transformation of the time did benefit indirectly from the more official initiatives in international relations. Nonetheless, it was private enterprise that guaranteed a regional role for Istanbul. The export drive was also successful, implying the establishment of a large number of world-market–oriented businesses in Istanbul. More importantly, foreign companies, which had shunned Turkey during the national developmentalist period, were persuaded by the liberal rhetoric of the government to invest and to open offices in Turkey. It was Istanbul that alone absorbed most of the foreign investment and accounted for a large proportion of the exports. As in other examples of liberalization, the financial sector was the first to be fully incorporated, with branch offices of foreign banks, foreign exchange dealers, leasing and insurance companies, fund managers, and a stock exchange opening in rapid succession (Oncu and Gokce 1991). On-line currency trading, electronic transfers, and ATM machines quickly followed. A new generation of small and specialized banks of domestic origin also entered the fray, to take advantage of the export boom and the increased ability of the economy to borrow from abroad. Five-star hotels, constructed in choice locations overlooking the Bosphorus, emerged alongside international banks and trading companies. Istanbul in the 1980s lived through its own version of casino capitalism and yuppie exuberance.

New arrivals in Istanbul's city core included, in addition to office buildings and five-star hotels, temples of luxury consumption, in the form of upscale shopping centers and boutiques of world brands. There was an upgrading of the main avenues in the upper-income neighborhoods; it became possible to stroll or sit in a café and to pretend to experience a decontextualized urban space of global homogeneity. New shopping centers were replicas of upscale urban malls in other world cities. The internationalization of retail trade, which started at the luxury end of the sector, continued with department stores and giant *hypermarchés* in the European mode (Tokatli and Boyaci 1997). Corresponding to the same demand, fast-food chains mushroomed (McDonald's, Burger King, Pizza Hut), quickly imitated by Turkish chains, adding local color to the same successful formula.

In addition to a proliferating fast-food sector, there emerged a diversity of ethnic and world cuisine restaurants to satisfy the most demanding cosmopolitan palates. Various European cuisines were always available; now there are regional Chinese, Japanese, Korean, Thai, Indian, Mexican, and Argentinian restaurants and those offering fashionable menus such as Californian. Along with native and expatriate restaurateurs, chefs on global rotation also grace Istanbul's eateries regularly. There has been an explosion especially in the entertainment sector. The night life is vibrant, with traffic jams until daybreak during weekends, leading the *Herald Tribune* to headline an article about Istanbul's night scene "The Best Kept Secret in Europe." Concert artists now include a stop in the city in their itinerary; annual international festivals of film, opera, classical music, jazz, and theater continue between April and October. There is a *biennale* of art that is beginning to occupy a place in the international exhibit calendar. The word is out that Istanbul is a preferred locale for international congresses. The *New York Times, Wall Street Journal,* and *Financial Times* all have permanent bureaus in Istanbul, and in addition to covering politics and the economy, their reporters regularly write on the festivals, arts, and daily life, in a tone that accepts the city on its own terms—beyond orientalist clichés. With ten million visitors to Turkey a year, most of whom pass through and stay in

Istanbul, the city has entered the global collective conscious as it never had since the Republic.

This mutual awareness between Istanbul and the world is what is new. Locals now choose from among more than twenty local TV channels, including those specializing in news, video clips, and Turkish and foreign soap operas. There is cable service in the middle-class residential areas of the city, carrying the world services of CNN, BBC, Eurosport, NBC, as well as German, French, and Italian channels. Dish antennas proliferate, offering more specialized menus. Dozens of FM stations, offering all kinds of Western and local music, serious talk shows, religious instruction, world business news, compete for the market. Foreign language newspapers and magazines are widely available, and the Turkish printed media, especially glossy magazines with niche readership, have exploded. These are generally produced in partnership with global media giants, carrying some translations and some local content. None of this happened smoothly; in fact, the national government was most ungracious and fought to preserve its prerogatives of broadcasting monopoly and information censorship. In the end, however, Ankara succumbed to technology and popular pressure: TV and radio stations that started as "pirate" undertakings eventually gained legal status.

PRODUCING GLOBALIZATION

Despite the considerable transformation at the market end with the rapid embrace of globalized consumption patterns and the signs that come attached, and the accommodation of cultural flows of all kinds, what is going on in Istanbul is ruefully inadequate from the perspective of the political economy of globalization. The pace of material change on the production and employment side, as envisaged in the conventional global-cities model, has been slow; rather, there has been a different kind of economic globalization with perhaps different consequences.

Liberalism of the 1980s had important political consequences for Istanbul—especially the changing attitude toward urban autonomy, which led to Istanbul's local government acquiring funds to rebuild the city. In the 1980s, Istanbul received a major influx of state funding—of much greater scope that at any time in the Republic's history (Heper 1987). The mayor at the time, B. Dalan, embarked on a brand of entrepreneurial restructuring that he forced on Istanbul. His projects supplied the impetus and created the framework for the transformation of Istanbul from a national primate city ravaged by rapid immigration into a newly imagined world city. A series of urban renewal projects that had remained on the drawing board for more than three decades were begun: large tracts of nineteenth-century inner-city neighborhoods were cleared, central city small manufacturing establishments were evicted from their centuries-old quarters. Boulevards were built along the Golden Horn and the Bosphorus—both massive projects involving large-scale investment. Istanbul was rapidly becoming a city designed for cultural consumption, easier to visit, with a well-defined tourist area containing monuments and heritage quotations in the form of restored neighborhoods, readily accessible from the newly built hotels. An internationalized business district was also shaping up, with modern, wired office towers designed to accommodate global functions. In the course of the 1980s, Istanbul emerged as the showcase and gateway for Turkey's new era of integration into the world scene.

The liberal mayor, however, had disregarded the overwhelming electoral weight of the new immigrants; in embracing the entrepreneurial dimension the popular had been forgotten. In the election of 1991, the social democratic candidate, a populist in the old vein, became the new mayor. Sözen was suspicious of the discourse of globalization. During his tenure an implicit amnesty was granted to illegal housing, and new migrants were encouraged. Resources of the urban government were mostly allocated toward bringing services to shantytowns. The social democrats in the early 1990s changed their earlier national-developmentalist outlook and veered closer to the European parliamentary left, accepting the parameters of the new world order. Accordingly, his own party prevented the populist mayor's candidacy in the 1994 elections; instead they nominated a well-known intellectual with impeccable global aspirations but no political or administrative experience. The candidate of the larger center-right party, a technocrat with World Bank experience, was also an outspoken proponent of the global vision for Istanbul. While they competed on a shared platform of making Istanbul a global city and received a total of two-fifths of the vote, and populist left- and right-wing parties along with splinter groups received over one-third, the candidate of the Islamicist Welfare Party won a plurality with 23 percent. Tayyip Erdogan, the new mayor, had run on a platform of anticorruption, public morality, and social justice. His stance toward the entrepreneurial dimension of the globalization alternative was, during the election, and also in his tenure, ambivalent (see chap. 3). This ambivalence, coming after left-nationalist populism, has been one of the elements preventing the emergence of a vision that might allow the city's elite to engage in effective urban entrepreneurship. From the point of view of the potential for globalization, the inability, manifest during the tenure of the last two mayors, to commit resources and rhetoric to a globalization project has led to a passive stance on the city's party. The globalization that has occurred since 1990 has not been assisted by urban entrepreneurship.

It was not only politics at the urban level that stymied a more rapid change. For all the development of civic pride and urban consciousness,

autonomy from Ankara has been an unreachable goal. The problem is not
so much at the level of administrative decision making or control over rev-
enues, as it is in the adverse effects of political ambiguity and instability on
the opportunities that Istanbul might otherwise benefit from. In fact, the
world and regional political situation provided Istanbul with a golden opportunity to emerge as the "global city" for the region as a whole, where
producers' services would be directed to markets beyond Turkey. This opportunity, however, was counterbalanced by the inability of the country to
provide the environment to create business confidence. Turkey always
looked unstable, its governments undecided and unwilling to allocate the
requisite funds to create the infrastructure for attracting capital, its ability
to construct an effective administrative and legal structure suspect. It was
ever embroiled in regional and internal conflict: Arab countries were suspicious because of its Western orientation, Russia saw it as a rival in Central Asia and the Caucasus, and Greece did its best to block all its attempts
to augment its European link. The uncertainty with regard to accession to
the European Union added to the appearance of instability; even when a
customs union officially came into effect at the start of 1996, Ankara governments gave the impression that they would soon ask for a renegotia-
tion (Keyder 1993). Because of a parliamentary system with a surfeit of parties and no clear majority, governments were always formed by brittle
coalitions, unable to take decisive steps. Internally, the war against an in-
surrectionary movement in the Kurdish areas continued, leading to budget deficits and inflation, and gross infractions of law by government mili-
tia. The legal system was in dire need of reform, with most business
interests giving up on recourse to the judiciary owing to its corruption,
slowness, and inability to dissuade violations. The lack of reform of the judiciary and the widespread belief in the total corruptibility of the police effectively negated all the good will that the government showed in legislation concerning foreign capital, trade, intellectual property rights,
environment, labor conditions, and human rights, as required by the
GATT, WTO, ILO, the European Union, or the European Human Rights
Court. All this reflected not so much an inability to act in the face of vested
interests and inertia of the social structure, as a reluctance of the political
elite itself to bring about an environment of legal predictability and civil
rights, where arbitrary interventions—hence the ability to strike patronage
deals for payoff—would be eliminated.

In its original formulation, the political economy of the global-city construct was based on a few assumptions (Friedmann 1986; Sassen 1991).
Capital was global, and its spatial organization hierarchical: the situation
of the cities of the world in which control functions of capital are located
and that house the labor force providing producer services would reflect
this hierarchy. Global cities supplied producer services at a supranational

level; those that were at the top commanded a second level of regionally important cities that in turn were linked to centers with only local importance. Within the cities in the upper levels, where global control functions and producer services catering to supranational clienteles predominate, such services are expected to constitute the most dynamic sector of the economy, providing investment and employing a greater than expected share of the labor force. This model assumes a postindustrial development where manufacturing employment declines and services expand. For global cities, it is the particular kind of high-value-adding services that are associated with control functions that become the index of success.

Istanbul has certainly experienced transformation in this regard. There is a flourishing service sector in marketing, accounting and management, telecommunications, banking and finance, transport, insurance, computers and data processing, legal services, auditing, accounting, consulting, advertising, design, and engineering. World transnationals have penetrated this sector through joint ventures, direct investment, and licensing. Some of this investment is, in fact, in the form of regional headquarters of transnational companies, rather than being entirely directed to the Turkish market. The next stage is when this producer service base established in Istanbul serves to mediate transnational operations elsewhere in the region. In the all important FIRE services (finance, insurance, real estate) employment has grown by one hundred thousand jobs between 1980 and 1990, from 10.3 percent to 13.9 percent of the services sector, or 5.3 percent to 7.1 percent in Istanbul's total employment (Aksoy 1996, 33) (compare to 17–18 percent that obtains in New York and London; see Sassen 1991). These are all located in the newly developing business districts with their tall office buildings encased in glass in the international mode. All this development, however, is slowed down by uncertainty, ambivalence, and lack of legislative and physical infrastructure.

A related dimension of the global-city position is informational infrastructure, serving the bridging needs that establish reliable conduct between the nodes of the global system of information flows (Castells 1989). Here, too, Ankara's reluctance and inability to undertake privatization in the transportation and communications sectors damaged Istanbul's chances. Keeping up with the technology in these two sectors is essential, but public agencies have proved inadequate in both. Despite obvious growing need (the rate of annual growth in the number of air passengers from abroad has been 15–20 percent during the 1990s; see Devlet Istatistik Enstitusu 1996, 443), airport capacities have not been expanded: a building completed fifteen years ago now serves a volume of traffic four times as much. A telephone system that was overhauled in the 1980s and was up-to-date at the time has been barely maintained, with no new investment, and is showing the strain. In a city where businesses move frequently, no telephone books were published between 1987 and 1996; and the 1996 one does not include business addresses or numbers. Perhaps most revealing has been the situation regarding the Internet. By law, the public telephone company has a monopoly over satellite connection, and it set up an autonomous unit to provide Internet access. Its trunk line, however, did not have sufficient capacity, and the connections, when they could be accessed, were exceedingly slow. Large companies had no choice but to set up their own direct (and illegal) satellite connections, and a number of "pirate" providers offered their services to the rest of the public.

These conditions have also kept foreign capital away. Foreign investors have been cautious; investment by transnationals fluctuated and was not sufficient to provide a self-sustaining momentum. Investment arrived mostly to exploit the opportunities of Turkey's internal market from the vantage point of its primate city. The customs union with the European Union, taking effect in 1996, was expected to attract foreign capital, essential for restructuring of the economy and for the securing of external markets. It was hoped that European companies would invest to profit from low wages and an experienced industrial labor force, and Japanese and Korean capital might be attracted because Turkey could serve as an export platform toward Europe. It should be remembered that there has in fact been a huge increase in the world volume of direct foreign investment during the 1990s, especially toward the "developing" countries of Latin America and Asia. In the case of Turkey, despite its geographic advantages and the access to European markets provided by the customs union, inflow of foreign capital has fluctuated below the $1 billion mark, and reached $1.1 billion in 1996, representing 0.3 percent of the world flow. Whereas foreign direct investment has been responsible for between 10 and 20 percent of capital formation in Chile, Argentina, and Mexico, in Turkey the figure is 2 percent. Portfolio investment, in the form of foreign individuals and funds buying shares in the stock market, was insignificant (United Nations 1997). Hence, the formal economy remained predominantly oriented to secure domestic markets; its restructuring along the expectations of economic globalization much below potential.

It was not only the reluctance of foreign capital that tipped the balance. The feeling that Istanbul failed to assume a new direction became widespread, and local capitalists stopped campaigning for a strategy pursuing global-city functions. The adoption of such a strategy, conjointly with the city's business and political elite, would have been crucial in convincing global capital that Istanbul provided the requisite material and legislative infrastructure accommodating global-city functions. This "positioning" of the city would help persuade overly irritable capital, which is technologically disposed to hypermobility, to locate or remain in the city.

INFORMAL GLOBALIZATION

Istanbul's transformation fell short of the expectations of the global-city model. Its regional role has been limited, and its service function is oriented predominantly to the national hinterland. Information technology has advanced slowly, and modern services have not become a leading sector accounting for significant accumulation or employment creation. Yet, the city is booming: luxury goods on display, the creation of office and upscale residential space, the conspicuous consumption exhibited on the streets cannot be fueled by the Turkish economy's internal growth alone. The answer lies in a different, informal, and temporary kind of intensification of transnational material flows, one shaped by the uncertainties in political environment and not envisaged in the global-city literature. There are two dimensions to this alternative globalization: the first has to do with "illegal" flows, with Istanbul emerging as a major center of money laundering and the drug trade. Istanbul is not unique in accommodating dirty money, but the government has been remarkably slow in responding to pressure from international agencies to comply with emerging world standards of transparency and financial sector accountability. Turkey has often been reprimanded for a too relaxed attitude toward money laundering through casinos and construction companies, and ultimately through the banking system; in other words, the bloat and high profitability in the financial sector are due in part to capturing a share of the billions of dollars of unknown provenance that daily circle the globe. In fact, political corruption, due mainly to the no-holds-barred competition over the payoffs involved in the circulation of dirty money, occupied the political agenda during most of 1998.

It is the coexistence of competing logics that permits corruption to flourish. The long experience with populism had created structures of political allocation that were difficult to give up. Incomplete liberalization afforded perfect opportunity to translate political position to market advantage. The old system was breaking up and there was much money to be made; for this reason, the political elite were slow to put in place the requisite regulations or, when forced to do so, to apply them with sufficient conviction. Part of the corruption translates to the formation of an environment that allows for various trading activities in illegal goods, notably drugs. The largest category of unaccountable money seems to derive from the fact that 75 percent of all drugs arriving in Europe are reportedly transported through Turkey. Figures in this field are not reliable, but a recent newspaper report put the annual volume at $55 billion (*Cumhuriyet*, December 29, 1997). It may be surmised that profit rates are high and that a good portion of the value added that remains in the country finds its way to Istanbul, which is the gateway and where, presumably, the principal players are located.

The second element of unexpected globalization in the economic realm is also an informal activity and derives from Istanbul's recapture of its status as a market place for Russian and Eastern European merchants. This is an entirely one-sided trade in which "tourists" come into Istanbul, buy mostly textiles, and take them back as "accompanied baggage" (Blacher 1997). It is because of the inability or the unwillingness of the political authorities to adopt legislation and regulations conforming to new world conditions that recourse to such fiction seems to be required. This trade, estimated at $5 to 10 billion dollars per year, is informal in the sense that for most part it is not recorded. (This figure must be evaluated against the level of formal flows: Turkey's recorded exports in 1996 were $25 billion, and GNP was estimated at $170 billion, with Istanbul's share in the national income as between $50 and $70 billion.) In fact, its distinguishing feature is small-scale, flexible organization where large numbers of competing merchants work with low profit margins. So far, authorities have balked at interfering with this trade because of the large constituency formed around it. It is not only the employment and income created by the five thousand or so shops that act as the exporting points but also the apparel manufacturers they are closely connected with, who are mostly small entrepreneurs employing ten to twenty workers in small workshops. (The textile sector has been and still is the most rapidly growing sector of employment in Istanbul's economy. It created 230,000 jobs in the 1980s, and its share in total employment increased from 10.7 percent in 1980 to 15.5 percent in 1990; it thus accounted for nearly half of all manufacturing jobs. See Aksoy 1996, 24.) In addition, there is a large service sector of hotels, restaurants, entertainment, transportation, and banking that caters to the Russian and other ex-Soviet traders. Nonetheless, because of uncertainty as to whether it will continue, more permanent structures do not come into existence. On the contrary, government functionaries with taxation in mind intermittently threaten to clamp down on "suitcase trading" with the full knowledge that any attempt to impose bureaucratic or fiscal restrictions will contribute to its flight to another world market city.

While such informal flows of money and goods undoubtedly shape Istanbul's new role in the world economy, this mode of internationalization hardly denotes a postindustrial or postmodern orientation in the economic realm—except in the sense of being postnational. In fact, its existence is due to the disintegration of control over national space and to the increasing absence of state regulation. However, it is an interstitial development benefiting from incongruity and what may be temporary arbitrage opportunity; it does not suggest the kind of structuring dynamic envisaged in the global-city model. What it points to is similar to the premodern function served by the city in its historical existence—as an international mart. Istanbul's comparative advantage in this trade derives from low profit margins and flexibility and access to the vast Turkish hinterland. It is due to manufacturing capacity and shopkeeping potential rather than a new breed of service or information economy.

The foregoing suggests that Istanbul experiences the impact of globalization, that it becomes globalized in the sense of a place where the intensification of global flows of money, capital, people, ideas, signs, and information is experienced; but it is not becoming a *global city* as envisaged in the model. There is some structural change toward providing producer services to the region beyond the national domain, but the transformation has not advanced sufficiently to claim that global rather than national functions, services rather than manufacturing, determine the direction of change. This is not because of a lack of opportunity; in fact, given its history and geography, the city would seem to be well placed to play a global role. Rather, it is the constraints imposed by the political sphere—the continuation of populist politics and the reluctance to institute a liberal framework at the national level, and the lack of coherent and unifying entrepreneurial vision at the local level—which limit its chances. What results from this juxtaposition is an appearance of private riches amid public penury: Ferraris and Porsches on mud roads, the latest architectural styles in business towers where there are regular brown-outs.

REALLY EXISTING GLOBALIZATION

The disparities in income, consumption patterns, and lifestyles brought about by the collapse of the Fordist welfare state in the developed world and of developmentalist populism in the periphery are well known. In the case of Istanbul, as in all global cities, the development is exceedingly uneven, both in terms of access of the denizens to globalized activities and in terms of the physical spaces under transformation. This unevenness seems to parallel and aliment a cultural conflict, revolving around the definition of locality and identity, between the globalizers and localizers—somewhat akin to the modern-traditional clash that an earlier literature described. Inequalities emerged through the rapid incorporation of one small segment of the population into the new dynamics provided by the world economy, while the majority witnessed and reacted to this incorporation without partaking in its material benefits. Entrepreneurs linking up with world markets, bankers, knowledge workers, data merchants, and professionals educated to be at home in the new paradigm quickly graduated to new salary and income scales on a par with their world counterparts, whereas the middle classes of earlier vintage and workers organized or informal, skilled or unskilled, permanent or casual, were left behind. Furthermore, the "decent" jobs of the previous era, promising middle-class incomes and status, were no longer being created. In other words, one segment of the city's population became corelike in the disintegrated spaces of the global order, while the majority remained excluded, with the additional awareness that the promises of assimilation that once held sway in the modernist era, were not to be reproduced in the postmodern one.

Social services that had catered to a wide spectrum in a relatively egalitarian mode were quickly privatized at the upper end, with a proliferation of private schools covering kindergarten through university education and expensive health services. Public offerings deteriorated: with shrinking public funds, schools and hospitals could not be maintained, teachers and health providers received low civil servant salaries, and buildings became crowded and inadequate. The spectrum of available services and consumer goods became much wider, and the disparities in consumption between the top and the rest too visible. A two-tier system emerged and the two spheres grew apart whenever lifestyles and consumption patterns could be segregated. Residential space also reflected this rift: new complexes built for the globalizers were landscaped, expensive, inaccessible, and forbidding to the outside population, while shantytowns continued to proliferate, especially for new immigrants (see chap. 8). Restaurants, night spots, concert halls, and exhibition spaces contributed to a situation in which class cultures were being redefined through the medium of consumption.

This is not to say that middle segments were not gradually absorbed into global patterns of consumption; this diffusion, however, was slow, and it did not make a visible dent because of the continuing influx of poor migrants from the Anatolian countryside. Driven out of their villages by the civil war in Kurdish areas, these migrants arrived in a city where the populist safety net was largely withdrawn. In the global-cities literature there is an expectation that such immigration (e.g., Central Americans in New York) will result in an ethnic division of labor and social polarization. In the case of New York City, for example, the number of immigrants per annum has been about seventy thousand, and the population of the city has not appreciably grown. As a result, it has been possible to absorb the newcomers into the employment hierarchy, and the population which is truly excluded (the "impacted ghetto" in Lash and Urry's [1994] terms) has remained stable. Istanbul, however, had to accommodate three times as many immigrants every year. There is an expectation that the emergence of the new informational elite at the top of the social hierarchy will create employment for a wide range of personal service providers at the bottom. This is only partially due to the demand generated by the business service firms where cleaning staff, couriers, and other less skilled personnel will necessarily be employed. It is due mostly to the differentiated consumption patterns of the highly individualized and high-income-earning professionals. They require unique luxury goods produced by labor-intensive methods; a wide variety of personal services ranging from five-star hotels, to tourism agencies and upscale boutiques, from ethnic restaurants to chauffeurs, bodyguards, and dog walkers; and provide the economic potential for the emergence of a variegated service sector. This "ripple" effect is limited when the primary—globalized—sector cannot provide sufficient momentum. Given the influx of two hundred thousand barely literate immigrants every year, it would be overly optimistic to expect a global-city dynamic, even if it had been more robust than Istanbul's, to provide sufficient gravitation in the labor market. Hence, the population in excluded positions, akin to the impacted ghetto but living in a very different cultural environment, grows and attains sufficient weight to color the urban political process.

Given this discussion, it might be more realistic to think of Istanbul, in terms of its economic transformation and employment structure, as not a "dual city" but a "divided city." In one part of it global material flows operate, whether they be formal or informal, and bring about the expected results of class formation, consumption patterns, and employment creation. However, there is also a second part in which denizens largely remain immune to these flows; material life is conducted under the old patterns of regulation, in the informal sector, in shantytowns, in centers in the periphery that might as well be separate towns, using networks deriving from the preimmigration world and its urban transformation (see chap. 9).

Within this separation of spheres conflict arises where the public space cannot be privatized, where interaction is unavoidable. All the big ideological battles of recent years have focused on the control of public space and its symbolism of public morality: head scarves in schools, location of mosques, nudity on billboards, taverns on sidewalks (see chap. 2), and rock music in squares are only the more blatant items in the catalogue of debates. While there is no one-to-one correspondence between exclusion and puritanism, political Islam has in large part been formulated to provide a vocabulary reflecting concerns about public morality and cultural clash (see chap. 4) and has been successful in capturing the adherence of many remaining on the margins. As a consequence, the secular discourse of modernization, which has historically defined the westernizers' platform, has been reduced to another factional and politicized discourse in the service of a positive appropriation of globalization. This polarity has obviously reduced the chances of formulating an oppositional agenda that is at the same time secular and that might potentially attract the marginalized.

It would be difficult to understand the intensification of social and cultural tensions outside the ambit of globalization and the differential access to the changes it has harbored. Perhaps more important, however, is the intensification of the flows of signs and symbols that qualitatively change the nature and the expression of conflict. The proliferation of media, of political ideas ranging from environmental concerns to human rights and world brands, of global styles, supply a range of symbols that may be appropriated for various platforms ranging from urban entrepreneurship to ethnic movements to political resistance. Globalization changes the political and cultural context, so that all expression must take account of and use signs with a global cachet, appeal to global forms of protest (the involvement of globally organized nongovernmental organizations in recent urban movements), appeal to global forums, and validate itself in global media. The local, the native, what various interests define as the real authentic, has to be redefined and contested in the light of global positioning of the city (see chaps. 2 and 4). This is why the modern and globalizing elites of the city require a new vocabulary of exclusion in the attempt to marginalize lifestyles that they feel to be the wrong and objectionable sorts of hybridities (see chap. 6). This is why the Islamic movement has to produce an alternative global-city project (see chap. 3) and cannot remain immune to the differentiation of employment and consumption that it experiences within the ranks (see chap. 5). It is also the reason that the music produced initially to express the woes of the immigrant now has to position itself vis-à-vis an emerging idiom of "world music" (see chap. 7).

At some level, however, the city remains "soft" and malleable, accommodating all the materially, culturally, and politically differentiated constituencies; tensions dissipate and interaction occurs. There is polarization of space but also cohabitation of heterogeneous populations. There is negotiation over cultural heritage, not outright war. Battles are waged, but compromises are also reached. In some ways the exposing of the illusion of common interest that statist nationalism had perpetrated has been positive: the new cultural, political, and symbolic communities that are forming under the impact of globalization permit conflicts to be aired out in the open. Acknowledgment of difference and the need to validate positions in the media bring a much needed transparency. New skills are learned to be able to operate in the new stage, with a new vocabulary. Perhaps this is the harbinger of civility: a civic culture without which urban life is impossible. Essays collected in this volume document various dimensions of the interplay between conflict and coexistence, between tension and negotiation. They show how globalization has increased the stakes and made the interplay more urgent.

REFERENCES

Aksoy, A. 1996. *Kuresellesme ve Istanbul'da istihdam*. Istanbul: Friedrich Ebert Vakfi.
Augustinos, G. 1977. *Consciousness and history: nationalist critics of Greek society, 1897–1914*. Boulder, Colo.: East European Quarterly.

Barillari, D. 1996. *Istanbul 1900: art nouveau architecture and interiors*. New York: Rizzoli.

Basu, D. K. 1985. *The rise and growth of the colonial port cities in Asia*. Lanham, Md.: University Press of America.

Blacher, P. S. 1997. Les "shop-touristy" de Tsargrad ou les nouveaux russophones d'Istanbul. *Turcica* 28: 11–52.

Castells, M. 1989. *The informational city*. Oxford: Blackwell.

Çelik, Z. 1986. *The remaking of Istanbul: portrait of an Ottoman city in the nineteenth century*. Seattle: University of Washington Press.

Cezar, M. 1994. Ondokuzuncu yuzyilda Beyoglu neden ve nasil gelisti? Pages 2673–90 in *XI. Tarih Kongresi. VI. Cilt*. Ankara: Turk Tarih Kurumu.

Criss, N. B. 1993. *Isgal altinda Istanbul, 1918–1923*. Istanbul: Iletisim.

Devlet Istatistik Enstitusu. 1996. *Statistical yearbook of Turkey*. Ankara.

Danielson, M. M., and R. Keleş. 1985. *The politics of rapid urbanization: government and growth in modern Turkey*. New York: Holmes & Meier.

Eldem, E. 1993. Review of S. Yerasimos ed., *Istanbul 1914–1923, capitale d'un monde illusoire ou l'agonie des vieux empires*, Paris: Autrement, 1992. *New Perspectives on Turkey* 9: 154–57.

Friedmann, J. 1986. The world city hypothesis. *Development and Change* 17, no. 1: 69–83.

Girouard, M. 1985. *Cities and people: a social and architectural history*. New Haven, Conn.: Yale University Press.

Heper, M., ed. 1987. *Democracy and local government. Istanbul in the 1980s*. Beverley, United Kingdom: Eothen.

Johnson, C. R., et al. 1922. *Constantinople today: the pathfinder survey of Constantinople*. New York: Macmillan.

Keyder, C. 1993. The dilemma of cultural identity on the margin of Europe. *Review* 16, no. 1: 19–33.

Keyder, C., E. Ozveren, and D. Quataert, eds. 1993. *Port-cities in the eastern Mediterranean*. Special Issue of *Review* (Winter).

Lash, S., and J. Urry. 1994. *Economies of sign and space*. London: Sage.

Mantran, R. 1962. *Istanbul dans la seconde moitié du XVIIe siècle: essai d'histoire institutionnelle, economique et sociale*. Paris: Maisonneuve.

Murphey, R. 1970. *The treaty ports and China's modernization: what went wrong?* Ann Arbor: University of Michigan Center for Chinese Studies.

Necipoglu, N. 1995. Byzantines and Italians in fifteenth century Constantinople. *New Perspectives on Turkey* 12: 129–43.

Öncu, A., and D. Gokce, D. 1991. Macro-politics of deregulation and micro-politics of banks. Pages 99–118 in M. Heper (ed.), *Strong state and economic interest groups: the post-1980 Turkish experience*. New York: de Gruyter.

Öniş, Z. 1993. The dynamics of export-oriented industrialization in a second generation NIC: perspectives on the Turkish case. *New Perspectives on Turkey* 9: 75–100.

Özmucur, S. 1976. Istanbul ili gelir tahminleri, 1950–74. *B.U. Ekonomi Dergisi* 4–5: 51–65.

Pamuk, S. 1987. *The Ottoman Empire and European capitalism, 1820–1913: trade, investment, and production*. Cambridge: Cambridge University Press.

Pentzopoulos, D. 1962. *The Balkan exchange of minorities and its impact upon Greece.* Paris: Mouton.

Rosenthal, S. T. 1980. *The politics of dependency: urban reform in Istanbul.* Westport, Conn.: Greenwood.

Sassen, S. 1991. *The global city.* Princeton, N.J.: Princeton University Press.

Tokatli, N., and Y. Boyaci. 1997. Internationalization of retailing in Turkey. *New Perspectives on Turkey* 17 (Fall): 97–128.

Toprak, Z. 1982. La population d'Istanbul dans les premières années de la République. Pages 63–70 in *Travaux et recherches en Turquie.* Paris: Peeters.

United Nations. 1997. *World investment report.* New York: Author.

Valensi, L. 1993. *The birth of the despot: Venice and the sublime porte.* Ithaca, N.Y.: Cornell University Press.

Van Millingen, A. 1910. Constantinople. Pages 3–9 in *Encyclopaedia Britannica.* 11th ed., vol. 7. New York: Encyclopaedia Britannica.

Part II

Culture and Politics of Identity

2

Who Owns the Old Quarters?
Rewriting Histories in a Global Era

Ayfer Bartu

The core of world history is no longer the evolution and devolution of world systems, but the tense, ongoing interaction of forces promoting global integration and forces recreating local autonomy. This is not a struggle for or against global integration itself, but rather a struggle over the terms of that integration. The struggle is by no means finished, and its path is no longer foreordained by the dynamics of western expansion that initiated global integration . . . These matters lead to the question of who, or what, controls and defines the identity of individuals, social groups, nations and cultures.

> Bright and Geyer,
> "For a Unified History of the World in the Twentieth Century"

Globalization does not signal the erasure of local difference, but in a strange way its converse; it revalidates and reconstitutes place, locality and difference.

> Watts, "Mapping Meaning, Denoting Difference, Imagining Identity"

On June 30, 1995, an international workshop took place in Istanbul called "City and Social History Museums." Organized by the Economic and Social History Foundation of Turkey, it confronted the issues surrounding the project of a social history museum in Istanbul. In his discussion of the "mental challenges" for such a museum, one prominent historian discussed the problems and difficulties of writing and representing social history in a museum context. He concluded his talk by suggesting that the only way to overcome such challenges was "to find a proper way of remembering what has happened in the past," adding, "it is almost impossible to exaggerate what a social history museum for the city of Istanbul, properly handled, can contribute to this kind of mental revolution."[1]

Recent scholarship has shown that history, memory, and the past are not objective and fixed notions but contested and negotiated entities within the politics of the present (Boyarin 1994; Herzfeld 1991; Lowenthal 1990). As Lowenthal (1990, 1) suggests, "memory, history and relics of earlier times shed light on the past. But the past they reveal is not simply what happened, it is in large measure a past of our own creation moulded by selective erosion, oblivion and invention."

Since the mid-1980s, there has been a gathering consensus on transforming Istanbul into a "global" city. In this campaign, which is also a competition with other cities, the image of a city and its cultural identity have become critical; it is important to emphasize the particular qualities of places (Harvey 1993). With its Byzantine and Ottoman-Islamic heritage, Istanbul seems particularly advantaged in this competition: it can be marketed once again as "the East in the West and the West in the East" and "gateway to the Orient."

Although the identity of the city and its distinctive qualities become more and more important in this process, these are also contested entities. Especially in a city like Istanbul with multiple and multilayered pasts, the question of which past to preserve, mobilize, and market, and for whom, become crucial political questions. In this chapter, I explore the contestation over Istanbul's heritage and how these multiple pasts are reworked in the politics of the present. My focus is on the ways in which different readings of the past inform and shape the present debates over cultural heritage; the contested meaning of the past and its relics. Through these debates, I also examine the ways in which cultural heritage is used as symbolic capital by different groups for both local and global audiences. I also attempt to bring into focus the complex meanings heritage and historical preservation acquire: What constitutes heritage and historical value? Which heritage is preserved and for whom? Who has the power to construct, preserve, and/or obliterate history? Who owns this history? In an effort to answer these questions, I examine contestations over the cultural heritage of Istanbul as they have been played out in recent debates over the preservation and revitalization of the first "Europeanized" quarter of the city, Pera/Beyoglu.[2]

PERA

Pera and Galata, the only busy quarters of Constantinople, are of no land and of all lands, each country administrating its own laws, exercising its own religion, circulating its own money, distributing its own letters. Here are the various banks, consulates and embassies, bazaars, churches and chapels, including the dancing dervishes, who display themselves on stated days. Water sellers, porters, sedan-bearers, who carry you out to dine in a delightful sedan-chair, like the old ladies at Bath; Albanians, wood-cutters from Asia Minor, Persian donkey-drivers, Croats and Native Turks, form a polyglot population unparalleled in the world. If I were to enumerate all the articles sold in the street, or all the languages spoken, I could fill pages which would interest no one. (Elliot 1893, 12)

Pera was established as a Genoese trading colony in the thirteenth century. It had autonomy from the Byzantine Empire and controlled the trade route in the area. Byzantines referred to this area as "Pera," which means "beyond," "far away" in Greek (Rosenthal 1980). It was "far away" because geographically, it was located on the other side of the Golden Horn from the imperial city, and because the Byzantines did not have control over the area. When the Ottomans conquered Istanbul in the fifteenth century, this Genoese colony formed an alliance with the new dynasty but still kept its autonomy as a trading colony. It was in the beginning of the nineteenth century that the native minorities of the Empire, Greeks, Armenians, and Jews started to move into this neighborhood. A predominantly non-Muslim population of the empire lived there along with "Levantines" (the descendants of Europeans settled in Istanbul, some of them the offspring of intermarriages with other minorities).

For the Ottomans, Pera represented the "Frankish" Istanbul; by the nineteenth century, it had become the financial and entertainment center of the city. It was the area where the embassies were located; the Pera Palace Hotel was built here for the passengers of the Orient Express. In the late nineteenth century, in the course of the Ottomans' efforts to transform Istanbul into a "Western" city, Pera was designated as the experimental area for urban reform. The reforms that would be enacted in this area were intended to be a model of urban planning for the rest of the city (Çelik 1986; Rosenthal 1980). Although planning was not successful, Pera became the first "Europeanized" quarter of the city, dominated by symbols of modern living such as office buildings, banks, theaters, hotels, department stores, and multistory apartment buildings.

With the transformation of the Ottoman Empire into the Turkish nation-state, Istanbul lost its status as the capital. In contrast to the new capital city of Ankara, which became the symbol of the new republic, of secularism and enlightenment, Istanbul symbolized the decadent capital of the corrupt Ottoman Empire and its entrenchment in Islam. But even during this period, Pera remained as the symbol of "civilization"—"Europe in Istanbul" for the Turkish bourgeoisie. Over the years, given the changes in its population (due to non-Muslim minorities leaving the area and the country), it can also be seen as a symbol, in itself, of the transformation from empire to nation-state (Arkan 1993).

REMAKING OF PERA IN THE 1980S

The new wealth and confidence of Istanbul are being translated into art and culture. There is a new passion for Islamic and Ottoman art, Istiklal Street is again becoming as elegant as it was in the nineteenth century, when it was the cosmopolitan, French speaking Grande Rue de Pera. (P. Mansel, *Financial Times* supplement, "Istanbul and the Olympics," June 24, 1993)

As Robins and Aksoy (1995, 6) argue, what this *Financial Times* reporter observed in Istanbul is what he was intended to observe: an "elegant," "cosmopolitan," sanitized image of the city "appropriate for international acceptance and recognition." As Harvey (1989) suggests:

under the speeded up circulation conditions of hypermodernity, where little escape commodification, there is nothing so big, so encompassing, so over-shadowing, so enormous in its implications, that it cannot be commodified, that it cannot be represented as a consumption spectacle. Through imagery and massive architectural projects, even entire cities or metropolitan areas may be served up as market objects and all-encompassing spectacles. (271)

This was the challenge taken up by the mayor Dalan in the early 1980s, who was keen on "transforming Istanbul from a tired city whose glory re-sides in past history, into a metropolis full of promise for the 21st century" (Keyder and Oncü 1994, 409). With the series of highly publicized urban renewal projects of the 1980s, Istanbul became a consumption spectacle.

Pera was a prominent part of these urban renewal projects. The massive architectural project offered for Pera was a revitalization plan. The project was to turn the main street, Istiklal (Independence—the name reflects the nationalist imposition on urban toponomy) Avenue, into a pedestrian artery and open a parallel boulevard (Tarlabasi Boulevard), which would connect the central Taksim Square (the main square in the area) with the old city, for car traffic. Opening up this boulevard would require the de-molition of a large number of nineteenth-century buildings and relocating thousands of people who lived in them, generally in slum conditions.

What was referred to as "Tarlabasi demolitions" dominated the public discourse in the 1980s. The most visible actors of this debate seemed to be Dalan and the Chamber of Architects (MMOB), the main organized oppo-sition to Dalan's projects all over Istanbul. Although this struggle was pre-sented at the time as one between "modernizers" and "conservationists," I will argue that one should go beyond this dichotomous model to exam-ine the more complex and multilayered meanings that were implicit. The struggle over what the architectural heritage meant can be read at differ-ent levels. At one level, it demonstrates how history, the past and its relics, and different readings of the past become a symbolic capital that can be used in contemporary political struggles. As with every revitalization attempt, this one also entailed a certain reading and interpretation of the past. Questions such as what Beyoglu looked like in the past, which Beyoglu to revitalize and for whom, and what Beyoglu represents and to whom became critical political issues. Different actors and groups had different narratives about the past and the present; stories about the physical landscape served as commentaries on the social, political, and cultural landscape. At another level, these struggles over built environment brought into focus the pressing problems that Istanbulites faced today where notions of urban culture, urbanity, and urban identity are contested, negotiated, and reformulated, in an attempt to answer such questions as what it means to be Turkish, European, or Istanbulite.

For the mayor, Beyoglu was a place that needed to be cleaned, rehabilitated, and, in parts, demolished. The proposed highway project was to take care of the traffic congestion in the inner city, and clear the area from illegal prostitution and drug traffic. Any canon of historical preservation was seen as an impediment to development and to the transformation of Istanbul into a "world city." "We are against the preservation of historical sites if they prevent development," he argued. "We will implement the plan and if needed, we are ready to undertake any penalty. There are no historical buildings in Tarlabasi, at least the ones we have demolished are not historical. We will continue the demolition" (Üçok 1987, 78–79).

For the Chamber of Architects, the struggle against the demolitions became a symbol of political opposition against neoliberalism represented by Dalan and his party. Although the main focus of their campaign was the illegal nature of the demolitions and concern about land speculation, positions within this group diverged, too. As the head of the chamber put it at the time, "what they are doing is selling the city to multinational corporations. These places will be sold to private speculators and some will turn into multi-storey parking lots which in turn will draw more traffic into the area rather than solving the traffic problem." Some were more concerned about the racist overtones of the demolition rhetoric: "Besides the fact that these people don't know anything about urban planning, they are also racists. They demolished these buildings claiming that they were the houses of Armenians and Greeks. One of them gave a speech next to a bulldozer covered with a Turkish flag."

Some argued that these buildings represented a unique architectural heritage. "This architecture is a synthesis," argued one of the architects; "it is neither European nor Ottoman, it is Levantine architecture." They came up with an alternative tourism project to save these buildings from demolition. Besides its architectural value, this "synthesis," they argued, could be an asset for the whole city: "This is the only area in the city where you can find well-preserved buildings from the same period. Istanbul is a city within Europe with Eastern culture, we have to use this potential" (author's field notes).

The debate becomes more complicated when we examine the split among left-wing circles. For some on the left, these same buildings connoted yet another past. Rather than a "synthesis," the architectural heritage of Beyoglu symbolized nineteenth-century European capitalism and its alliance with the local population. It was the reminder of Europe in the Ottoman Empire. Here is what one of the prominent left-wing novelists at the time had to say about the demolition process:

> There are people who think that old Istanbul is destroyed, [but] the thing which is destroyed is Pera and Pera has nothing to do with Turkishness. . . . All of [the buildings] were designed by Armenian architects. They are built in Western style. All are imitations. Their demolition will not be a great loss. They are the product of slavery years. Just as in India today British buildings are irrelevant, it is really unnecessary to preserve these buildings where the managers of the Ottoman Bank, Jewish families, and Turkish compradors used to live, and which are now being used for illegal prostitution. . . . [T]hese places, which were all inhabited by foreigners, reminders of Europe in the Ottoman Empire, are not the product of Turkish culture. (Arkan 1993, 27)

This account is striking in its blunt nationalism and xenophobia, demonstrating both the power of the Turkish nationalist project and its ambivalent relationship with Europe. Until the 1980s, the left in Turkey was dominated by third-worldist nationalism; in fact, at times it became difficult to distinguish between left- and right-wing reaction against westernization. Although the Ottoman Empire was never colonized directly, it was articulated with the European markets through the intermediary positions acquired by the indigenous (local) non-Muslim communities, who were involved in trade. Their involvement allowed for the penetration of European influence in the absence of direct colonial presence. Galata and Beyoglu, being the financial center and the residential area for families who were involved in these commercial activities, symbolized this penetration. Although the Turkish nationalist project was willing to identify with European civilization, it was also defined as a struggle against European imperialism. As a result, the local non-Muslim minorities became the symbol of this imperialism and the targets of "ethnic cleansing."

When we turn to another set of narratives, which have been very much part of the public debate over Beyoglu, we see different versions of what Beyoglu symbolizes—Beyoglu: a symbol of "civilization" and "elegance"; Beyoglu: a "brothel"; Beyoglu: a "foreign" heritage. For people who consider themselves the real owners of the city, the real Istanbulites, Beyoglu, like many other neighborhoods in the city, represents the "peasantization of the city."[3] Although the Turkish nationalist project was and continues to be based on the glorification of the peasant as the core of the new nation-state, for the urbanites it was a different story when those peasants came to the cities to stay. According to this chronology, the change in the city started in the 1950s with migration from the countryside. The city was "conquered" by immigrants from Anatolia. Here is the way an older man, who comes from a well-known Istanbul family, describes this change:

> Istanbul was conquered again in the 1950s, five hundred years after Sultan Mehmet's victory, by the Anatolian invasion. These people brought their own civilization to my city, instead of trying to adapt to ours. I am sure that none of these people have ever been to an exhibition in their lives, all they think about is getting enough money for a summer house. We became a nation of *lahmacun*[4] eaters. Fifty years ago no one in Istanbul knew what lahmacun was, or, if we did, we called it pizza.

This was a "lost city," "conquered by the Anatolian invasion," and Beyoglu could no longer be identified with the Grande Rue de Pera, where one once saw "only well-dressed and well-behaved ladies and gentlemen." In this highly sanitized history, Beyoglu became the site of nostalgia in this "lost city." This sanitized and nostalgic version of Beyoglu's past is very much in line with the genre of "nostalgia" literature that became very popular at the time. Since the 1980s, there has been an abundance of best-selling books on old Beyoglu. The authors of these books and their audience agree that something had to be done to revitalize the district, to re-create the elegance of old Beyoglu. As a result, they would not object to demolitions, if these helped in this kind of revitalization. One of the writers, who used to live in the area, said:

> Beyoglu used to smell of perfume and sesame, now it smells of lahmacun. When I was a child, "to go to Beyoglu" was something. We would wear clean and neat clothes, and shave. Beyoglu was a mark of civilization. If these demolitions and closing down Istiklal Street to traffic will help to return the old ambiance, I don't have any objections to them.

But most had reservations about this revitalization attempt through what might be called a sociological critique. What had once made Beyoglu unique was its people; preserving or restoring the buildings was a futile attempt, because they were not populated by the same people anymore, and thus the "spirit" of the place was lacking. Disappointed with the revitalization project, one of the old inhabitants complained:

> [T]hese were places like the cafés in Paris, where people would sit and talk with friends, hold meetings, do business, and make appointments. These new cafés in Beyoglu are trying to re-create this era, but they are just not the same.

The spirit is lacking. I would like to live back in the golden days of Pera at the turn of the century; the days when Jewish, French, Greek, and Armenian people all lived together.

Another popular narration on Beyoglu was the "brothel" version. Some were puzzled by the rhetoric of elegance regarding Beyoglu. An actor, who lived in Beyoglu for twenty-three years, said, "Beyoglu has always been one of the most popular red-light districts of the city and still is. I don't really understand what elegance these people are talking about, and I don't see any reason why this neighborhood should not be cleaned up. I don't have any objections to the demolitions."

A compromise position was offered by an activist who was highly critical of Dalan's projects. He suggested that

we need neither the nostalgic nor the brothel version of Beyoglu. We need a national and clean Beyoglu. One cannot argue that since people are gone, we should also get rid of the buildings. We are neither Franks nor Levantines. We have to restore these buildings and open them up for tourists. We should be the hosts and Levantines should be the guests. (Gülersoy 1987, 46)

This heritage which has been identified with "Franks" and "Levantines" could be appropriated to create a "national" Beyoglu.

All these different positions reveal a complicated picture of the various meanings people attributed to this environment. What was Beyoglu all about? What did this built environment represent? Could one think of it as "heritage"? If so, was it worth preserving? Who was the audience for any kind of preservation and/or revitalization of this area? Some argued that it should be demolished because of what old Beyoglu was. Some suggested that it should be demolished to re-create old Beyoglu, although most had reservations about this revival. Some argued that it should be preserved because of what it was, emphasizing its architectural value and potential for tourism. But the questions of which Beyoglu, whose Beyoglu and for whom, still remained relevant.

THE LEGACY OF ISTANBUL AND PERA
IN THE ISLAMIST IMAGINATION

Within the Islamist discourse, the popularity and resurgence of the Ottoman past and of Istanbul take on a very different form. As a movement that challenges the Turkish nationalist project (which defines itself in opposition to the Ottoman past), the Islamic movement attempts to revitalize and resurrect that past. In this reading of Ottoman history, everything Ottoman becomes a symbol of Islamic ideology and can be utilized as a powerful political tool to challenge the Turkish secular enterprise. The Islamist aim is to resurrect the lost "glorious Ottoman past." Istanbul, the glorious capital of the empire, is a key symbol for this revival.

The Islamist discourse contains a chronology of the changes in the city in a form that is quite different from the one proposed by secularists. For them, the "real" history of the city starts with the conquest of Constantinople in 1453 by Sultan Mehmet. In this historical narrative, Istanbul represents the organic unity and justice of the Ottoman (read "Islamic") rule. The city embodies a pristine purity prior to the westernizing reforms of the nineteenth century. This view is blatantly expressed in a recent photograph album on Istanbul published by the Research Center for Islamic History, Art, and Culture called *Istanbul: A Glimpse into the Past:*

> These are the images of a period in which this city of the secret tales and unknown beauties was just beginning to be westernized. The city of Istanbul, known as "Der Saadet" (the door to happiness) in those days, was truly *a realm of happiness*, where the aesthetic taste of life which matured with time, made its inhabitants happy. . . . In this city, where each neighborhood had a different beauty, atmosphere, and view, buildings and people made up *a magical unity within the simplicity of daily life.* The disturbing pressure of a geometric order made up of grand boulevards, large parks, monumental fountains, palaces, memorials and stone bridges laid out in the logic of urbanism, and shared by so many famous contemporary cities was absent in Istanbul. . . . You will see in these photographs, Istanbul in its *authentic beauty* which survived until the beginning of the process of westernization. (Ihsanoglu 1992, 6–7; emphasis mine)

Given that Pera was the symbol of order and modernity for the Westernizing reformers when the first urban reform took place, it is not surprising that, within the Islamist discourse, this is exactly the place where the old harmony was first corrupted. As one Islamist intellectual suggested, "Pera, which is marketed as the symbol of Istanbul's civilization and elegance with words like 'culture,' 'civilizational heritage' and 'nostalgia,' is actually the place where our contemporary urban problems emerged" (Müftüoglu 1995, 9).

THE "RECONQUEST" OF THE CITY: THE MUNICIPAL ELECTIONS OF MARCH 27, 1994

> For cultural analysis and criticism, the contesting of the meaning of things or events is what centrally constitutes politics.
>
> Marcus and Fischer, *Anthropology as Cultural Critique*

As one might expect, the tensions described above take their most overtly political form during political contest. The municipal elections of March 1994 played extensively on these issues of identity and ownership. The following section is not intended to be an exhaustive analysis of the elections but rather a partial discussion of campaign themes pertinent to these issues and their specific ramifications for Beyoglu.[5]

During the election campaign, all the parties except Refah embraced the global city project. The candidate of the Social Democratic Party summarized what the election was about in terms of people choosing between making Istanbul a "Middle Eastern" city or a "European" one. Refah, with slogans of "just order" and "a new world," was the only party that alluded to the groups that were excluded by the global city project. Refah called for the "conquest of the city the second time" by those they referred to as the "real owners of the city."

The election results were a scandalous development for the secularist circles. Refah won the elections in most of the big cities, including the greater municipality of Istanbul and most of its districts. The destiny of the city would no longer be determined by the previous "owners of the city" but by the "outsiders" who had settled in its peripheries. Although there was a general sense of shock among the secularist circles after the elections, the results in Beyoglu were the most controversial of all. It was difficult for secularists to believe that in this entertainment center of the city, with its many bars, restaurants, and nightclubs, Refah could win. This victory meant different things for different groups. For secularists, it was the fulfillment of their worst nightmare. It was seen as a rupture in Beyoglu's history. The area was flooded with journalists trying to capture the "new" Beyoglu—Beyoglu "after Refah." Mainstream secular newspapers were full of articles and series titled "Now What in Beyoglu?" "Beyoglu until Refah," and "What Next in Beyoglu?" It was the end of Istanbul as they had known it, and Beyoglu was to be the most visible public space of this transformation.

But for Refah, the symbolism of Beyoglu took an interesting turn. Although it represented cosmopolitan degeneration, Beyoglu also became an essential symbol combining many of their campaign themes. For party officials, it was a crucial opportunity to demonstrate the "Ottoman model" of government, which they defined as the coexistence of different lifestyles in peace and harmony. Given this version of history, Beyoglu was the perfect place to resurrect the Ottoman model. For party officials, it was this model that had enabled people from different ethnic and religious backgrounds to live in peace and harmony for centuries. Beyoglu has been the symbol of this cosmopolitan coexistence of different groups under the tolerant Ottoman (read "Islamic") rule, and it was still the perfect place to resurrect the harmonious Ottoman past. Refah's self-representation was that it, just like Beyoglu itself, would embrace everyone. The new mayor, N. Bayraktar, was keen on underlining this theme both during the campaign and after the elections. His visits to all the synagogues and churches in the area were one of the highlights of the election campaign. After the elections, in an April 13, 1994, interview in the *Turkish Daily News* underlining this theme of tolerance and pluralism, Bayraktar noted, "The first thing I ordered was to clean the garbage around the Armenian church. Now how can you say that Refah is the party of Islam alone?"

CLAIMING THE QUARTERS BACK: DIFFERENT STRATEGIES

The postelection period manifested different strategies of various groups to claim Beyoglu and to inscribe new meanings in this old quarter. Through the analysis of these different strategies, one can see how discourses on the identity, the past, and the present of the city are both embedded and played out in social practice.

One of the fiercest political battles was over the Islamist party's proposal to build a mosque and Islamic cultural center in Taksim Square located in Pera. The choice of this square and the specific location of the mosque were not coincidental. It was to be located across from the Greek Orthodox Church and would also be competing with the Atatürk Cultural Center, a powerful marker of the Turkish nationalist ideology. As Ashworth (1990) argues, the relationship between nationalism and historical preservation has been particularly intimate. Nation-states have been forged by nationalist interpretations of the past, and what is considered to be "heritage" is largely determined by these interpretations. The Islamist movement, challenging the secular nationalists' interpretation of history and their version of Istanbul's legacy, established an alternative version of national heritage apart from, and in opposition to, the official one. This alternative reading of Istanbul's legacy and identity was emphasized by the mayor of the greater municipality in his defense of their mosque project. He pointed out that the idea was to highlight the Islamic identity of Istanbul. In an interview in *Yeni Zemin* on March 30, 1994, Erdogan argued, "Taksim is a crucial region for tourism in Istanbul. While visiting this area, one will have a sense of being in an Islamic city. When we gradually bring out the historical and cultural texture of our city, tourists who visit Istanbul will understand that they are in a city populated by Muslims."

The messages around this mosque were complicated and embodied different possibilities. For the party officials, the mosque represented the real mission and legacy of Istanbul, and it became a cultural resource that was mobilized for both their local constituency and a global audience. For the secularist circles, it was the last blow to the secular ideals of the republic, "an identity battle which would be played out in Taksim," as the head of the Chamber of Architects put it. For the financial sector and the government, which were interested in resurrecting and marketing a sanitized version of the Ottoman past, building a mosque in Taksim would jeopardize Turkey's chances of membership in the European Union.

People involved in tourism were not very convinced about the touristic potentials of this project. Here is what a travel agent had to say:

> Tourists who want to see the Islamic heritage go to the historical peninsula, anyway; the real and monumental Islamic architecture is there. The mayor is just trying to please his constituency, and he is using tourism as an excuse for that. Moreover, who says that tourists come here to see the mosques? They visit Istanbul to see the Byzantine heritage or Christian heritage. When they come to Beyoglu, they visit some churches and Galata Tower—that's it.

The controversy over the Taksim mosque took place at a time when the party officials declared that they were going to demolish Byzantine city walls surrounding the historical peninsula. The motivation was put rather bluntly by one of the party officials: "We don't want a Byzantine Istanbul." At a time when historical preservation has been an increasingly common phenomenon globally and has usually been framed as a sign of tolerance where everyone is expected to "join the global drive to preserve the great architecture of all periods and civilizations" (Herzfeld 1991, 121), this proposal of Refah led to a series of debates both within and outside Islamist circles. Many issues were at stake: whose heritage would be preserved, and for whom; cultural liberalism and tolerance (the main issues worrying the secularist circles, fulfilling their nightmare); potentials for tourism (demolishing part of the Byzantine heritage in a city that caters to tourists who visit the city mostly for the Christian heritage). Proposing this demolition at a time when official Turkey was trying to gain a stronger foothold in the European Union made it even more problematic. The prime minister at the time, Tansu Çiller, flew to Istanbul the following week and held a press conference in front of the city walls, in which she focused on the historical value of this heritage.

Refah's victory in Beyoglu meant different things for different groups. It was a chance for Refah to revive the "Ottoman model." For others, it was the end of Beyoglu as they knew it. But for both, Beyoglu was a key symbol. Most of the inhabitants of the area, however, were highly critical about this sense of rupture. For them it was politics as usual. Most preferred to talk about this change through a rhetoric of corruption. One of the inhabitants, a shop owner in the area, was furious about the activities of the secularists:

These people who try to save Beyoglu do not live here, and they don't know what it means to live here. That's why they see this as rupture. . . . All of these people steal, they are corrupt, but I guess Refah is just more clever. There is no such thing as "post-Refah" here. That's the problem of the outsiders. Life just goes on here.

"Yes, a lot of students come here. They tell us that these are historical buildings, but what is the use? That's what I want to know," the owner of the coffeehouse near the Galata Tower complained. His coffeeshop was crowded with students of architecture who were in the neighborhood to document and measure the buildings. He told me that this was routine. Students would come here, take pictures of the buildings, draw, and chat with him about the "historical value" of these buildings. Although he appreciated the students' efforts, he had a more utilitarian approach to the "historical value" of these buildings. "Tourists come here, but they just go up the tower—that's it. There is no place where they can spend money. These buildings have no use for us."

CONCLUDING REMARKS

Although in the new race between cities, "cultural identity" of a city becomes essential material and symbolic capital, these identities are "far from being eternally fixed in some essentialized past, they are subject to the continual play of history, culture and power" (Hall 1989, 70). Cultural heritage, preservation, and conservation become contested domains through which the past, present, and future are (re)worked and (re)formulated. The different positions, alliances, and strategies that I describe in this chapter bring into focus complex meanings heritage and historical preservation/revitalization acquire. These struggles are shaped not only by the (re)imaginings of the past but also by the forces of global politics and local identities in the present. Globalization is inscribed within particular localities and is reworked within particular social, cultural, and historical contexts. "To find a proper way of remembering what has happened in the past," as suggested by this historian during the museum workshop, would be a simpler question were the past, present, and future more uniform.

The struggle over Beyoglu brings up the issues of "who we are/who we were." What it means to be Turkish, European, "modern"; what becomes "local" and "global" are negotiated and contested around this built environment. Simultaneous (re)workings of local and global converge around the discursive and material practices around these buildings. Sometimes these buildings are "Turkish"; sometimes "European"; sometimes they are "Levantine"; sometimes they are "our own"; sometimes they are the "other."

In this era of global integration, as one of the nineteenth-century travelers to Istanbul suggested, Beyoglu is still "of no lands and of all lands." It embodies different pasts and presents for different actors. What Herzfeld (1991) has suggested in another context is relevant for Beyoglu, too. Monumental history has its place in Beyoglu, but Beyoglu has, and is a place in, many histories.

ACKNOWLEDGMENTS

This chapter has been presented in various forms at seminars at the Department of Anthropology at the University of California, Berkeley, and at the Middle East History and Theory Conference at the University of Chicago. I am grateful to the participants of these seminars and the conference for their comments on earlier versions of this essay. I am particularly indebted to Nezar AlSayyad, Sandra Cate, Nadim Copty, Kathleen Erwin, Chris Ertel, Mia Fuller, Aleks Göllü, Nelson Graburn, Aylin Küntay, Laura Nader, Alan Pred, Nancy Scheper-Hughes, Seteney Shami, and Sibel Zandi-Sayek for their critiques and encouragement. I would also like to thank Çağlar Keyder for his interest and patience.

NOTES

1. This and further references and descriptions come from my field notes unless indicated otherwise.
2. I use the names *Pera* and *Beyoglu* interchangeably to refer to the same area. Although these terms connote different meanings and histories, space limitations preclude any discussion here of the relevant politics of naming and boundaries.
3. A more common term used for the description of this change in the urban scene is *Arabesk;* see Stokes 1992 and chapter 7 in this volume.
4. One of the characteristic foods of southeastern Turkey, identified with Arab cuisine, *lahmacun* became a popular fast food among the new migrants into Istanbul and simultaneously an expression of resentment among middle and upper classes in the city.
5. See chapters 3 and 4 in this volume for a detailed discussion of the politics of local elections of March 1994 in Istanbul.

REFERENCES

Arkan, O. 1993. *Beyoglu: kisa geçmisi, argosu.* Istanbul: Iletisim Yayinlari.
Ashworth, G. J., and J. E. Tunbridge. 1990. *The tourist-historic city.* London: Belhaven.

Boyarin, J., ed. 1994. *Remapping memory: the politics of timespace*. Minneapolis: University of Minnesota Press.

Bright, C., and M. Geyer. 1987. For a unified history of the world in the twentieth century. *Radical History Review* 39: 69–91.

Çelik, Z. 1986. *The remaking of Istanbul: portrait of an Ottoman city in the nineteenth century*. Seattle: University of Washington Press.

Elliot, F. 1893. *Diary of an idle woman in Constantinople*. Leipzig: Collection of British Authors, Tauchnitz Edition.

Gülersoy, Ç. 1987. Dogu'ya giden teknede bati'ya kosuyoruz. *Sehir*, July 17, 46–49.

Hall, S. 1989. Cultural identity and cinematic representation. *Framework* 36: 69–70.

Harvey, D. 1989. *The condition of postmodernity: an enquiry into the origins of culture change*. Oxford: Blackwell.

Harvey, D. 1993. From space to place and back again: reflections on the condition of postmodernity. Pages 3–29 in J. Bird, B. Curis, T. Putnam, G. Robertson, and L. Tickner (eds.), *Mapping the futures: local cultures, global change*. London: Routledge.

Herzfeld, M. 1991. *A place in history: social and monumental time in a Cretan town*. Princeton, N.J.: Princeton University Press.

Ihsanoglu, E. 1992. *Istanbul: geçmişe bir bakiş*. Istanbul: Research Center for Islamic History, Art, and Culture.

Keyder, Ç., and A. Öncü. 1994. Globalization of a third-world metropolis: Istanbul in the 1980s. *Review* 17, no. 3, 383–421.

Lowenthal, D. 1990. *The past is a foreign country*. Cambridge: Cambridge University Press.

Marcus, G., and M. Fischer. 1986. *Anthropology as cultural critique: an experimental moment in the human sciences*. Chicago: University of Chicago Press.

Müftüoglu, F. 1995. Istanbul'un perisan hali ve islah calismalari. *Nehir* (March): 8–12.

Robins, K., and A. Aksoy. 1995. Istanbul rising: returning the repressed to urban culture. *European Urban and Regional Studies* 2, no. 3, 1–13.

Rosenthal, S. T. 1980. *The politics of dependency: urban reform in Istanbul*. Westport, Conn.: Greenwood.

Stokes, M. 1992. *The Arabesk debate: music and musicians in modern Turkey*. Oxford: Clarendon.

Üçok, A. 1987. Hepsini yikacagiz. Interview with B. Dalan in *Şehir*, March 1, 78–79.

Watts, M. J. 1991. Mapping meaning, denoting difference, imagining identity: dialectical images, and postmodern geographies. *Geografiska Annaler* 73B: 7–23.

3

Istanbul of the Conqueror
The "Alternative Global City"
Dreams of Political Islam

Tanil Bora

The 1994 local elections were widely regarded as the test whether Istanbul would be able to seize the opportunity to become a global city. The big bourgeoisie, along with the media and rising professional groups who fully subscribed to the global-city project, judged the preceding five years under the social democratic mayor Nurettin Sozen as lost due to his populist policies. That the candidate of the Islamic Welfare Party (WP) won the 1994 elections aggravated the defeatist spirit. The belief that the global-city project could no longer be revived became widespread. According to the pessimist prognosis, there would be a reversal of Istanbul's modernization, a turning inward that would delink the city from the world economy, leading to cultural provincialization.

There does, in fact, seem to be a contradiction between the global-city project and WP's political rhetoric; WP's practice, however, belies this facile expectation. Just as in their attitude toward modernization, the WP seems to be ready to appropriate the project while transforming its cultural signification. In this attempt, the more specific confrontations of the universal global-local dialectic become manifest and gain further complexity due to tensions and conflicts within political Islam itself. This chapter describes the attempt by political Islam to construct an alternative version of the global-city project and shows that in doing so, political Islam exhibits its own internal contradictions and is subject to dilemmas in terms of social and cultural policies that parallel the ones beleaguering the global-city project.

I will treat the subject at three complementary levels. In the first part I will analyze the location of Istanbul in Islam's grand narrative. Istanbul carries a symbolic burden in Islam's struggle with modernity, because of its special location in the frontlines of the "clash of civilizations." The second part concentrates on questions of cultural identity and describes the conflict and complementariness between Istanbul's "eastern" and "western," traditional and modern, dimensions. In the third part, I discuss whether these different aspects of Istanbul are regarded by the Islamic movement as irreconcilable.

CONSTANTINOPLE-ISTANBUL

In the popular historical narrative of both political Islam and Turkish nationalism, Istanbul is promised land. It is believed that had God wanted it, the prophet would have conquered the city; but Mohammed actually did give the good news that a great commander and his soldiers would take the city for Islam. Istanbul thus attains holiness, both because the prophet predicted its conquest and because it served as the capital of the Islamic Ottoman Empire. Istanbul is *the* Islamic city, the jewel of the Islamic universe. Within the same Islamic discourse, however, Istanbul is also believed to be lost, divorced of its true essence because of its experience of westernization. Westernization, according to this lament, has degenerated the city and has led to its forfeiting its soul and beauty. Thus, the construction of the westernized quarters of the city starting in the late eighteenth century is taken to signal the beginning of the contamination process (Muftuoglu 1995, 8–12). Republican policies in the twentieth century only added to this process by encouraging Western-type development and denuding the city of its authentic character.

Islamic ideology stipulates that Istanbul needs to be conquered again, owing to its degenerate state. In both Islamic and conservative-nationalist literature since the 1950s, the reconquest of Istanbul has been a popular theme. This theme first came on the agenda in 1953, on the occasion of the five hundredth anniversary of the Ottoman conquest, when one of the important centers of the right-wing intelligentsia, the Association for the Conquest of Istanbul, articulated an entire nostalgic discourse on Istanbul, the Islamic city. They thus laid the groundwork for an internal irredentist movement aimed at reconquest. The theme of "waiting for the generation that will reconquer Istanbul" was constantly on the agenda, and a right-wing student march of the time exhorted the youth, reminding them they were the same age as Fatih when he conquered the city.[1] Tayyip Erdogan, the WP candidate who won the elections for mayor with 23 percent of the vote in 1994, talked in the daily *Hurriyet* on December 26, 1993, about "the second taking of Istanbul, in the sense of bringing light onto darkness."

Since March 1994, Istanbul municipality, under the direction of an Islamic party, has been attempting to complete Istanbul's political capitulation with reconquest at social and cultural levels—to transform Istanbul into the object of Islamic nostalgia. How can the modern city be remade in the original Conqueror's image? The principal strategy is to emphasize Istanbul's identity as an Islamic city, through such symbolic acts as constructing a mosque and an Islamic cultural center in the middle of the city's modern window that opens to the West, Taksim. "This is the point of attraction of Istanbul's tourism. The person who comes there should be able to tell that he has arrived in an Islamic city. . . . As we succeed in uncovering the historical and cultural texture of our city, its Muslim character will become apparent to the visitors," said Erdogan in the March 1994 issue of *Yeni Zemin.*

From the point of view of Islamic ideology, two symbolic aspects are involved in this discourse of Fatih's Istanbul. One, the city signifies Ottoman (Islamic) hegemony, and this is what appeals to WP's constituency. Two, it also symbolizes Islamic justice and pluralism—of course, under Islamic domination. In this latter version espoused by some Islamic intellectuals who might be termed "liberal" or "civil society oriented," Istanbul is the ideal city of a multicultural society. Some intellectuals articulating this position in a neo-Ottomanist vein want to see Istanbul as a Balkan metropolis:

> It has to be underlined that the religious and spiritual center of the Orthodox world with its 250 million adherents is still the Patriarchate in Istanbul. Fatih, after his conquest of Istanbul, in his broad and farsighted vision, decreed that the Patriarch wear the Byzantine emperor's purple cloak, and that he should become the religious and political leader of Orthodox Christianity. In accordance with this position the Patriarch was accorded an equal status as the Islamic Sheikh-ul-Islam, and in official ceremonies carried the specter given to him by the Sultan. This privilege and its political implications are still important in our day. In Balkan languages Istanbul is still referred to as Tsarigrad, that is, the city of the Caesar. . . . Istanbul today is a central city which has the requisite character to again become Tsarigrad. (Bulac 1992, 17–18)

In the discourse underlining the Turkish-Islamic character of Istanbul's past hegemony, what is stressed is the generosity of the rule that accommodated a certain pluralism in the city. Thus, the city becomes a proud example of Islamic justice that allowed foreign and non-Muslim groups to live in peace. For E. H. Ayverdi, the president of the Conquest Association mentioned earlier, this is the epochal element in Istanbul's conquest: in the Middle Ages a conquered city's inhabitants would be sold as slaves, but Fatih allowed freedom to the people of Istanbul by decreeing a long-term payment of nominal ransom. He visited the Greek patriarch in his offices and engaged him in philosophical discussion, he accorded religious and commercial freedom to the Genoese who had enjoyed extraterritorial status under the Byzantines, and the Armenians probably owe their survival to Fatih's creation of a new patriarchate for them (Ayverdi 1985, 332–35). This extolling of a pluralism under Islamic hegemony simultaneously derides the pre-Ottoman city. Thus, the same author relates how the Ottomans found Byzantine art "valueless and artificial" and chose to rebuild the city from scratch and beautified it with their own works of art. It was the Muslim Turks who gave Istanbul its characteristic style in harmony with its essential structure. Ayverdi describes even the Byzantine church of Hagia Sophia (Ayasofya) as too monumental, with an unnecessary hugeness, and lacking the internal harmony and peaceful simplicity of Ottoman-Turkish architecture.

The arguments concerning Ayasofya and the Greek patriarchate, which have ever been on the Turkish political agenda, also reveal the conflicts between the two aspects of the discourse on "Fatih's Istanbul." The patriarchate in the nationalist and religious discourse is, on the one hand, the proud example of Islamic justice that allows it to survive in its bosom (and even a diplomatic card to play in gaining centrality for Istanbul in the Orthodox world, as mentioned earlier). On the other hand, the patriarchate is seen as an instrument, a fifth column of revanchism, of a Christendom that still cannot accept the loss of Istanbul to the Muslims. In the 1994 elections, WP candidates both paid visits of respect to the patriarchate and participated in demonstrations, chanting slogans designed to instill fear in the same. This contradiction reflects a real schizophrenia; it cannot be simply explained through the conjunctural demands of electioneering. The discussion on Hagia Sophia is even more revealing and constant. Fatih did not convert all the churches in Istanbul to mosques; he selected a few to do so, above all the cathedral of Hagia Sophia. Thus, Ayasofya became a symbol of Islam's victory over Christianity and the West; this is why political Islam never forgave Atatürk for decreeing Ayasofya a museum in 1935. This act was not a gesture of generosity akin to the pluralist tolerance of the Ottomans; it was a capitulation to the Christian West, a reversal of Islam's victory. Hence, its reconversion to a mosque has been a constant demand and mobilizing platform of the reconquest discourse. In fact, this demand, in the form of draft legislation to be discussed in the parliament (and guaranteed to incite passions), remains in the arsenal of Islamic deputies and is brought on the agenda as it becomes tactically expedient.

As a final example of the conflict between the beliefs of Islamic tolerance for diversity and victory over the Christian world, I will relate the discussion on the Byzantine walls of Istanbul. The subject was launched when the WP general secretary declared that "those Istanbul walls that are intact should be protected, but the ones that are lying in a rubble should be cleared away." The mayor added that those who disagreed with this statement were "on the side of the enemy" and that to defend the walls was "to

defend Byzance. We do not want an Istanbul in Byzantine appearance."
Referring to alleged destruction of mosques in western Thrace (where the
Muslim minority live in Greece), he said in the December 27, 1994, *Milliyet*,
"I will respect their houses of prayer only as much as they respect ours."

This reduction of the cultural heritage of Istanbul to something that
could be used as a diplomatic weapon in negotiations with neighboring
countries received much reaction and was widely interpreted by the secular media to show that under WP administration Istanbul would lose its
chance of becoming a world city. Metin Sozen, a professor of architectural
history, declared in *Hurriyet* December 30, 1994, that it was the Byzantine
walls which had led UNESCO to include Istanbul in the world heritage list.
Among the Islamic intelligentsia there were reactions also. Fehmi Koru,
writing December 27, 1994, in *Zaman*, said, "Istanbul is our greatest trea-
sure with its mosques, schools, and monuments; to say that these [Islamic
buildings] are our heritage should not mean to discard the rest. We have
to pay our respects to our right to live in these lands." The mayor retreated
in front of this onslaught and declared in *Hurriyet* on January 8, 1995, that
what he had said about the walls had to do with priorities: "The walls are
a historical presence; of course, we have to protect them. But, we should
first restore and bring to light Islamic monuments; only after that we will
repair the walls."

The construct of Fatih's Istanbul is one where Islamic and nationalist
ideology intersect; it is one of the key motifs in the definition of the cultural identity targeted by the politics of these groups (Tapper and Tapper
1987). National pride in Islamic discourse presents Istanbul as the "last
and only capital city of the Islamic world" (as reported in *Ittihad-I Islam*,
May 1995), thus pointing to the special place of Turkey and the role Turks
play in the glory of Islam. The Ottoman nostalgia mentioned earlier feeds
into this privileging argument. Second, the Islamic wing, like its nationalist counterpart, shares in the paranoid existential fear that posits a
chronic Western conspiracy aimed at "the last Turkish state," with the
revanchiste goal of recapturing Constantinople. Thus, the idealized fan-
tasy of "Istanbul of the conqueror," ever present in Islamic discourse, is
tinged with a nightmarish perception of threat and conspiracy that
requires constant vigilance and militancy.

FATIH-HARBIYE

Dream city versus nightmare city: this tension is reflected in political Islam's approach toward Istanbul not only because of the city's symbolic situation but also because it is simply a large metropole, a chaotic jungle.
Thus, it is a world of loneliness and alienation, of "false sociability," full of

individuals "who have lost their social identities and relate to each other mechanically" (Akdogan 1995, 32). Political Islam shares this communitarian theme with other conservative movements. In addition, however, Istanbul is suspect because in its heritage is something "Byzantine," with all the duplicity and conspiracy that implies. In the Islamic imagination this contamination is compounded because, as the premier locale of Ottoman modernization, Istanbul was the outpost of the West. As such it was the scene of dualities representing the modern-traditional, East-West conflicts. Both the modernists and the traditionalists found in Istanbul the concrete correlatives to their arguments. Naturally there were those who argued for the elusive "synthesis" of the East and the West, also deriving their arsenal from the world of Istanbul. Hence, the city was the backdrop to the ever-lasting debates on Turkish modernization. The novelist Peyami Safa, himself initially a proponent of "synthesis" then becoming a traditionalist, based his *Fatih-Harbiye* (1931) on this conflict. Fatih is a Muslim neighborhood where traditional culture survives, whereas Harbiye symbolizes all those districts that are in the throes of modernization/westernization. The hero of the novel wavers between the two localities, symbolizing Turkey's own dilemmas of cultural identity. It is this duality that political Islam would like to highlight today.

During the municipal elections of 1994, WP's campaign addressed the losers in the metropole, those in the periphery of Istanbul.[2] The poor of the shantytowns who were excluded spectators of Istanbul's globalization, with the fear of getting lost in the metropolitan labyrinth, and betrayed by the social democrats because their campaign and mayoral candidate were also identified with the globalization strategy, turned to WP, whose candidate expressed all their frustration, anxiety, and resentment (Coskun 1994). Only the future mayor defended the legitimacy of shantytowns; it was revealed that he himself had been convicted of attempting to clear a forest area to build six illegal houses. The press uncovered that this particular *gecekondu* was going to be luxury housing; it was called a *villakondu* by the journalists. This led to a media campaign that argued that the builders of shantytowns were not the poor and the downtrodden but thugs pillaging land and appropriating urban rent, thus attempting to identify the land mafia with the new immigrants they exploited—the poor and the downtrodden. The accusation leveled against Erdogan, that he was, in fact, wealthy, was seen by the people of the shantytowns as an elitist slur. When Erdogan declared that he actually lived in a rented house and that people building illegal housing should not be blamed until the problems leading them to migration were solved, the contest was clinched in favor of WP.

The fact that Erdogan originated in a neighborhood in "deep" Istanbul, combining elements of traditional and lumpen, and that he used to be a minor soccer star in the amateur league (his sobriquet was "Beckenbauer," indicating that he had attained Western levels in technique), completed his profile that was so attractive to the metropolitan periphery. While the election campaign was continuing, Cem Ozer reported in *Hurriyet* on October 30, 1994, that an anti-WP talk show host, in an attempt to deride the candidate, declared that Erdogan represented those who benefited from what Istanbul offered, without becoming citizens of the city. This was on the mark: WP's strategy concentrated on the attempt to impart a new cultural identity to those excluded and marginalized by the imagery of the global city, on the basis of a new symbolism building on the imagery of a folk Istanbul or deep Istanbul.

In terms of his location within the Islamic Welfare Party, the mayor of Istanbul is a social democrat and redistributionist toward the urban peripheral poor. When tinged with resentment against the "global" lifestyle, however, the social-democratic allusions of the platform become populist-fascist. The reaction against extreme inequality in consumption patterns exhibited by the contrast between "globalized" neighborhoods and the shantytowns becomes a severe moralism against any kind of entertainment and fun. Islamic ghettos in marginalized shantytowns may well be mobilized to a blind anger against the wealthy "sites," gated compounds within which the globalized population engage in hyper-consumption. That the urban elite found the funds for conducting international culture and art festivals but the money was not forthcoming for the celebration of the anniversary of the conquest was one complaint of the nationalist-conservative intelligentsia in the 1970s. Now, the mayor banned the selling of alcohol in restaurants owned by the municipality; he declared that ballet is immoral and would not be funded if the municipality has anything to do with it; he announced that celebrating the new year is a Western and decadent custom. All this makes for a confrontation where the symbols of globalization are vilified as cultural signs of a foreign/infidel invasion.

This is a cultural *"jihad"* against the modern and cosmopolitan facet of Istanbul and, from the point of view of the Islamic movement, part of the reconquest. It glorifies the resistance of deep Istanbul against the revival of Byzance and its intrigues by the westernizers. Istanbul has been able to preserve its profound essence against all onslaught: "Do not despair when you watch young girls running from one discotheque to the other. . . . Istanbul is a city of meaning which cannot be contaminated by any evil or damnation. Thousands of holy men lie in its cemeteries, and the ezan is chanted thousands of times in its skies" (Haluk Nurbaki in *Vakit*, November 20, 1994). It is thus that political Islam expands and reproduces the Fatih-Harbiye duality. The secular political class play their own allotted part in this process: immediately after the elections, *Sabah* reported on April 1, 1994, that the governor of Istanbul (appointed from Ankara) declared that Istanbul was Turkey's window to the West and he would not allow the Islamic party to disturb the denizens' peace, thus contributing to reinforce the elite-mass dimension of the Fatih-Harbiye conflict.

The fact that WP won the elections in Beyoglu (Pera), which has been the singular district encapsulating the Western facet of Istanbul, has imparted new momentum to the Fatih-Harbiye duality. In traditionalist literature Beyoglu has always been seen as the stronghold of foreign cultural invasion and cosmopolitan degeneracy. One popular nationalist-Islamic agitator of the post–World War II era had described Beyoglu as a "den of disease." In this conception Beyoglu was the temptation to contaminate the Turkish-Islamic purity, it was a whore, an enclave of evil:

> Istanbul has been in the hands of the Turks since 1453. . . [but] Beyoglu has remained a tumor in the Empire's brain, a syphilitic presence. . . . Beyoglu is the entryway of western imperialism. . . It is a dagger on its side that sucks the blood, the labor, the essence of the Turkish nation, of all eastern nations. . . It is a disease that eats away at national unity. (Serdengecti 1992, 112–13)

Hence, the "taking" of Beyoglu was of as much symbolic import as the victory in metropolitan Istanbul itself. In addition, the votes that brought victory to the WP mayor originated in the margins of the district that the visitors to the entertainment centers, the *flâneurs* of the grande rue, and the cinema, theater, restaurant, and café goers hardly ever see, thus underlining the center-periphery conflict that underpins WP's victory. Meanwhile, the WP mayor has in fact left the bars, taverns, and other dens of entertainment alone, much in the spirit of the Conqueror, who permitted the survival of the Genoese-controlled district in the fifteenth century—one inference from this generosity being the implicit statement that the new Genoese, the infidels, are being tolerated.

How should this tolerance be interpreted? Is it the proud generosity of the victor, a pluralism theme park, a pragmatic tactical stand, or is it the seduction of the modern that attracts the Islamic politicians into the soft and accepting metropolis? An Islamic romantic of the 1930s had already pointed to the danger when he compared the freedom, indulgence, and the privacy accorded by the metropole to the spiritual bliss that the believer could find in the courtyards of the great mosques (Arik 1974, 181–20). Is it possible today to mystify the dynamism and awe of the great city in the name of an Islamic imperial mission? Can the profane aura of modernism be instrumentalized for purposes of representing the Islamic sacred? If such an option is even remotely possible, it is again because Istanbul's potential as a global city is first admitted.

CENTER-PERIPHERY

As the power of modernity makes Istanbul into a world city, the nodal export commodity in the increasingly globalized economy, the Islamic imaginary engages in the dream/nightmare ebb and flow described earlier. During the election campaign, the WP candidate for mayor was the only one to be able to distance himself from the global-city project. While all the other candidates, including the social-democratic, were trying to criminalize immigration and illegal housing, blaming the newly urbanized for lowering the quality of the human stock, Erdogan's rhetoric was in the direction of legitimating the peripheral population. His party's organizational superiority in the shantytowns and its anticosmopolitan stance was interpreted as another instance of embracing the popular against the global-city project.

But the attainment of power changed everything; the logic of economic rationality came to dominate and soon altered the new local government's thinking about the city as a business enterprise. Six months after the election, the mayor declared in New York (during an international conference he attended) that "in order to prevent migration to Istanbul, an entry visa may be imposed as they used to have in Ottoman times" (as quoted in *Sabah*, August 24, 1994). In a special issue of the Islamist journal *Nehir*, to commemorate the first anniversary of the elections, Islamic intellectuals and municipal technocrats wrote about "Istanbul: a city in search of identity," but the principal concerns were material problems such as infrastructure and migration. Articles argued that illegal housing should never be given amnesty, that secondary centers outside the metropolitan area should be encouraged as buffer zones against migration. "The lawlessness, normlessness, and absence of order and priority that dominated the world of the migrant," which made it impossible for him to be truly urban, was deplored. Authors warned that populism would lead to fiscal crisis. Other Islamic intellectuals led a campaign to recover the aesthetic values of Islamic elitism against the populist version. In fact, the job of reconfiguring historical buildings now used as cafés and restaurants and operated by the municipality was given to an outspoken Islamic aesthete. The WP had initially complained that these were managed with the intention of "protecting Istanbul from Istanbulites"; in their critique they ended up resorting to another elite sensibility.

These attempts to save Istanbul from provincial barbarians, coming so soon after the "reconquest," carry a dimension of obtaining accreditation for the WP with the system and the state. The new Islamic elites thus broadcast the message that they will not allow ruffians and peasants to upset established balances or to challenge the all-important appearance of stable power. Istanbul is the key to WP's bargain with the established structures of power—primarily because the city is the locus of capital. As the Islamic movement seeks to come to an understanding with the Turkish bourgeoisie, it also has to accept the global-city project of big capital. In fact, there is no possibility of aligning with a "small and medium-scale" Anatolian capital against Istanbul's big bourgeoisie, because the more successful pro-Islamic bourgeoisies have already scaled the ranks of big capital and cannot any longer oppose the global-city project whose economic rationality is apparent.

A second factor drawing the WP to the global-city project follows from the party's developmentalist ideological heritage. Industrialization (preferably heavy), high technology, and the goal to become an "Islamic superpower" always occupied a prominent place in Turkish Islamic thought. Although the older generation of WP grandees continue to espouse these pre-"postindustrial" goals, the more contemporary technocrats in the party have succeeded in transforming the economistic goals to adjust to the new world economy and thus to conceive of Istanbul as a potential source of accumulation in high-technology sectors and in services. Thus, the mayor wanted to clean a red-light district in the city's center and to establish there "the largest electronics center in the Balkans" (as quoted in *Hurriyet*, December 26, 1993). Another Islamic ideologue went further, beyond a productionist thought, and mused about "Istanbul leaving behind its industrial role in order to become an international commercial center. It should become a center of learning as it was in Ottoman and Byzantine times. It should also house the world's largest [financial] exchange" (Cakir 1994, 147). Another Islamic author is more concrete in his expectations that Istanbul should become "the center of attraction of the Balkans, the Black Sea basin, and Turkic states" and will thus take its place

among second level world-cities such as Los Angeles, Chicago, Paris, or Frankfurt. . . . For this to be achieved, Istanbul should become secure, clean, and livable. It should also be able to attract a high-skilled labor force. This should be the immediate goal: to make Istanbul into an international center of science, art, and culture. (Kutlu 1995, 29)

According to the author, this would mean that Istanbul would reattain the status that it held during Ottoman times. It appears that the global-city project is readily internalized by Islamic politicians, with the addition of an alternative signification. The alternative meaning requires that the global city formula serve the purposes of an Islamic or neo-Ottoman hegemony over the region; in fact, Istanbul may be conceived of as a geocultural[3] focal point in the "clash of civilizations." The intention, however, is not to attribute a role to the metropolis that would isolate the Islamic cultural area from the rest of the world. On the contrary, because the catchment area is supposed to include the Balkans, Transcaucasia, Georgia, and Ukraine, it is difficult to understand how this cosmopolitan conception and its probable implications in population movements accord with the conception of an Islamic global city.

Islamic commentators seem also to pay attention to the fragmentation and decentering that accompany globalization. An Islamic author distinguishes between a Byzantine, an Islamic-Ottoman, and a modern Istanbul and argues that we cannot talk about a single category of Istanbulites. He points to the Istanbul of the provincials as the source of the problems but accepts the existence of a "modern" city, and he argues for the preservation of the old city within the walls as the real Istanbul that "reflects the Ottoman-Islamic identity." He refers to the tolerance toward 'the people of the book' in the Koran to advocate a post-modern collage—a position very much in conformity with the image of the global city, which may be summarized as 'to each their own Istanbul' (Dursun 1995, 14–15). A final instance of appropriating the global-city project surfaced in the mayor's angry rejection of an attempt by the government to take back some municipal authority. He argued that corrupt and clientelistic Ankara, in attempting to strengthen its hold on Istanbul, was an impediment to the city's success in becoming globalized.

All this willingness on the part of Islamic politicians to accommodate the global-city project carries certain risks in terms of its mass support. The victory of modern Istanbul over folk or deep Istanbul implies a marginalization of WP's electoral base, who also wanted to participate in the division of the massive urban rent that the city generates. If Islamic populism remains symbolic (e.g., at the level of circumcision ceremonies for the poor), a popular resentment against the ready acceptance by the Islamic elite of the global-city project, with all the attending cultural contestation mentioned here, may not be too far off.

CONCLUSION

The great conservative novelist Ahmet Hamdi Tanpinar, an unabashed lover of the city, had acknowledged that Istanbul's future would be determined by its economic prospects: "it is certain that its geography and resources will confer a new life, the life of freely laboring inhabitants, to the city. . . . Istanbul is impatient for this new life and its new values" (Tanpinar 1972, 149, 259). The Islamic administrators of today also bow to economic logic and to the requirements of the global-city project. Their anti-systemic radicalism that was so prominent during the election period retains only a symbolic presence. The seduction of world-city status articulates with imperial dreams and grandeur and becomes an element of

Islamic-nationalist rhetoric. As elitism gains over populism, Istanbul also becomes a mirror of the fragmentation and uneven development of Islamic politics. Within this fragmentation it will be difficult for the WP to retain the allegiance of its electoral base, because its populism finds no counterpart in its increasingly economic- and logic-driven policies. Its only offering directed to its social base is a radicalized identity politics that can only go so far in covering over the material polarization that global-city–oriented policies necessarily imply. This might well lead to a realignment where within the polarized cityscape, the marginalized and the criminalized attempt to find a new expression of their plight in a new radical politics, of either an Islamic or traditional left coloring.

NOTES

Translated by Çağlar Keyder.
1. The poem is by Arif Nihat Asya. It asks, "You are at the same age as Fatih when he conquered Istanbul, why are you torn internally when you are of the stuff that is a banner on ramparts?"
2. This political inclination in poor and/or proletarian neighborhoods was registered in the research conducted by Boratav et al. in 1991; see Boratav (1995).
3. See Wallerstein (1991) for this concept. The Turkish translation of this book has been published by an Islamic publisher.

REFERENCES

Akdogan, Y. 1995. *Nehir* 18 (March).
Arik, R. O. 1974. *Meseleler*. Istanbul: Hareket Yayinlari. (Originally published 1932)
Ayverdi, E. H. 1985. *Makaleler*. Istanbul: Fetih Cemiyeti.
Boratav, K. 1995. *Istanbul ve Anadolu'dan sinif profilleri*. Istanbul: Tarih Vakfi.
Bulac, A. 1992. *Yeni donemin esiginde*. Istanbul: Bosna Dayanisma Grubu.
Cakir, R. 1994. *Ne seriat ne demokrasi*. Istanbul: Metis.
Coskun, Z. 1994. Istanbul neyi seçti? *Birikim* 60 (April): 11–29.
Dursun, D. 1995. *Nehir* 18 (March).
Kutlu, M. 1995. *Nehir* 18 (March).
Muftuoglu, F. 1995. *Nehir* 18 (March).
Safa, P. 1931. *Fatih-Harbiye*. Istanbul: Semih Lütfi.
Serdengecti, O.Y. 1992. *Mabetsiz Şehir*. Istanbul: Görüş Yayinlari. (Originally published 1949)
Tanpinar, A. H. 1972. *Beş Şehir*. Istanbul: Basbakanlik Kultur Mustesarligi.
Tapper R., and Tapper, N. 1987. Thank God we're secular. Pages 51–78 in L. Caplan, ed., *Studies in religious fundamentalism*. London: Macmillan.
Wallerstein, I. 1991. *Geopolitics and geoculture: essays on the changing world-system*. Cambridge: Cambridge University Press.

4

The Historical Construction of Local Culture
Gender and Identity in the Politics of Secularism versus Islam

Yael Navaro-Yasin

WHO IS "TURKISH"?

I will begin with an anecdote of an encounter between two women who independently went to visit the Ayasofya museum in Istanbul on a March afternoon in 1994. At that time, there had been some public controversy over Ayasofya, which had originally been built as a Byzantine church, transformed into a mosque upon the Ottomans' conquest of Istanbul, and finally converted into a museum in Turkey's early republican period. Islamists have been demanding ever since that Ayasofya be turned back into a mosque. Ayasofya is at the top of the must-see list in tourists' itinerary of Istanbul. While for most secularist Turkish visitors, it represents a museum of "a time past," an Islamist visiting Ayasofya would most likely be lamenting its former state as a mosque.

On the day on which my account takes place, two women, one veiled, the other not, were standing in line to enter the Ayasofya museum. The short-haired one, dressed in a skirt to her knees, a trimly fit blouse, and a short coat, asked the other woman, dressed in a black veil from head to toe, whether this was the line for tickets to the museum. The veiled woman was surprised. "You speak Turkish?" she asked in amazement. "Yes, I am Turkish," asserted the short-haired woman, put off by the question. "Oh! You don't look Turkish. You look like a Westerner," said the veiled woman. "You don't look Turkish either," said the other. "I thought you were an Arab." "Oh!" said the veiled woman, "thanks to God, we are Turkish and Muslim." "Well, we are too," said the short-haired woman. Both these women were claiming exclusive "nativity" through their own respective manners of dress and public comportment, mutually ascribing "foreign-ness" to one another.

I start my chapter with this anecdote only to emphasize that this sort of voiced disagreement about the content of "Turkishness" is extremely com-monplace in the public culture of contemporary Turkey. Not only living out their everyday practices with the lack of consciousness that Pierre Bour-dieu's notion of "habitus" suggests, people in Turkey also abstractly think and comment about their "culture." This chapter explores the implication of politics of gender in competing discourses of "nativity to Turkey." The Turkish term for *nativity* (*yerellik*) was overinterpreted in the period when I was doing my field research. *Yerellik* contains an implicit reference to place, signifying "locality" or ingrainment to the land. It also, in contem-porary Turkish, is used to signify "local culture." In the 1990s, *yerellik* was used as antonym for *yabancilik*, standing for "foreignness" or "the state of being alien." Yet there was no consensus on the content (the signified) of this notion. There was, in the 1990s, a proliferation of arguments over the meaning of nativity in Turkey. There was intense public discord over what "being native to Turkey" or "acting like a native" meant. The debate was at its most acute on the axis of secularist/Islamist politics of identity.

It is no secret that in terms of the public presentation of life worlds, Is-lam's challenge of secularism focuses on the position of women. In fact, how women are dressed, how they behave in public, how much they are covered becomes the most important index of adherence to Islam, and the rejection of the secularist order. As they were coming to sort and argue the differences among themselves, secularist and Islamist women found that they had to justify their lifestyles in claiming to organically belong to Turkey. In doing so, women often wrote their opponents' ways of life out of their own respective narratives of "nativity to Turkey," or what could also be termed "locality" or "authenticity." In the 1980s, Islamist women legitimized their assumption of the veil through a version of a nationalist discourse (i.e., the Turkish-Islamic synthesis).[1] They argued that they were reviving what was "Turkey's local culture," which they said "had been re-pressed through years of westernization." Those women who did not cover, Islamists argued, had lost their authenticity, were copying the West, were no longer behaving like natives.

In political and ethical struggle with Islamists, secular feminists did not at first realize that they had to justify their lifestyles through a competing discourse of "being native to Turkey." For many feminists, westernization signified women's liberation, freedom from the constraints of Islam. Yet, as they interacted with and lost ground to Islamists in the activist arena, secular feminists realized that they had to claim an organic belonging to Turkey to be convincing. They had to create their own discourse of Turkey's local culture. Women found that their concerns about their rights and freedoms had to be articulated through narratives of belonging, nativity, or autochthony.

If we were to endeavor writing a social history of the concept of culture in the Turkish domain, in the manner that Raymond Williams did for England, we would be able to point to historical periods when a public contestation over the concept of culture rose to the surface. At certain points in the history of Turkey, culture was transformed from something to be unconsciously practiced to an abstracted concept to be also publicly discussed, dissected, theorized, and contested. My ethnographic work is based on one such important period, the mid-1990s in Istanbul, when, with the rise of a significant branch of the Islamist movement to assume municipal power, the concept of local culture was reproblematized in public debates. The foundational years of the republic, the 1920s and 1930s, had been an important period for the debate of the question "What is Turkey's culture?" So have the 1990s been, with the rise of the Islamist Welfare Party to represent an electoral plurality in Turkey's version of "democracy." Once again, people across class, gender, and ideologically based differences have become anthropologists of themselves, arguing over what *nativity* signifies, what sort of everyday comportment, manner of walking in the streets, dressing, or talking to strangers the idea of "Turkish authenticity" requires, or what sort of worldview, belief, or statecraft "Turkish locality" calls for.

Because time runs so fast and change is so emergent in Turkish public culture, the ethnographic material I will present in this chapter should be understood to be about a particular historical contingency: on March 27, 1994, the Islamist Welfare Party won municipality elections in Istanbul and a majority of other cities throughout Turkey. This chapter is an account of a dominant public discourse on "local culture" in the one month that preceded and the one month that followed the municipal elections of 1994.

Before I present ethnographic detail, I would like to voice my theoretical, political, and existential discomfort with a certain genre of "progressive" or relativist studies on Turkey, which in wanting to be critical of the devastating cultural effects of westernization on the Ottoman Empire and Turkey ends up by almost celebrating the Islamist movement in opposition to secularists. Kevin Robins (1996, 66), for example, writes, "As much as it has been shaped by the assimilation of western culture, modern Turkish identity 'is also a product of various negations': Turkish society became practiced in the art of repression." Later he argues that in the 1980s, with the rise of the Islamist movement, "once the psychic repression had been lifted, lost identities and experiences began to be recovered" (74). There is a discourse of "authenticity" in this account, one that resembles Orientalist accounts that, while appreciating Turks well above other Muslim groups for their efforts to "civilize" themselves, always suggested that

Turks were not and could never really be European, that in westernizing their ways they were putting aside what was essentially true (i.e., Muslim/Eastern) about them.

In this chapter, I take issue with "nativist ethnography," a term coined by Adam Kuper in critique of the work of a whole lineage of anthropologists who have institutionalized the task of anthropology as the description of "native culture" (that which is presumably unbeknown to the natives themselves) or as the unearthing of "the native's point of view" (Kuper, 1994, 544). Recent nativists have been especially influenced by the work of Edward Said (1978) (perhaps the favorite Western author of Islamic intellectuals in Turkey), where they have endeavored to challenge Orientalist depictions of native lives, paradoxically implying and describing a prediscursive "truth" about the "local culture" under study. While Orientalist or Western depictions of "local culture" have been criticized as constructions in this literature, native articulations, native voices, practices, and worldviews are presented almost as "the truth" or as "the reality" behind the prejudiced images. Thus, the former representations were misrepresentations, and the anthropologist's task is to create a narrative that will be loyal to "the truth of native culture." Yet, what is native or what is local culture are highly contested issues.[2] Indeed, as my introductory anecdote reveals, there are competing discourses produced and consumed by the very people whose actions we were enjoined to study as transparent reflections of nativity or "the cultural or structural truth of a certain place." As the natives of different places, we may enact nativity; we may assume it, begin to wear it like a veil, an embroidered blouse, a fez, or a long beard. In such circumstances, what the nativist ethnographer identifies as local or native might only be the effect of a (nationalist and/or revivalist) discourse that disciplines certain "truths" about local culture and nativity and rejects others perhaps as deeply rooted and "authentic."

This is not to say that the existential potency of assumed nativity for those who practice it or those who have internalized it is irrelevant. Consciously or unconsciously assumed identities are lived and felt as if they are real and authentic.[3] This is why Turkish women who have only recently assumed the veil feel so poignantly assaulted when they are ousted from secular institutions on the grounds of their identity, as do women whose mothers and grandmothers used to cover and who have assumed pants and T-shirts as their own manner of presenting themselves in public. These women do not feel that they have "repressed their true selves"; they consider jeans and blouses as also part of their authentic selves. Thus, nativist anthropologists have unwittingly reproduced certain versions of nationalism and cultural revivalism in the non-Western places that they study.[4] Taking the "East versus West" dichotomy to be real, they have mostly identified those elements least transformed by westernization as examples of "the native's point of view" and their "progressive" cultural relativism has dangerously over-lapped with indigenous cultural conservatisms.

My ethnographic strategy is to study the discursive enactments and con-testations over "native culture." The question, therefore, becomes not what is (or was) culturally indigenous to Turkey given its history of state-enforced westernization and secularization but what is being reformu-lated as "local" after years of westernization. Undoubtedly this reformu-lation gains urgency owing to the accelerating impact of globalization that forces the inhabitants of Istanbul to come to terms and to take position vis-à-vis all the crosscurrents of material and cultural flows that engulf them.

TALES OF NIGHTMARE

The municipal elections of March 1994 did not merely consist of a compe-tition between political parties in promising to better manage the city's in-frastructure. The campaign was a rivalry in politics of culture. As the win-ning potential of the Islamist Welfare Party became obvious in early 1994, all the other political parties claimed to be the sole guarantee for the future of secularism in Turkey. It was one of the first times that an Islamist group was going to assume significant official power in the history of republican Turkey. Its political rivals charged that the Welfare Party was threatening the meaning and unity of "the State of Atatürk" as founded in 1923 and in-stituted through decades of secularist and modernist practices.

When the election was won by the Welfare Party, there was an atmo-sphere of uncertainty, sometimes ridden by panic and serious anxiety. What would happen to life in Turkey now that an Islamist political party had obtained the municipality? An older woman who grew up under the strictly secularist regime of the early republic was complaining of higher blood pressure.[5] A young university student said that she was walking around with "zero morale." For a few days, many people were fearful of passing through places that were to be administered by the Islamist Wel-fare Party. No one was sure as to what to expect of public life on the streets of Istanbul next.

Times of social hysteria incite much creative imagination. Fearfully awaiting what was upcoming for Istanbul, people exchanged many jokes and stories; Welfare's victory was largely and more significantly received through the medium of humor or, more precisely, black humor, on the part of its opponents—the sort of humor that exaggerates an anticipated calamity to render it ridiculously funny in order to lighten up the seriously anxious. I observed that it was in the domain of this informal production and sharing of humor and rumor that secularist discourse on Islam had its force. Moreover, Islamists were aware of this mode of discoursing about them. And they, in turn, joked about what they called secularists' exaggerated "nightmares."[6]

The domain of humor and rumor reflects discursive knowledge in the form of "flashes," in Walter Benjamin's (1968) sense of the term. The jokes and the gossip are like glimpses of "memory as it flashes up at a moment of danger" (255). More than in seriously contemplated talk, humor and rumor reveal a precipitation of past republican discursive forms in the present. My ethnographic examples reveal that Islam was conceived, on the part of secularist jokers and gossips, as a plea for the rejuvenation of "local" and "native" (*yerel*) as against "contemporary" and "civilized" values (in Turkish the word *çağdas* encompasses both these notions). What I will now recount are examples of humorous secularist projections about upcoming Islamist mayors' notions of locality and nativity.

On one of those first few days after the election results when the Islamist Welfare Party won, a secularist businessman ironically said, "My attire is set. I already have a beard. I will buy prayer beads to carry and I am fine!" A small shop owner asked his employees, "Tell me what color veils you want, so I order them wholesale for you to wear from now on!" Some joked with female acquaintances on the street suggesting that they would no longer be able to stroll around without proper Islamic cover. A famous writer said that he would volunteer to wear a turban: "at least no one will see the bald spot on my head!" Like this, many of the humorous comments on the part of secularists had to do with dress and appearance. Indeed, one of the main things that secularists imagined Islamists would do was to impose "Islamic" attire in place of versions of European-style clothes now customarily worn by many of Turkey's urbanites. In their discursive association, Islamic attire was mapped onto tradition and local authenticity—the past—against westernized attire that was linked with the modern and contemporary.

In the week that followed the elections, Istanbulites made many ironic remarks in reference to "the Islamist takeover": "how nice—Turkey sleeps after midnight! No more fun in bars or drinking places!" "We'll sure find some new ways to entertain ourselves. Perhaps we can learn to chant and whirl like dervishes!" They feared they would be forced to resort to "Islamic" or "local" ways of socializing and entertaining themselves against the lifestyle that was available to people like themselves in the bars, restaurants, cafés, moviehouses, theaters, and discotheques of Istanbul that were said to match those of the world's biggest metropolises. Mostly, secularists projected about possible restrictions on women's lives with enforcement of "Islamic ways." Islam was associated with polygamy and covering: a young bank employee complained with a grave-looking grin, "they won't allow women to work, women will sit at home, will not vote, will cover themselves." She was sitting alone in an inexpensive bar. "This must be one of my last nights out like this!" she ironically gasped. Shocked by the election finale, secular Istanbulites were attempting to relax, by humorously getting themselves ready for what they perceived was the worst that could happen.

Humorous projections about a dystopian future reflected genuine unease. Concerns revolved around a cluster of central issues. Islam or local culture signified only specific things for those anxious at that time. As the jokes reveal, covered public appearance, especially for women, was central to the resonance of "Islamic order" in the stream of secularists' consciousness. Restrictions on drinking and public entertainment was another conviction about Islam. And most important, there was projected imagination about control over women's public lives. All these markers of everyday public comportment had been surpassed, secularists thought, with national leader Mustafa Kemal Atatürk's westernizing cultural reforms, which they took to have moved Turkey to a more "modern echelon of culture." A revivalist movement, they imagined, would want to unearth local, premodern, or Islamic cultural ways that had historically been overcome. And, somehow, "cultural authenticity" had to do, in the making of these secularists, again and again with the public disciplines of (especially) the female body (see Gole 1991). Islam, in their construction, was primarily about that.

What is more interesting to point out in this particular ethnographic context was the excess of emphasis on gender. This should not be much of a surprise to anyone attuned to the gendered component of social formations—that cultural difference between secularists and Islamists at that time of crisis should especially be mapped onto the question of gender. According to secular Istanbulites, Islamists were "different" particularly in the disciplinary and moralist ways that they would impose on women. Curiously, in international othering discourses on Islam, constructions that implicate Istanbul's secularists and Islamists, Islam surpasses other sociocultural domains in its attention to women. Islam is portrayed as obsessed with gender, as if other domains were less so.

Those unfamiliar with Istanbul might not comprehend why the imagination of such things as enforced veiling and polygamy or as controlled public space could be so outrageous for citizens of a Muslim country if they maintain such a preconception about what is native or authentic to Muslim cultures. Curiously, many citizens of Turkey share versions of such Western prejudice about what is normal to Islamic administrations. Yet one thing native secularists knew was that as far as they could remember, the religious order that they demonized did not exist in their country. In their mental association Turkey was different from other Muslim countries, and especially distinct from Iran and Saudi Arabia. In the mid-1990s, a common slogan chanted by secularists in counter-Islamist demonstrations in Turkey was "Turkey will not become Iran." Under

cultural reforms paved by the country's national leader Atatürk, in
Turkey, as secularists had been schooled to remember, there had been a
clothing reform in 1925, when the wearing of the fez, the turban, and the
robe was abolished and that of the veil officially discouraged. Since then,
Turkish urbanites mostly followed domesticated versions of European
fashion, variable by class. In fact, it would be wrong to classify such habits
as "westernized" or "European," for they are so much part of Turkey.
Women's pants, trimly fit skirts, and sweaters are as "authentic" to Turkey
as the veils and overcoats worn by contemporary Islamist women. But, in
the construction of those brought up under republican institutions, not
only secularists but also Islamists, such clothes as the turban, the robe, and
the veil symbolized Islam or what was "local" to Turkey in opposition to
European modernity into which Turkey had been slowly assimilating
throughout years of westernization. The voters for the March 1994 elections were not used to encountering too many veiled or turbaned people
on the streets of Istanbul. Even though many women wore scarves in public at that time, there was no official imposition to do so, and many of the
scarves worn by immigrants from small Anatolian towns or villages did
not necessarily indicate religiosity. Secular Istanbulites knew the city as a
metropolis with numerous locales for public entertainment, including bars
and restaurants, cafés, casinos, and nightclubs. Drinking alcohol was part
of social life. Most of the public spaces they frequented were open to
women especially in daytime, if not also at night, and most women
worked outside the home. It was from the vantage point of such marks of
urban middle-class sociality that secular Istanbulites used their preemp-
tive imagination about what could happen with enforced "authentication"
or a "return to Islam."

There is, of course, also a historical explanation for secular Istanbulites'
mapping of their difference with Islamists especially onto the question of
the public disciplines of women. In the formative years of the Turkish nation-state, Atatürk had successfully tried to differentiate "the new Turkey"
from its past and from its Muslim neighbors especially in instituting two
important reforms for women: the granting of voting rights and the institutionalization of Western dress for Turkey's women—again a symbolic
move (Kandiyoti 1987). In the historical consciousness of today's secularists, "the culture of Turkey" had been differentiated from its Ottoman-
Islamic past especially on the axis of gender. In this secularist narrative of
progress, Turkey had rejected its local culture to ascend to "civilized
ways," especially in "liberating" women. So much symbolic bearing had
been burdened on the question of women in the period of the new nation-
state's character formation vis-à-vis other states and histories, that it is no
surprise for contemporary secularists to once again differentiate themselves from local culture or Islam, especially on the basis of gender.

The public imagination about Islam that I untangle here, in studying the secular middle class of Istanbul, might seem to resonate with versions of Orientalist constructions of Islam, especially as articulated in mass media produced in contemporary Western societies. Compare, for example, Turkish-secularists' notions of Islam with the matter of Said's criticism in his *Orientalism* (1978) and *Covering Islam* (1981). One can indeed argue that images of Islam that were institutionalized and popularized under secularist regimes in republican Turkey, as well as contemporary secularist ideas about Islam, have been influenced by past and present Orientalisms. What is even more curious to note is the comparable implication of Turkish-Islamists in Orientalist discoursing on Islam; in other words, in wanting to be more loyal believers, Turkish- Islamists have been Orientalizing themselves. There is so much emphasis on gender in secular-Islamist politics of culture in Turkey because internalized Orientalist discourses on Islam are so significantly gendered.

It must also be remarked that secular Istanbulites, much like white Europeans, tended to think at that time that their ways were not "cultural." "Culture," in their construction, was what Islamists had: praying five times a day, celebrating religious festivals, reading the Qur'an in Arabic script, dressing in Islamic gear, and so forth. In contrast, secular Istanbulites thought that they themselves had transcended culture. They were modern; they were civilized; they had attained global norms, leaving behind a local aberration. It is hence that secularists thought that the Welfare Party's campaign for the municipalities, unlike that of other political parties, was about "culture." They thought that Welfare would force them to "localize." In fact, however, as time went by after the initial two months of Islamist municipal rule, secularists shifted their discourse on local culture and found that to be publicly convincing, they had to argue that their ways were "local," too.

RUMOR OR REALITY?

The period after the elections produced not only humor and story but also much rumor. Within the two weeks that followed the announcement of election results, rumors spread in the city that Welfarists were harassing people in public. Many people returned home with stories, either experienced in person or heard from someone else, of street confrontations.[7] On March 29, 1994, two days after the election, I heard, via word of mouth, that "some men approached women without head covers as they were walking in a central district of the city and told them that they would no longer be able to promenade in that [unveiled] fashion." One middle-aged man said that "a woman who went to a children's park was told by some

covered women that she couldn't enter that place without covering her
head." On those tense days that followed Welfare's electoral victory, many
people were sitting around, exchanging overheard stories of street events.
I heard, for example, that "a woman who was getting on a public bus in
the neighborhood of Sariyer in Istanbul was not allowed in because she
wasn't properly covered." Then there was a story about men dressed in
turbans and robes attempting to separate train passengers traveling from
a suburb of Istanbul by gender into different compartments.

Mass media, print or broadcast, also had a role in spreading or catalyz-
ing the dispersion of hearsay. The secularist left newspaper *Cumhuriyet* reported on April 1, 1994, "Fanatics kidnapped a bus in Istanbul." "Four turbaned and robed aggressors who halted a public bus in [the neighborhood
of] Ortakoy ordered the women passengers out and threatened the men to
abide by the order of the segregation of genders (*harem-selamlik*)," the article read, adding, "After the Welfare Party won the municipality of greater
Istanbul, gangs in favor of Islamic order have been continuing their attacks
against young girls and women." Similar coverage appeared in mainstream secular newspapers and TV stations as well. The news items were
based on calls made to press offices by people who had experienced the
events. But, on top of word of mouth, press coverage had the further effect
of confirming, validating, and enhancing the power of rumor.

Hearsay is not produced or consumed in a cultural or historical vacuum.
My argument is that if opponents of Welfare were complaining, then, of
attacks on their freedom of movement in the city or if they were spreading
such warning from ear to ear, it was also because they were already afraid
of exactly this before the event. Long before Welfarist officials made any
first moves to institute change in the urban domain, secular urbanites had
made humorous projections about "what would happen with an Islamist
administration." Like Zizek (1995), I will argue that the time was ripe at
this historical contingency for secular urbanites to interpret the success of
the Welfare Party in this way. Was there fear about the flimsiness of the
modernization project in the seventy-year-old Turkish state? That was
there, for sure. But what is significant to point out is that the Welfare Party,
before it even realized itself in practice, was received with a preexisting
discourse about "Islamism" on the part of secularists. Secularists projected
their fears about restrictions on public life across gender; they imagined
that Welfarists would institute Islamic law where they thought justice was
delivered through the severing of bodily parts; they feared that all
Muslim-born Turkish women would be forced to cover themselves and to
keep themselves to the private sphere of the home. When the Welfare
Party won, the context was already there for this sort of interpretation.
There is a dimension of self-fulfilling prophecy operating as well. Othering discourses about Islam and Islamism to an important extent preceded

Welfare's bureaucratic practice, and they proved to have power in inciting historical consequence. Indeed, much of the humor was exchanged before the happening of event. When rumor and actual information arrived, this struck a familiar cord in the cultural imagination of a certain secularist public about Islam. For many people, the stories matched a preexisting structure of feeling about Islamists and their quests for the enforcement of a certain locality and nativity. This is an argument, *pace* Foucault, about the intricacy or inseparability of discourse and event, construction and truth, abstraction and the concrete. The incidents narrated here are in part about the truth effects of discourse. A dominant secularist discourse about Islam had managed not only to imagine but at least to a certain extent also to produce truth about Islam.

In the everyday life of Istanbul in March 1994, women were used to being subjected to sexual harassment on the street, but not especially on the basis of their abidance by Islamic prescriptions to cover. Men and women ordinarily used the same vehicles for public transportation, standing or sitting beside one another. There were few public places, among them traditional coffee shops, certain restaurants and bars, certain schools, and mosques, that had informal gender-based rules of entry.

The rumors I have mentioned revolve around the public separation of men and women, either through women's attire or through the physical segregation of space. Is this "Islam"? Is this "Turkish local culture"? Does this reflect what is "native" to Turkey or what "was there" before Turkey moved to westernize? I would argue that this is not "the repressed native" striking back, as certain cultural critics of Turkey have argued, but it is what has been reconstituted, reformulated, or constructed as "native" on the part of both secularists and Islamists after years of westernization in Turkey. For the new habits of Islamists are very much contemporary and have little to do with lifestyles in the Ottoman Empire or in the times of the Prophet. Yet, at the moment, word of harassment, discourse, and event were indistinguishable. So much symbolic bearing had been given to women's public appearance that, at time of crisis, the notions of Islam and locality came to be identified with it, even for some of their Islamist proponents.

There were others who reacted to secularist prejudice in a different way. "It is not us [Welfare's cadre] who are doing this," a municipal police officer of the neighborhood of Beyoglu complained to me one day. We were sitting in a corridor of Beyoglu's municipality building a couple of days after the election finale. The building was crowded with Welfare Party officials joyously settling in. The officer had just returned from a call to work on the main street of Beyoglu. "We were called because there were four men walking around with turbans, robes, and sticks hitting women with miniskirts on the street," he said. "They are accusing us [Welfare's

workers] for this sort of event. In fact, these turbaned men are provocateurs. They are doing this in order to divert public opinion against us."
With a few other officers of the new municipality, this man had turned the
harassers in to the central police station. Welfare officials were worried
about these events, especially because they did not want to be associated
with them. Having just assumed power, they wanted to show that they
would be effective in managing urban affairs, what municipalities were
supposed to be about. The "provocateurs," however, served to actualize
secularist discoursing on "the essence of what would happen under an Islamic order." Among some officials of the winning party, more pragmatic
about sustaining rule, it was important to disproving the fears of their opponents. In fact, many of the Welfarist administrators and workers with
whom I spoke at the time were attempting to escape secularist pigeonholes
on the issue, by diverting attention away from controversy over veils or
miniskirts, Coca-Cola or lemonade.

THE ISSUES AT STAKE

During the first couple of months after the election results, journalists of
"secular" mass media were preoccupied with the affairs of the new municipalities. The new leaders, victoriously sitting in their democratically
earned seats, indeed provoked much attention. In awe of the first Islamist
takeover of significant official power in the history of republican Turkey,
the new leaders then seemed to be amused in declaring their projected
dreams for a more "Islamic" Istanbul. In those first interactions between
journalists of "secular" mass media and the new "Islamist" mayors, all
broadcast nationwide on TV and published in detail in newspapers, the
secularist discourse on Islam and locality was at play once again. When
Welfare administration became reality, journalists posed only certain sorts
of questions to the new mayors: "What will you do with the brothels in Beyoglu?" asked a young TV reporter in one of the very first public addresses
of Istanbul's new mayor Tayyip Erdogan. "I will shut them down and send
their workers to resthomes," responded the victorious mayor, seeming to
enjoy the pleasure, at that time, of announcing his most provocative vi-
sions. A day after the election results were formally announced, an article
appeared in a secular mainstream newspaper in which Istanbul's police
chief assured readers that "municipalities can only inspect brothels' hy-
giene, they have no authority to shut these down by themselves" ("RP'ye
Oy Vermedik," in *Millyet*, April 1, 1994). The question of brothels was also
high on the agenda of foreign journalists who had flocked to Turkey at that
time to report on what they thought were the outrageous election results
in the only secular state in the Middle East. I was present when a reporter

for the French news magazine *L'Express* was interviewing Nusret Bayraktar, the new mayor to the district of Beyoglu on April 2, 1994, in the municipality building. When the question was put differently, a different answer was produced. "Is the problem of brothels one of the main issues on your agenda, or is the press exaggerating this?" proposed the French journalist. The mayor attempted to make it clear:

> Brothels are not our first, not even our second, but one of our very last preoccupations. Our first acts will be routine ones. We will visit different neighborhoods and ask, "what are your needs?" and we will meet those specific needs.

Yet, despite the mayor's intentions, such a big deal had already been made out of the shaky future of brothels on the part of secular mass media that, indeed, one of the very first acts of the mayor turned out to be a general inspection of the brothels of Beyoglu.

"Are you going to remove the portraits of Atatürk from office buildings?" journalists queried the new mayor of Beyoglu, imagining he would do so as the Welfare Party defined itself against the national leader's secularism. "Or will you hang a portrait of Fatih Sultan Mehmet by it?" suggested the French reporter, referring to the Ottoman conqueror of Istanbul much reified by Welfarists. "We are not bothered by such obsessions with form," Nusret Bayraktar snapped, irritated by the questions. "If there are people who have served our society in the past, we remember them, but we are not into such formalisms." In a press conference, the state-appointed governor of Istanbul reassured the public that "in case the photographs of Atatürk are removed from municipality buildings, he [would] take legal action. In official buildings people are obliged to have a picture of Atatürk on the wall" (*Milliyet*, April 1, 1994).

As the new mayors assumed office, much uproar was made about inaugural ceremonies. "Welfarist mayors took power by praying and offering sacrificial animals," was the news, "while mayors of the Social Democratic People's Party (SHP) and the Republican People's Party (CHP) placed flowers by Atatürk memorials" (*Cumhuriyet*, April 1, 1994). The new mayor's manner of inaugurating the municipal parliament of Istanbul also came under criticism. While the normal procedure asked that members silently stand in respect to Atatürk and sing the national anthem, the mayor opened the ceremony by reading aloud a prayer. Outraged by the incident, the social democratic mayor of the district of Besiktas tried to move people to stand in respect to Atatürk. As members of the parliament began to chant the national anthem, the Welfarist mayor felt obliged to stand but could not keep himself from criticizing the ordeal by saying that standing in respect to the deceased was a Western tradition. "What good does it do to the dead if we stand for them?" (*Milliyet*, April 16, 1994).

Notice that a similar discursive distinction between "foreignness" and "locality" as mapped respectively onto "secularism" and "Islam" runs in this controversy as well. A revivalist movement would, in the imagination of secularist journalists, replace secularist symbols such as the portrait of Atatürk and the national anthem with Islamic ones such as the picture of Fatih or the prayer. It turned out, in this case, that the Welfarist mayor himself reproduced this dichotomous discourse in action. In defining the habit of standing in respect to the deceased as a "Western tradition," against the Islamic prayer as supposedly "authentic" to Turkey, the mayor was putting secularist distinction between the foreign and the local to effect.

In another exchange, "Will you bring restrictions to women's clothing?" a TV reporter asked, addressing the representative to the ladies' commission of the Welfare Party, and "Will women still be able to wear miniskirts if they want to?" "We will ask social scientists to do research on the moral values of the average Turkish citizen, and we will study the results and bring regulations accordingly," Welfare's representative, Sibel Eraslan replied. She was suggesting to normalize public appearance on the basis of a supposedly objective evaluation of "general local values." Implicitly, miniskirts would have to fall outside this category of Turkish "authenticity."

Indeed, the future of brothels, Atatürk portraits, and miniskirts was on top of the agenda of secular-mainstream journalism on those first days after Welfare won. And through media, the concern trickled down to anxious viewers to an important extent. These issues were discussed as the markers of cultural difference between secularists and Islamists. Discussion was geared over and over again to the future of such symbols of modernity and "the state of being civilized" or of "being up-to-date with the world" (in Turkish, *çağdaşlik*).

Part of the anxiety of secularists indeed turned out to be well founded, but in this case the attack was easily repelled. One of the very first measures taken by Beyoglu's new mayor was to order the removal of tavern tables that were set out on the street or sidewalk. Restaurant owners were asked to put opaque curtains on their windows to conceal indoors. This interdiction was justified with a rhetoric of populism, arguing that the street would become more accessible to pedestrians who could not afford to eat out. A few days after the event, a group of secularists organized a sit-in on Nevizade Street, moving the tables outdoors and drinking beer, raki, and wine in public. They demanded their right to socialize and drink in public space. There was no conceivable way the outdoors facilities of Beyoglu locales could be forced shut, for the scope of demand for these to remain open was vast. In a few weeks the mayor had to allow tables out onto the streets once again.

This incident shows that in crafting an ethnography of the effects of "discourse on locality" on the actualization of municipal actions, one has to be very specific historically, for the first months that followed the election results were different from later ones. In the first month of intensity, discourse had much effect of truth; in the later months of sharing space and institutions, discourse began to dissipate, leaving the ground to negotiations where a popular notion of culture could emerge. In other words, starting postures were loaded with former structural projections about Islam and locality. But as cross-cultural relationships inevitably developed on the site of the management of urban affairs, issues were negotiated on a more concrete basis. As time passed and as the new municipality settled in, new issues came to the fore that could not have been premeditated by either parties of the struggle before or during the time of the elections.

An example was the issue of the rain bomb. The city of Istanbul has had a chronic problem of shortage in water, especially during the past decade. The distribution of water is among the most important duties of the municipality. During the reign of the Social Democratic People's Party for the five years that preceded the March 1994 elections, the mayor of Istanbul ordered the use of the rain bomb (seeding rain clouds) to fill up dams close to the city. In mid-April 1994, it was reported that the level of water in the dams was seriously low. With recorders in hand, journalists rushed to interrogate the new Welfarist mayor as to what he was planning to do. "Will you continue the use of the rain bomb?" he was asked. "That [technology] was used last year, to no avail. Today a group of our citizens are going out on a prayer for rain," was his answer. "Welfarist mayor goes for rain prayer" was the mocking headlines in the following day's newspapers and TV. "Instead of wasting money in vain, we will go out to pray for rain. In Anatolia rain prayer has always given positive results. Throughout history this has proven effective," the mayor said in an interview in *Cumhuriyet* on April 19, 1994. The matter was turned into an object of ridicule on the part of Welfare's critics, who took the mayor's refusal to use this technology as proof of what they conceived to be his "backward mentality." Thus, a new issue created a new controversy around which cultural difference in identities was defined anew. The matter was not, this time, about women's public appearance or use of space but about the use of technology. Around the signifier of "rain bomb," secularists constructed discursive difference between "civilization" and "backwardness." At the time, a symbolic rain prayer was held; but the past few years have been very fortunate in terms of rainfall, for which nobody has taken credit.

THE HISTORICAL CONSTRUCTION OF LOCAL CULTURE

According to whom is Islam "local culture"? What has turned Islam into a sign of control of women's public appearance and of public space? By focusing on the first sites of cultural controversy when Welfare administration became Istanbul's reality, I have argued in this chapter that Islamist municipal administration takes place within the conditions of possibility yielded by an established secularist discourse on local culture. I argue that, to a certain extent, Islamist policy is the making of the secularists; it is a relational and reactive effect of secularists' othering. The examples offered earlier display the dilemmas of Islamists working within the parameters and language of culture set up by a dominant secularist discourse on culture, one that (in time) shifted as secularists realized that it was self-defeating. Indeed, more often than not, Islamists in the first months of their rule were actualizing the fears of their opponents.

My ethnographic data also reveal that the process of everyday municipal practice produces shifts in conditions of possibility. At several moments, Islamists attempted to escape the pigeonholes in which secularists locked them. Welfarists have been taking contradictory strategic moves at every point, at times fulfilling and at others countering secularists' worrisome anticipations. Yet they have always been doing so relationally. As recent work on identity politics has put forward, identity formation and everyday practice are always relational, always in reference to a negative other (Devji 1992). In the process of municipal practice, Welfare administrators have had to come to terms with a multiplicity of lifestyles also customary (or "local") to Istanbul. In other words, the "authenticity" they prided in representing exclusively did not match the everyday experience of many inhabitants of the city. The present process of cross-cultural interaction in the municipal domain, then, opened some possibilities outside a former dominant discourse on authenticity. The event of sharing institutional and public space across cultural, ideological, and religious difference put the very notion of Turkey's culture into question, whether it be in its secularist or Islamist productions and enactments. This has been enhanced, as I suggested, by secularists' shift of discourse, in coming to assert the authenticity of their own lifestyles to Turkey. Anthropological sensitivities to local or native culture often overlook the historical dynamism in which cultures take shape and tend to leave out of the picture the domain of everyday contestation and debate in which the notion of local culture is implicated. The foregoing is an attempt to place power and history in the center of our inquiries about native culture.

NOTES

1. "The Turkish-Islamic synthesis" is a version of Turkish nationalism that has developed in Turkey in the twentieth century. Advocated by certain Islamists as well as by certain activists of pan-Turkism, it maps out a Turkish and Muslim heritage for Turkey, externalizing Europe as well as all elements deemed "non-Turkish" or "non-Muslim" within Turkey.

2. Rena Lederman (1989) draws attention to internal contestation among the Mendis, taking issue with ethnographies that produce wholesome cultural accounts. My line of thought passes through her work as cited here.

3. Vincanne Adams (1996) approaches Sherpas, in their ongoing relations with Europeans, in this way. Rather than looking for "the authentic Sherpa" underneath the "Sherpaness" that contemporary Sherpas have assumed to please the gaze of Western tourists, Adams studies what she calls "virtual Sherpas" to be authentic.

4. For an excellent critique of the overlap between anthropological work and nationalist discourses, see Spencer (1990).

5. This and further references and descriptions come from my field notes taken at the time of the events.

6. For example, the monthly magazine *Bulten,* published by members of an educational foundation for young Islamist intellectuals (Bilim ve Sanat Vakfi), entitled its postelections issue of March-April 1994 (vol. 5, no 34) "The Nightmare: The 27th of March, the most Exciting Adventure after Friday the 13th."

7. The Turkish language has two forms of past tense. One, expressed with the suffix *-di,* is used in speaking of past events that were either experienced firsthand by the narrator or that are known to have certainly taken place. The other, expressed with the suffix *-miş,* is used in the narration of stories, fairytales, and past events overheard only secondhand from someone else. History is always written with the suffix *-di;* rumor is exchanged with the suffix *-miş.* The specific gossip that I cite here reached my ears in the *-miş* form and was inscribed in my notes in the form of *-di.* In other words, I am saying that these pieces of rumor certainly did (*-di*) revolve around saying that such and such an incident was apparently experienced by such and such person (*-miş*).

REFERENCES

Adams, V. 1996. *Tigers of the snow and other virtual Sherpas: an ethnography of Himalayan encounters.* Princeton, N.J.: Princeton University Press.

Benjamin, W. 1968. Theses on the philosophy of history. Pages 255–266 in *Illuminations.* New York: Harcourt, Brace, & World.

Devji, F. F. 1992. Hindu/ Muslim/Indian. *Public Culture* 5, no. 1: 1–18.

Gole, N. 1991. *Modern mahrem.* Istanbul: Metis.

Kandiyoti, D. 1987. Emancipated but unliberated? Reflections on the Turkish case. *Feminist Studies* 13, no. 2: 317–38.

Kuper, A. 1994. Culture, identity and the project of a cosmopolitan anthropology. *Man: The Journal of the Royal Anthropological Institute* 29: 3.

Lederman, R. 1989. Contested order: gender and society in the southern New Guinea Highlands. *American Ethnologist* 16, no. 2: 230–47.

Robins, K. 1996. Interrupting identities: Turkey/Europe. In S. Hall and P. du Gay (eds.), *Questions of cultural identity.* London: Sage.

Said, E. W. 1978. *Orientalism.* New York: Pantheon.

Said, E. W. 1981. *Covering Islam: how the media and the experts determine how we see the rest of the world.* New York: Pantheon.

Spencer, J. 1990. Writing within: anthropology, nationalism, and culture in Sri Lanka. *Current Anthropology* 31, no. 3: 283–300.

Zizek, S. 1995. *The sublime object of ideology.* London: Verso.

5

Islamic Chic

Jenny B. White

On an Istanbul city bus, three teenage girls in long pastel coats and volu-minous silk head scarves, the dress of the urban Islamic conservative, clutched the worn metal pole and discussed the previous night's install-ment of a television serial about the Turkish War of Independence in the early twentieth century. They agreed that what they loved most were the scenes with horses and Ottoman tents. The film, shown on state television, paid the usual homage to the heroic deeds of Turkey's secular modernizer, Mustafa Kemal Atatürk, but contained Islamic scenes as well. This was in 1987; for most of the Republican period, it had been unusual for carefully secular state media to include overt reference to Islam. The combination of Islam and Republican values was, of course, nothing new to viewers. As in many other countries, the majority of Turks combine seemingly incom-patible sets of beliefs seamlessly in their daily lives: they pray and vote; they learn science and civic virtue at school and Muslim values at home and in their community; they give alms and pay taxes; they ask local imams for advice and take legal matters before the government represen-tative or the court. A banner on a government building in Istanbul reads, "Taxed income is holy."

What was new in the 1980s was state sponsorship of Islamic images and ideals. For over half a century, secular education in the new Republic had attempted to fashion from the loosely woven ethnic fabric of the Ottoman Empire a new tapestry of Turkish citizens, "individuals free from com-munal restraints and active members of a contractual society dominated by instrumental rationality" (Kazancigil 1991, 355). Islam was to be a pri-vate affair and nationalism the integrative fiber.

The vast secularist reforms instituted by Atatürk became naturalized to varying degrees in different parts of the population. The flat cap replaced the fez, after a brief flirtation with the European hat, whose brim caused it to tip off during prayers. Elite urban women began to wear Western styles of clothing, enter college, and vie for professional and government positions. Women in the countryside continued to wear their kerchiefs and loose clothing, suitable for heavy labor in the fields, and covered their faces only against the infrequent stranger visiting their villages. The westernized uncovered female schoolteachers sent out by the state served as models, to be copied or gossiped about.

Most important, Islamic law, courts, and other religious institutions were abolished, and religious affairs came under state control. Women, in particular, gained the right to vote, better access to divorce, inheritance, and other family and civil rights, at least on paper. Lack of education, mobility, and resources; low literacy rates; and lack of knowledge of and formal connections to the coda and implements of law and state kept rural people in thrall to traditional norms of conduct and patron-client ties to wealthy landowners and local bureaucrats. Women rarely sought divorce, and both men and women had little knowledge of or access to their new "rights." Under these conditions, Islam continued to provide a moral framework for daily living.

Islam rediscovered a legitimate political voice in 1950, when Turkey ventured its first multiparty elections. The opposition Democrat Party came to power in part by appealing to traditional regional and religious affiliations and by harnessing landowner/peasant patron-client ties. Since then, through three coups in 1960, 1971, and 1980 and within a wide spectrum of political parties in power or in coalition, these elements of society have participated in Turkish governance either openly, as part of a political party, or as unacknowledged silent brokers of or partners in power.

In the 1980s that silence was definitively broken as the military government, which had stepped in to recast the violently fractured political and social fabric, decided to dust off Islam as a coherent mold to shape society away from feared socialist and communist designs. Huge budget increases for the Directorate of Religious Affairs led to a proliferation of officially propagated religious schools and seminaries. A balance was attempted that preserved secularist values despite the state's inoculation with Islam. Official television stations allowed Islamic content. At the same time, they serialized American soap operas and loosened strictures on sexual content and nudity to compete with the private commercial stations springing up.

There is strong government support for women's issues, a continuation of the state feminism that, since the founding of the Republic, has given women rights and established supportive public policies. Some government departments, however, through their publications and projects, support the traditional role of women that is favored by Muslim conservatives. Government television also broadcasts weekly sermons, some of which emphasize women's primary role as mother and homemaker. These contradictory activities reflect the momentary distribution of power among political parties with opposing views of women's role in society but also are the legacy of Turgut Özal's administration in the 1980s. Özal, a key architect of the political liberalization of Islam, incorporated Islamist politicians in his government at all levels, resulting in a diverse ideological makeup of the government bureaucracy and institutionalizing the Islamist/secularist debate.

In the 1980s, the strategy of first the military and then the elected government of Özal that succeeded it was to encourage the expression of Islam as an alternative to Kurdish separatism in the east and the perceived threat of communism from the north and within Turkey's own borders. The resulting policy decisions, and the decimation of the Turkish left by the military and by the end of the cold war, encouraged and legitimated the verbal and symbolic expression of Muslim conservatism. Under Özal Turkey also abandoned its policies of controlled economic development and import substitution, opening its economic doors to the global marketplace. Through the doors came opportunity but also aggressive consumerism and heightened perceptions of social inequality, compounded by ever more marked differences in income distribution (White 1994).

This inequality was most noticeable in Istanbul, a megacity of nearly ten million people. In many ways, Istanbul is emblematic of the multifaceted and multilayered postmodern city, growing from the ashes and embers of modernist experiments: the mechanization of agriculture, which led to a mass rural exodus that glutted the cities with migrants; city planning, with its triumphs of engineering and failure to predict and ameliorate human needs; the belief in rational progress and technology challenging human desires for eternal values and local belonging. In the 1980s the remaining embers of modernist hopes flared anew, fanned by the winds of capitalism that swept through Turkey's newly opened economic doors. Economic liberalization created new wealth but also new expectations for upward mobility among millions of hopeful migrants to the cities. Since the 1980s Istanbul has become the Turkish gateway to the world, in terms of creation of wealth in the global marketplace but also as an entry point for modernization and the global culture it drags in its wake, which some perceive as a threat to local cultural values. Thus, the hopes of many Turks, while focused on material and technological progress, are shaped through symbols and beliefs that privilege faith over rationality. Islam, symbolized by Islamic dress, has become a credible route for upward social mobility in the postmodern city. It has become not only acceptable to be openly devout and politically Muslim but also (in some circles) chic.

Herein lies a major difference between political Islam, or Islamism, in the 1970s and the 1990s. In the 1970s Islamist activists expressed anticonsumerist attitudes and struggled for power mainly through one, comparatively marginal, political party (National Salvation Party, or MSP). In the

1990s, Islamic activists have several power bases in the government, either through the Welfare Party, or as counterweights in center-right parties. They have attained legitimacy in other ways too, in popular culture and intellectual discourse, as well as in the economic sphere.

Turkey's Islamic groups, in all their diversity, have taken to the printed word and the media to spread their messages. They have organized and professionalized their networks in such a way that they provide credible paths for upward mobility for men and, increasingly, for women. They provide loans, business contacts, social services, and avenues for political and media expression. Women in religious dress work and attend college, publish their own magazines, write columns in pro-Islamic newspapers, read the news on an Islamist television station, and canvass voters door to door. These activities would have been out of the reach of many young women from restrictive traditional families before 1980. The new era of Islamic respectability makes it possible.

It has become chic to be politically (and, increasingly, economically) Islamic, and it has become associated with the road to success. This is expressed and even flaunted by the more and more common wearing of a new, distinctively urban Islamic garb. *Tesettür* fashion, the fashion of long coats and large silk head scarves that signal the new urban Islamic conservatism, can be expensive. Tesettür fashion shows are held, with models on runways, the Islamic elite taking notes below, and the press in the wings. Islamic chic has now spilled to the streets, a sign of growing success and legitimacy; success breeds success. The sight of women in tesettür browsing the expensive shops of westernized Bagdad Boulevard in Istanbul sends a message to those under economic pressure that political Islam works. Adopting Islamic dress has become a sign of status, more than a marker of personal devotion, but less than a political statement. It is now necessary to make a distinction among political Islam, socioeconomic Islam, and, of course, personal Islam.

The leaders of political Islam, the Islamists, are for the most part urban intellectuals interested in reforming both Islam and society. Their followers object to the economic injustice and moral decay they perceive has resulted from treading the path to the West. They point to the results of opening Turkish culture and economy to global market forces without an accompanying ethical framework through which to channel modernity: nudity in the media, crass displays of wealth and materialism in the face of poverty, the breakdown of family values as young men and women mingle freely in the ubiquitous urban bars and restaurants. The Islamists are actively engaged in reformulating Islamic thought, sometimes with reference to Western literature and thought, to fit modern problems.[1] Many are active seekers of an alternative Islamic road to modernity.

Islamist elites are suspicious, however, of the influence of the market, even as they participate in it, and of the Faustian allure of images, even their own. This is not an idle concern. The marketplace of ideas fractures, multiplies, and ultimately dilutes their messages, and the convergence of modernizing interests and defensive antimodernist motivations leads to a multiplicity of meanings represented in one set of polyvalent signs—tesettür. Global and local converge, not in a coherent agenda or image but in a contingent syncretism of cultural traditions and social discourses.

Islamists represent a spectrum of thought, from liberals interested in economic justice to fundamentalists intent on replacing the secular state with one based on Islamic (*shari'a*) law. Islamic symbols and Islamic values in the service of political ideology can take many forms, from mystical Sufi orders (themselves ideologically diverse) to political parties, such as the pro-Islam Welfare Party. However, not all women adopting Islamic garb or all devout men belong to a religious order or vote for the Welfare Party. There is a deep strain of pragmatism, nationalism, and belief in the democratic process in all but the most radical of the population.

The increasing internal differentiation within the Islamic set has resulted in a profusion of symbolization through Islamic dress, with the same dress evincing different meanings and location of identities, while other styles of symbolic dress converge. Although tesettür is adopted sometimes in conjunction with adherence to Islam as a political ideology, it is also deeply conditioned by socioeconomic status as well as by socioeconomic aspirations. As time has passed, many devout Muslims, especially young women, have begun to adopt the style without evincing any overt interest in politics or in political Islam. Socioeconomic differentiation has become increasingly more obvious as the political intent has receded and the styles proliferated. Tesettür is a process, not a category, and, as such, it has been the victim of its own success.

Fatma, a devout middle-aged woman whose husband owns a small automotive repair shop, takes me to a wedding in Ümraniye, a sprawling working-class Istanbul neighborhood, populated in large part by migrants from the Black Sea coast. The women celebrate out of sight of the men in a mosque hall. They are almost all covered, the villagers in their black cloaks and white cotton scarves, their regional dress, the rest in the citified and Islamicized version of the village cloak. There is music and a little tentative, modest dancing by the young girls. The women eat nuts and pumpkin seeds and chat over the growing piles of hulls.

Another wedding in the same neighborhood is held at a restaurant, the men on the upper floor, the women on the second floor, screened by curtains. These women are also wearing Islamicized garb, but the quality and style of dress are strikingly different. The groom's father owns a taxi

company and other businesses and is quite well off. This success is mirrored in tesettür style—colorful pastel linen coats and silk scarves with
gold accents—and in the tenor of the wedding as a whole. Instead of villagers, the room is filled with young contemporaries of the bride and
groom and their families. They take off their coats and sometimes their
scarves to dance seductively and even wildly to lively, piped-in Oriental
music. The groom's sister and brother's wife wear intricately draped and
folded turbans of dazzling pink or blue material, called *peçe*, a revival of
the Italian-derived Ottoman term for *veil*, with artfully styled long
dresses of the same material, the turban blending seamlessly with the
dress into an opulent sheath. The overall effect is startlingly unlike the
usual tesettür.

Tesettür also may be nothing more than an expression of personal devotion. Fatma explains that she has always worn a long coat and scarf; it
is the dress of her village. But the specially cut cloth coats and oversize
headscarves are a new style, learned in the city. For Fatma and her Ümraniye neighbors, tesettür is the dress-up city version of their traditional
dress and an expression of their belief that a good Muslim woman is covered. It has no political overtones whatsoever. In fact, Fatma has consis-
tently voted for political parties of the center-left because she felt they
were the most responsible in issues that concerned her, such as municipal services and consumer prices. In the 1994 municipal elections, she
switched to Prime Minister Tansu Çiller's True Path Party. She felt that
the center-left parties had failed their mandate, taken bribes, and not
delivered services. She admires the uncovered and thoroughly westernized Çiller.

By 1995 Fatma's family and neighbors all were disillusioned with Welfare's performance and were weighing alternatives. In fact, Welfare's mix
of politics and Islam disturbs them. They are suspicious of political Islam
and doubt its legitimacy. "We were Muslims before. Where were they?"
exclaims Fatma, whose grandfather had been the village imam. "This has
always been a nation of Muslims. It's as if *they* were the only good Muslims. What are we?"

Other Turkish Muslim groups, such as the Shi'a Alevi and mystical Bek-
tashi, whose approach to Islam is more liberal than traditional Sunni practice, also are put off by the Islamist insistence on Sunni rituals and beliefs.
They express this discomfort through votes for non-Islamist parties. Some
members of conservative Muslim groups, such as the Nakshibendi and
Nurcu, are impatient with the Welfare Party's pragmatic concessions to
party politics and are moving toward founding their own parties. The
seeds of the fracturing, dilution, and co-optation of the Islamist message
were sown during the first heady period of Islamist political, economic,
and social success in the 1980s.

POLITICAL CHIC

The oversize scarves worn by the *tesettürlü* women are usually made of Bursa silk handprinted or painted with delicate floral designs. The lovely, flowered scarves, a sea of silk and polyester, some of the triangles of cloth with beautiful bouquets of flowers, many in abstract pastels, centered in the middle of the back, are fascinating. I remember in the 1970s being equally fascinated on market day by the seemingly endless variety of stitched beading edging the white cotton scarves of the working-class migrant women filling their shopping bags with fresh produce. Simple cotton scarves, of the kind worn in their villages of origin, were much more common in the 1970s than even polyester squares, the next step on the aesthetic path to an urban culture. Long coats and oversized scarves were extremely rare. The latter were different too, in that the coat was almost ground level, the scarves undecorated, often a simple blue, and the wearers young, probably students showing political support for the National Salvation Party. Now, the *kiyafet* (costume, attire) is a real "style" with chic and careful attention to details of coat design, scarf pattern, and angles and intricacies of wrap. It is a true fashion, not merely a protest symbol.

I remember a young woman at an engagement party held in a mosque building in 1987. At first glance, she looked much like the other women, dressed in voluminous thin black coats and large white cotton headscarves, their regional dress but also, in this urban migrant community, a signal of their personal devotion to Islam. This dress is usually worn over loose trousers and unostentatious jewelry. No makeup is ever applied, since Islam discourages personal display. As the woman came closer, I noticed that she wore high heels, a dress, an enormous gold medallion, at least four inches in diameter, on a chain, and over this a black leather coat, obviously designed to mimic the village coats. Her face was lightly made up. A very large silk scarf hung down her back to below her waist. Very chic—Islamic chic. Someone whispered to me that she had married a very wealthy man. She didn't stay long, only long enough to speak to a few people, and I soon lost sight of her. Many of the symbols of political Islam had already become naturalized as signs of socioeconomic status.

This progression is mirrored in the language used to refer to the various styles of scarves. In the 1970s the common term for the cotton scarf, worn both by villagers and new migrants to the cities, was *başörtü*, literally "head covering." In the late 1970s some young women began to challenge the government's ban on wearing head scarves to university classes. The blue head scarves and long coats symbolized dissent and challenge of the status quo, as well as alignment with the Islamic political party. It was the first major symbolic manifestation of political Islam through dress since the banning of the fez and discouragement of veiling at the founding of the

Republic. Men also displayed personal signs of political ideology, primarily shapes of moustaches and beards, still today an accurate indicator of political position. Covering and shaping hair is a time-honored display of political values (Delaney 1994; Olson 1985).

The increasing differentiation within "Islamic fashion" is more than simply a difference in clothing. The Turkish scholar Ali Yasar Saribay (1994) argues that this differentiation and the lack of a meta-image to encompass a coherent Islamic style is a reflection of eclectic postmodern consumer culture. In postmodern consumer culture, the meaning and power of Islamic symbols can be transferred to support or create a limitless number of images in a collage. This unease and the search for a meta-image was taken up in a discussion reported in *Izlenim* (July-August 1995) among three young Muslim intellectuals, two of them women, on the culture of dress in the context of traditional and modern culture.[2] In the modern mentality, several of the discussants argued, aesthetics has pushed ethics into the background. While modern clothing is made with the possibility of aesthetic choice, this is done for profit only, with no regard for the ethical component of dress. The discussants warned that the problem in seeking an individual image was that if the image is of primary concern, an internalized group culture will not develop. A woman discussant explained that, as the Muslim elite began to participate more in social life in modern five-star hotels, circumcision celebrations, and engagement parties, they began to be disturbed by "typical" clothing and desired to make an impression and to communicate through their dress. In traditional society, there are fewer people, and it is not as important to be seen or to make an impression. But in the anonymous mobility of modern life, "when you come face-to-face with a total stranger in a bus, whether you want to or not, in some respects that person enters your world with his or her appearance." According to her, women had a dress language until the Republic, but fashion is dictated by the upper class, and the new Kemalist upper class, the bureaucrats and wives of officers, began to wear their hair uncovered. Now Muslims are trying to regain the dignity of the clothing styles that had been taken from them and to recapture the fashion belonging to the upper class.

In Turkey, language, clothing, hair, and music all have been indentured to political ideology, historically as well as in contemporary society. The Islamists have resuscitated Ottoman imperial symbols and *mehter* music, the military music of the Ottoman Janissaries. Secularist elites support Western classical and popular music as a political statement. Working-class urbanites listen to Arabesk, popular music whose lyrics express the woes and longings of a hard life (Stokes 1992), and Turkish pop singers who draw their inspiration from the West and the East. Islamist newspapers use a form of Turkish replete with Arabic-derived words, much closer to Ottoman Turkish. Atatürk had founded the Turkish Language Institute specifically to purge elite Ottoman Turkish of such "foreign" influences to create a language closer to the Turkish spoken by the common people. Non-Islamist publications use this "new Turkish." Islamist students pack the Ottoman archives to satisfy their interest in pre-Republican history while the secularist elite debates civil society and the fate of the Republic.

CLASH OF CIVIL SOCIETIES

What has happened since the 1970s to change and enhance the symbols and language of urban Islam to such an extent? A sea change can be traced to the Özal government's policies and the continuing fallout from the social, political, and economic liberalization and opening of the early 1980s. Economic liberalization has encouraged Islamic elites to organize and compete openly in the political and economic arenas. The appeal of Islam in the 1980s, however, is also a result of the repression of the left by the military, which encouraged Islam as a panacea for healing divisions in Turkish society. This depletion of the left allowed Islamic groups to take up the critique of social inequality and exploitation that had traditionally been the message of the social democrats. Left-wing intellectuals were in disarray; the Islamists, on the other hand, were consummately organized, combining evidence of economic success with a message of social justice, a balancing act that has eluded other groups.

Despite the military's leash on political expression, which is still jerked from time to time, civil society in general is flourishing. This is due, in part, to the rise of an Islamist, secularist, as well as pragmatist business elite after the opening of the economy to foreign investment and trade in the 1980s. Business associations are being set up or strengthened. There are also history and art foundations; civil and human rights groups; environmental groups; women's groups; friendship, culture, and charity associations; and regional and religious associations. Ideological divisions in society are expressed as different associations. Different groups with Islamist, liberal, and nationalist messages compete in trying to influence public opinion through printed matter, periodicals, books, research institutes, and so forth. Some of these groups are interested in pluralist compromise; others, on both sides of the Islamist/secularist debate, are less tolerant and work to exclude the other from the national platform. Most, however, pursue these goals within a democratic and ultimately pluralist framework, thereby adding to its strength. Liberal secularist groups (although not the traditional left) and Islamist groups, in particular, have gained in popularity and become the main competitors for determining the direction of Turkish society.

After the Welfare Party's success in the 1994 municipal elections, urban middle-class women in particular began to mobilize, because it is their lifestyle that they feel is most vulnerable to the presumed social agenda of the religious right. Membership in women's organizations boomed, and the organizations themselves united under umbrella councils. I attended a meeting in Istanbul of the new Besiktas branch of the Association for the Promotion of Modern Living (*Çağdaş Yaşami Destekleme Derneği*). The association was founded in 1989 with a feminist and environmentalist orientation. Since 1993, like many other feminist organizations, it has placed more emphasis on secularism, democracy, and antipolitical Islam. The Besiktas branch, one of six, opened shortly after the municipal elections. The meeting was held in a fairly large well-appointed auditorium in the basement of a grade school. In the anteroom was an exhibit of prize-winning artwork by city school-children. A table was set up amid the panels of artwork with a bowl of red fruit punch, savories, and cake. The sixty-five attendees (seventeen of them male) were between the ages of twenty and fifty. Everyone was well dressed and extremely well coiffed. During the break, I spoke to several of the women as they were sipping punch. All were housewives; none had ever participated in politics before; all were energized by the election results.

They had invited a professor of law to explain the basics of lobbying and organizing, a kind of crash course. Future meetings were announced, with one speaker on secularism and another on the Turkish search for identity. The lawyer, a distinguished looking man, spoke slowly and clearly, without notes, for over two hours. He pointed out that it surprised him to find people of their background and status here in this situation, "because, before, these kinds of questions were represented by political parties. Now no longer. Let's get to work. . . . We liberal, civil people feel the need to become more active. . . . You need to be professional; you need to be concrete, learn technique; you need to spend money." He gave examples, discussing how one can pursue one's rights by means of lawsuits. He emphasized, however, that civil society means open debate, education, living together.

The audience listened intently and, in the second half, asked many concerned questions. A young man asked, "How can we take the head scarf to court?" A woman from the audience broke in, "But I don't agree. They don't force me—why should I force them [to wear certain things]?" Another woman: "That is dangerous; it leads to our being soft on these people." People all began to speak at once, revealing the fear and the intolerance, the ambivalence and, ultimately, the pluralist nature of contemporary Turkish debate: "If there's a law, it should be obeyed." "If I go naked, is this democracy?" "These people use democracy's flexibility to force a different ideology on us."

At 9 p.m., the audience was still paying rapt attention. The lawyer reassured them that "there are certain secularist things in the constitution that can't be changed. Therefore, theoretically, even if religious parties come to power, the law can't change certain things. It would lead to a suit before the Constitutional Court. To defend against social changes, we need education and economic changes."[3] The meeting clearly would have gone on into the night if the organizer, a university teacher, had not intervened.

The most organized civil societal groups are those of the Islamists. The Islamists are no longer marginal. Islamic groups, like their secularist counterparts, tend to be participatory in nature, rather than antagonistic toward the system, despite intolerance on the part of some of their members. They have a counterelite and a counterculture; they are in positions of power in several center-right political parties and have their own party, the Welfare Party. That means that they are represented in parliament and control many municipal governments; they have jobs in state bureaucracies; they control several newspapers, journals, and radio and television stations; they have a widely read and respected intelligentsia, and graduates of schools giving religious education, both male and female, are increasingly entering the universities and bureaucracy; they have their own labor confederation and businessman's association; they run Islamic banks and Islamic businesses. Islamist women have also become mobilized. Taking part in Islamist activities has allowed religious women of the lower classes to attend university and to become upwardly mobile and politically active. They organized and demonstrated in universities for the right to wear the veil. They write and publish their own magazines (Acar 1991; Arat 1991).

The Welfare Party uses and benefits from civil society. It owes its popularity to the representation of civil societal issues: access to education, employment, protecting the environment, the dispute about the right to wear a head scarf in universities. But its organizational methods have been crucial in its success. It maintains many types of clubs to bring together potential voters and offers free or subsidized services ranging from communal circumcision ceremonies to sewing and Koran classes. Unlike other parties, Welfare does not rely primarily on the media to get its message across but works face to face. Activists are matched to voters by age, gender, and regional origin. The party takes full advantage of neighborhood, regional, and cultural bonds that tie people to one another in mutual assistance, as well as its flip side: mutual obligation. This, in a sense, privatizes public space and brings into the political process people, such as working-class women, who would not have been able or willing to deal with strangers in a public arena or a formal organization.

Along with its old constituency of traditional, nationalist Anatolian merchants, the Welfare Party now represents many of the recently urbanized and educated newcomers on the political and economic scene. It capitalizes, therefore, as much on rising expectations as on the frustration of the lower and middle classes. This is the source of its strength as well as its

Achilles' heel. As Fatma's neighbors demonstrate, people expect their lives to improve under a Welfare Party administration; when they do not, voters will look elsewhere. Socioeconomic and personal Islam are independent of political Islam and provide their own impetus for change.

Nevertheless, Fatma and her neighbors are representative of a wide and growing constituency. Since the 1950s, increasing mechanization of farm labor, government support for industry at the expense of agricultural development, and the building of networks of roads linking the countryside to the cities have led to massive migration to urban centers. In 1950 only 18.7 percent of Turkey's population lived in cities; today over 60 percent of the country's sixty million inhabitants do so. These new urban classes share with the provincial lower middle class a lifestyle rooted in Islamic values as well as a desire to live in a prosperous, technologically advanced society. From their ranks arose Islamic technocrats, who came to power in the 1980s in Özal's government and are now leaders in the Welfare Party; they are people who until recently had been at the margins of a nation dominated by secularist elites. They have a desire, as much as these elites, to participate in the material welfare of a modern nation. However, while they are interested in the technology of the West, they do not espouse the westernization of moral and social values. The Welfare Party is not the only party able to represent these views and is now slowly being jostled aside by old and new parties bearing a similar message, in yet another example of the fracturing of meaning and identities in the postmodern marketplace of ideas.

FRACTURED MESSAGES

In a former squatter area recently incorporated into municipal Istanbul, the Denizli family has undergone a transformation in just six years, along with their own and their community's economic advance. Taking advantage of the export boom of the 1980s, Osman Denizli and his wife, Hatice, ran a piecework atelier from their home, commissioning neighborhood women to knit sweaters that were then passed up the subcontracting hierarchy and exported. The money they earned was modest by entrepreneurial standards but sufficient for improving their economic and community status. They built a squatter home, bought better furnishings, and eventually added a second story to their home, for which they had obtained a deed. The family dressed conservatively. The mother and all three daughters wore loose, modest clothing (skirts, sweaters) and covered their heads with cotton village scarves whenever men, including their fathers, were present. Like many other Turks, they fasted on religious holidays and sent their daughters to Koran lessons once a year, but they did not pray daily or pay much verbal attention to Islam as religious practice, much less as a religious ideology. Their neighborhood was fairly homogenous in its symbolic standards, with only an occasional woman in tesettür and a few with uncovered hair.

When clothing exports declined in the 1990s, partly as a result of trade barriers and changes in government policies, the Denizli family changed tack, moved to the second story, and turned the ground floor into two shops, rented out to a grocery and a fast-food stand. In other words, they became landlords, fairly prosperous by local standards. On my last visit in 1994, I was startled to see that the oldest daughter, Emine, now married, moved around the neighborhood bareheaded, in tight jeans and a loose but low-cut sweater. Her engaged sister, on the other hand, had become tesettürlü. A young unmarried woman from the neighborhood dropped by dressed in shorts and a short-sleeved shirt! The entire neighborhood had risen economically, almost to the point of unrecognizability—new buildings, shops, roads. Its inhabitants, like the members of the Denizli family, expressed their new economic mobility in different ways, representing symbolically the two competing languages of success and status that are now available to the urban migrant. These languages are neither local nor global, but a creole of local and global cultural elements, modernist goals made comprehensible within a traditionalist grammar and traditionalist goals made accessible through a modernist grammar, all their contradictions intact; Islam and McWorld sweeping tides across the symbolic face of modern Turkish culture like two powerful moons.

Emine Denizli, who defied an arranged marriage by eloping, only to find herself in a restrictive traditional marriage, still is enthralled by romantic love stories and pop songs that present images of women as sexually attractive, if passive, objects of romantic interest. These images of women, along with the accompanying expectations and boundaries, are global images, with little reflection in local Istanbul reality. Yet they motivate Emine to act out a creolized synthesis of contradictory cultural traditions.

Despite the increasing polarization of Turkish society along the Islamist/secularist divide, the symbolism of clothing tells clearly the story of both the hardening of the center line and a blurring of the borders. The Islamist political stand is being absorbed by its success in supporting socioeconomic mobility and diluted by the spread of its message. While upward mobility strengthens the Islamist appeal, it also dilutes and fractures its political message, setting the lure of Islamic chic, and its interest in wealth and consumption, against Islamist principles of anticonsumerism and social justice.

The poor remain pragmatic, as they have been for decades, voting left or voting right, depending on the message and the opportunities. Despite the recent swing to support the Islamists, the message of symbols, even in the heart of the ultraconservative neighborhood of Fatih, demonstrates this pragmatic ambivalence. There is more tesettür, but there is also the occasional young resident in a sleeveless dress, uncommon in Fatih even now, but unheard of a decade ago. In the newer and less ideologically colonized squatter areas and working-class neighborhoods (areas increasingly difficult to distinguish on any formal basis), the symbols speak of an even greater ambivalence.

The Islamist girls on the bus were drawn to symbols of power and nationalist identity rather than to romance. Yet their symbolic domain is as fraught with contradictions as Emine's. Other tesettürlü girls flirt, kiss and hold hands with boys on the street and in the park, dance seductively at parties, and long for lavish turbaned dresses and a wealthy husband and well-appointed home. Both "open" and "covered" lifestyles are credible paths to status and mobility: both potentially open doors to women of the working-class, and both circumscribe women's roles in different ways, not always predictable along local/global lines. As Turkish women look in the modernist, or as Saribay would have it, postmodernist mirror, they see, as we all do, the image of their desire superimposed on the image of their need, the symbolic language of "I" competing with the multiple languages of "we."

NOTES

1. See, for example, Meeker's (1991) discussion of Turkey's new Muslim intellectuals.

2. Participating in the discussion were Peyami Gürel, owner and director of the Payami Art Gallery; Fatma Karabiyik Barbarosoglu, author of *Fashion and Mentality during the Modernization Process* (*Modernlesme Sürecinde Moda ve Zihniyet;* Istanbul: Iletisim Yayinlari, 1994); Ayse Böhürler, journalist and writer; and Ilhan Kutluer, *Izlenim* editor, who acted as moderator.

3. Indeed, in 1995, the Welfare Party pushed unsuccessfully in parliament to have the article of the constitution rescinded that forbids basing the state on religious principles.

REFERENCES

Acar, F. 1991. Was die Islamische Bewegung für Frauen so anziehend macht: Eine Untersuchung über Frauenzeitschriften und eine Gruppe von Studentinnen. Pages 73–92 in A. Neusel, S. Tekeli, and M. Akkent (eds.), *Aufstand im Haus der Frauen: Frauenforschung aus der Türkei*. Berlin: Orlanda Frauenverlag.

Arat, Y. 1991. Zum Verhältnis von Feminismus und Islam: Überlegungen zur Frauenzeitschrift *Kadin ve Aile*. Pages 93–106 in A. Neusel, S. Tekeli, and M. Akkent (eds.), *Aufstand im Haus der Frauen: Frauenforschung aus der Türkei*. Berlin: Orlanda Frauenverlag.

Delaney, C. 1994. Untangling the meanings of hair in Turkish society. *Anthropological Quarterly* 67, no. 4 (October): 159–72.

Kazancigil, A. 1991. Democracy in Muslim lands: Turkey in comparative perspective. *International Social Science Journal* 128: 343–60.

Meeker, M. 1991. The new Muslim intellectuals in the Republic of Turkey. Pages 189–219 in R. Tapper (ed.), *Islam in modern Turkey*. London: Tauris.

Olson, E. A. 1985. Muslim identity and secularism in contemporary Turkey: "The headscarf dispute." *Anthropological Quarterly* 58, no. 4 (October): 161–69.

Saribay, A.Y. 1994. *Postmodernite, sivil toplum ve Islam*. Istanbul: Iletisim Yayinlari.

Stokes, M. 1992. *The Arabesk debate: music and musicians in modern Turkey*. Oxford: Clarendon.

White, Jenny B. 1994. *Money makes us relatives: women's labor in urban Turkey*. Austin: University of Texas Press.

Part III

Contested Positions

6

Istanbulites and Others
The Cultural Cosmology of Being Middle Class
in the Era of Globalism

Ayşe Öncü

Who is an Istanbulite? Or, for that matter, a Beiruti, or a Parisian, or a New Yorker? Akin to all cosmopolitan cities with heterogeneous populations and intermingling of diverse cultures, Istanbul is a study in contrasts rather than uniformity. A plurality of social groups and cultures coexist in Istanbul, often separated from one another as the hard-edged pieces of a mosaic. It is a city of immigrants, with three-quarters of its population born elsewhere. In this sense, the question of who is an Istanbulite is a rhetorical question. A true Istanbulite is a "myth."

Contemporary myths, suggests Barthes (1972), are not expressed in long, fixed narratives of the primitive epic but in phrases and forms of speech whose meanings appear self-evident and hence "natural." They are linguistic expressions through which a dominant cultural discourse floods the hidden corners of everyday existence, presenting itself as universal and ideal. An "Istanbulite," then, is a myth in the Barthian sense of the term. It is a figure of speech that insistently and repetitively circulates through daily life—in conversations among friends, in newspaper articles, television commentaries, captions of photographs in weekly magazines, films, jokes. The Turkish word *Istanbullu* appears to simultaneously condense and connote an array of distinctions, refinements, competencies that are already "known" from daily experience and hence understood without saying. In a metropolis of numerous and fluctuating plurality of cultural hierarchies, the word *Istanbullu* stands guard over the boundary between high and popular culture.

It can be argued perhaps, that most cosmopolitan cities of world stature, ancient or modern, have similarly developed such mythical significance around their names—as the repository of multiple and nuanced distinctions of refinement and taste emblematic of "high" culture. In this sense, being an Istanbulite is part of a more general phenomenon, the linguistic manifestation of cultural hierarchies that are subject to power relations in all metropolises, everywhere. Yet, an Istanbulite is also a specific myth, one that requires thinking in terms of a distinctive set of cultural mediations located in historical time and place. For contemporary myth making is a cultural activity that presumes the existence of makers and users, who are not themselves a homogeneous collectivity. The discursive constructs of a hegemonic culture are continuously undermined and actively renegotiated within the contours of lived experience and practices of everyday life; the ways in which the linguistic term *Istanbullu* acquires cultural content and meaning is bound with the city's changing sociopolitical landscape.

My interest in the phenomenon of an Istanbulite is located in the present, a moment in time when the dynamics of everyday existence is penetrated and shaped by a diversity of cultural flows from different corners of the globe. A dizzying array of "glocalized" (global-local) icons, images, and sounds intermingle in the landscape of contemporary Istanbul, threatening to overwhelm established cultural hierarchies, at least in the public realm. The kinds of issues posed by this new order of complexity have inspired a prolific literature that emphasizes the "flux" and "fluidity" of contemporary metropolitan experience, the erosion of boundaries between high and popular cultures, and its implications in terms of "fragmentation" and "crisis of culture" in cities across the world. My purpose here is not to review all the issues prompted by this literature.[1] Instead I will simply focus on the discursive construct *Istanbullu* and try to show how it lends coherence and political logic to cultural boundaries that threaten to lose their clarity in the texture of living reality.

How does the word *Istanbullu* acquire content and meaning as it circulates through daily life in present-day Istanbul? One way of seeking answers to this question is to explore how multiple and changing typifications of "others" operate in different textual contexts. Thus, following Bakhtin, I will depart from the premise that the meaning of the word itself is never sealed, or finalized, because it necessitates the existence of "others" to imagine, even if temporarily, the imagined unity and wholeness of Istanbulites. But the processes of "othering" that are hidden in the trivia of everyday life and renegotiated in the experiential world of humdrum existence are difficult to capture and understand through "authoritative" texts such as histories, biographies, poems, and so forth . The strategy I will adopt here is to turn to popular humor where the "pretentious" universalist claims of the dominant social order are debunked through ridicule and parody. Popular humor, which intervenes in the polite world of privileged utterance, to transgress established symbolic hierarchies and invert them through play, belongs in what Bakhtin referred to as the realm of "carnevalesque."[2] Bakhtin's metaphor of "carnival" derives from the ribaldry and irreverence associated with popular festivities—Mardi Gras, Fasching, fairs—that involve a temporary, licensed suspension of order. In the popular culture of Istanbul, the oppositional view of the world that Bakhtin associated with the "carnival square" (where formal hierarchy is suspended, and the sacrosanct and dignified elements of official-serious culture are deprived of their authority through unrestrained festivity and gaiety) finds its counterpart in the seemingly inexhaustible fund of jokes produced and reproduced as part of everyday sociability, as well as an immense variety of cartoons in the pages of daily newspapers, popular journals, and satire magazines.

In this chapter, I will turn to the lively and prolific scene of graphic humor in Istanbul and ground my discussion on a series of cartoons that poke fun at the pomposity and dignity of prevailing distinctions and hierarchies in the discursive realm. While such cartoons are a constant feature of Istanbul's graphic scene, their *humor* is time bound. Cartoons that were funny yesterday become stale today. This is because cartoons, akin to all humor, draw upon an inventory of *familiar* signs and symbols, play with the predictable meanings to evoke an instant of surprise, and elicit a chuckle on the part of the reader. In this sense, graphic humor "interferes" with the cultural discourses of the moment; that is, it captures, distills, and accentuates the "authoritative" codes that shape and organize the mixture that is everyday consciousness, so as to debunk or unmask them through parody and humor. Humor is always in dialogue with the enclosing cultural discourse. It evokes, simultaneously, both common sense and also its ambivalences and inconsistencies.

Using this double-voiced discourse of humor, I will try to develop three interlinked points of argument. My first point derives from the insistence and repetitiveness of cartoons that parody stereotypes of "immigrants" in the graphic scene of Istanbul. By drawing upon cartoons chosen from different time periods in the history of the city, I will try to show how parodies of refinement and distinction, as well as parodies of belonging and authenticity, are built around prevailing stereotypes of "immigrants." The argument I will develop here is that the immigrant combines, within a single typification, two central components in the dialogical imagination of an Istanbulite. On the one hand, the immigrant operates as a repository of negative attributes, through whom the refinements and distinctions of being an Istanbulite is reflexively understood. On the other, the immigrant operates as the invading outsider, whose unjustified presence in the city establishes, by extension, a seamless chronology for Istanbulites as the basis of their authenticity and moral superiority.

Based on recent typifications of "the immigrant" produced and reproduced over the past decade, I will then show that in the cultural cosmos of contemporary Istanbul, "the immigrant" has become an absolute other, activated to gather all accents and nuances of cultural hierarchy and distinction, into a single, total, and totalizing category of exclusion. I will thus venture to suggest that the mythology of an Istanbulite has lost its cultural moorings in the realm of taste and distinction emblematic of high culture, shorn of its connotations of belonging and authenticity. It merely negates and excludes. It thus operates at the level of everyday, to cut and reshape the living texture of reality into a rigid dichotomy of Istanbulites and immigrants.

My last point will be a broader one, having to do with myth making as a cultural process that presumes the existence of makers and users. Contemporary myths are not anonymous like the bricoleur of primitive myths. The prevailing stereotypes and typifications of immigrant culture cannot be conceived apart from a "mainstream" middle-class culture that defines them. But a "middle-class way of life" is not something solid and immutable; it is based on an elaborated system of distinctions and differences that have become increasingly subject to erosion in the era of globalism. Hence, I will argue that constructions of the immigrant as the absolute other in the neoliberal ethos of Istanbul is part of an ongoing struggle to redefine the boundaries of middle sectors or classes.

I will try to lend substance and content to these points of argument through readings of cartoons chosen from different time periods. Before turning to Istanbul and processes of "othering" within it, however, a few words of explanation about the use of cartoons as textual material seem required.

A METHODOLOGICAL CAVEAT ON READING CARTOONS

All humor—pranks, wit, comic strips, cartoons—is essentially a play on established, commonsense hierarchies of meaning. The humorist begins with taken-for-granted, established categories of meaning that inform our commonsense order of reality as ordered and predictable. By juxtaposing desperate frames of reference, the artist exposes the impurity and arbitrariness of all categories, blurring the hierarchical impositions of order to elicit a chuckle. In an instant of surprise and laughter, fragments and emblems are dissociated from one cultural discourse and reassembled in another, conveying the inextricably mixed and ambivalent nature of all cultural life, the reversibility of cultural forms, symbols, meanings. In this sense, humor builds on established symbolic hierarchies and subverts them through play.

The specificity of graphic humor resides in bringing together a rich inventory of images and signs of metropolitan life and articulating them in powerful visual condensations. It must be kept in mind, however, that visual sign systems operate only in indirect relation to the material world of reference. This seems especially important when dealing with cartoons and comic strips that initially appear to be much more directly and clearly accessible than linguistic forms. But as current theory suggests, the visual is mediated and controlled linguistically (Jenks 1995, 1–24). Hence, language is a crucial mediator of the visual, regardless of the absence or presence of words or narratives. The visual entails a complex process of generating meanings that cannot be divorced from linguistic-discursive forms. This is another way of saying visual signs are polysemic (i.e., open to different meanings depending on the linguistic-discursive realm in which they operate).

When attempting to interpret cartoons, the complexities of working with visual texts are compounded with the play upon meanings that is the essence of humor (e.g., Palmer 1994, 93–103). The graphic artist uses the polysemic nature of visual signs to simultaneously invoke and play with their common sense meanings in everyday discourse. For humor to work, the humorist and the viewer must share the same symbolic maps and sign systems. Graphic humor at its best is a sophisticated play, one that the cartoonist sets up and invites the viewer to participate.

The cartoons on which I focus in the present study are noteworthy for the mundane repetitiveness and predictability of their humor, rather than the sophisticated play on meanings they evoke. Such humdrum cartoons lie about in pages of daily newspapers, magazines, albums, or pamphlets, requiring little effort beyond a glance to elicit a smile, precisely because the situations and typifications they evoke are interwoven with the experience of daily life in Istanbul. Their humor is based on incongruities hidden in the trivia of daily life, the politics of everyday, rather than politics writ large. Hence, they are not political cartoons in the conventional sense of the term: their humor is grounded in the culture of everyday Istanbul.

What renders such cartoons interesting for the purposes of this chapter is that taken together, they provide a continuous stream of "irreverent" conversation, in graphics and words, in a city where the majority of the population is semiliterate. But to the extent that their humor is situationally grounded and based on verbal-visual codes that rely on instant association with the concrete, the specific, the here and now of experiential reality, "translating" them into written words, in a language other than that of its intended audience, becomes fraught with pitfalls. It seems important to acknowledge these pitfalls from the very beginning, however impossible it may be to avoid them. My own selection and "authorial voice" in the rereadings offered here is simultaneously that of a researcher who has been working on a large archive of cartoons on daily life in Istanbul and also that of a person who enjoys the work of particular graphic artists and the flavor of their humor.

HACIAĞAS INVADE THE GRAPHIC SCENE OF ISTANBUL

Graphic humor has a lengthy historical lineage in the cultural and political life in Istanbul, spanning more than a century. From within this history, I will choose to begin with the early 1940s, when the haciaga makes his appearance on the graphic scene of Istanbul. The haciaga is a culturally and historically specific version of a breed often encountered in graphic humor—the arriviste, the social climber, the nouveau riche—characterized by having too much economic and too little cultural capital. Genres of humor based on conspicuous display of wealth, flawed by absence of "cultural taste," has its variants in all societies. The usual theme of such humor is overconsumption combined with a notion of shallowness or fakeness. The forerunners of this genre of humor in the graphic scene of Istanbul date all the way back to the late nineteenth century.

The cultural specificity of the haciaga in Istanbul of the 1940s resides in his origins and his fake piousness. The lexical term -*ağa* signifies a traditional landlord, connotes wealth as well as power and patronage, with its reciprocal obligations of loyalty and protection in agrarian Anatolia. The prefix *haci*- indicates that he has been to pilgrimage in Mecca—an obligatory voyage for every pious Muslim, but a voyage only a privileged few could afford at the time. How this traditional figure of power, wealth, and piety from Anatolia becomes a "fish out of water" in Istanbul (to translate from Turkish directly) diminishes in stature despite his wealth, not only provided rich material for cartoonists but also afforded much pleasure for Istanbulites of the 1940s, to judge by the number and repetitiveness of haciaga parodies.

In cartoons, the haciaga's wide girth and double chin, accustomed to the comforts of baggy pants and loose clothing, defies the strictures of trousers and ties. His wife, whose body bulges out of her new dresses, is equally uncomfortable but luxuriating in her new "urban" role in displaying and consuming family wealth. It is no longer the largesse of the haciaga that enhances family honor and prestige in Istanbul but conspicuous consumption controlled by the wife. Regardless of how powerful in Anatolia, his abundant money fails to gain him entrée among Istanbulites, in the absence of requisite social graces and "cultural taste." He simply becomes ridiculous through lavish but "uncultivated" spending. In Istanbul, the "aga" is cut down to size. But he also merits some sympathy, because he now shares in the common fate of mankind in Istanbul. He suffers from the tireless ambitions of an assertive wife, who sheds her subservience upon arrival in Istanbul and begins to nag her husband into ever increasing consumption. The haciaga's loss of power in Istanbul thus extends into the private sphere, where his wife gains the upper hand in consumption (see Figure 6.1).

Fig 6.1

Mr. nouveau riche: "We should spend the summer on the island."

Mrs. nouveau riche: "Really?"

Mr. nouveau riche: "Yes, I am told that five hundred lira houses go for five thousand."

Fig 6.2

Man: "Darling, they say that for Istanbul beauties, money comes before everything else, is that right?"

Woman: "I don't know. I am not very materialistic. It is alright if money comes
afterwards."

An equally significant theme in haciaga cartoons is his fake piety. Playing on the connotations of the *haci-* prefix, the haciaga is depicted as a lecherous fat man, lusting after young girls, whether they be belly dancers, revue starlets, call girls, or secretaries (see Figure 6.2). To emphasize the incongruity between the professed religious piety and conservatism of the haciaga and his lascivious yearnings, he is repetitively portrayed in bars, nightclubs, and dance halls. His fakeness resides in espousing Islam's strictures on alcohol and illicit sex, while at the same time liberally imbibing or engaging in both. In the "dirty mind" of the haciaga, all unattached women are sex objects and hence easy prey; the night life of cosmopolitan Istanbul is associated with vice and sin.

Viewed from a broader historical vantage point, many of the individual motifs that appear in haciaga cartoons can be traced all the way back to the late nineteenth century in the graphic humor scene of Istanbul. In its earlier forerunners, especially at the turn of the century, the genre was often used to negotiate the cultural boundaries between the Europeanized elite of the metropolis and its more modest middle classes. The ambiguities associated with practicing European manners correctly—that is, within the bounds of modesty and decorum befitting a middle class way of life, as distinct from "super-Westernization," which is aping European customs uncritically—was a prolific source of parody from the very inception of graphic humor in Istanbul. Later, in the earlier decades of the Republican era, innumerable cartoons explored the ambiguous line between modesty and immodesty by focusing on nuances of proper comportment in public space, on the street, on beaches, on tram cars. Parodies based on the etiquette of gender relations in public space were closely bound with the question of how far the newly emerging middle classes of the Republican order could go in adopting European customs, and still remain within the bounds of respectability.[3]

The stereotype of the haciaga is important, because it powerfully combines a series of existing motifs—money/taste, false piety/true morality, provincialism/cosmopolitanism, Anatolia/Istanbul—and condenses them into a single, negative "other." In Istanbul of the 1940s, the haciaga cartoons are not simply parodies of taste and comportment but guard the cultural capital of "authentic" Istanbulites against the vulgarism of new wealth flowing in from Anatolia. Thus, the invasion of haciagas in the graphic scene of Istanbul coincides with a historical moment in time when Istanbul's middle classes were waging a cultural battle against a particular breed of overconsumers, the new rich.

Today, the cultural battle lines have shifted to a new front—the vulgarities of overconsumption among the lower strata of the city. Thus, although tasteless overconsumption continues to be a very potent theme in the graphic scene of Istanbul, the haciaga stereotype, as the symbolic embodiment of vulgarism associated with new wealth, has receded into the background. Various reincarnations of the same typification, produced and reproduced, are no longer funny but simply stale.

ARABESK CULTURE INVADES ISTANBUL

The next set of cartoons I turn to are from the 1980s when parodies of Istanbul's *arabesk* culture provided fresh material for young graphic artists of the decade, distinct in style and flavor from earlier decades. Throughout the 1960s and 1970s, graphic humor had become synonymous with radical social criticism in the art scene of Istanbul, and many artists with formal university training in fine arts, architecture, and graphic design had turned to cartoons as a potential means of reaching the urban poor. Universal themes such as capitalist injustice, exploitation of labor, and oppression of the masses had taken over the graphic scene, delivered in the "abstract-minimalist" graphic styles of the period.

In the shifting political mood of the 1980s decade, graphic humor of the 1960s and 1970s, with its direct mode of delivering significant political messages, seemed out of tune with the prevailing neoliberal ethos of the times. Istanbul was now the emergent growth pole of Turkey's rapid integration into world markets, riding on a wave of foreign investment and buoyant exports. Almost overnight, the consumer markets of the city were flooded with goods from around the world—available for purchase on installment. In open-air vegetable and food markets that dot the poor neighborhoods of the city, stalls now displayed electronic goods from Taiwan and tableware from Germany, beneath overhanging racks of cheap clothing of every imaginable variety, ranging from lacy women's underwear, to T-shirts and jeans with fake designer labels. Everybody seemed to be on the move: in the language of Istanbulites, arabesk culture had invaded the city.

The epithet *arabesk* denotes impurity, hybridity, and bricolage and designates a special kind of kitsch.[4] The word was first coined in the late 1960s and early 1970s to describe a hybrid music genre that emerged and acquired immense popularity among recent immigrant populations of Istanbul (Özbek 1991; Stokes 1992; Markoff 1994). Banned from state radio and television for defying the established canons of both folk and classical Turkish music, by intermixing rhythms and instruments from popular Western and Egyptian music, arabesk music soared in the expanding cassette market of the 1970s. Films featuring famous arabesk singers as the star–popular hero achieved immediate box office success in local movie houses on the urban fringes of Istanbul as well as other large cities of the country. In the process, the label *arabesk* acquired a wider chain of associations, denoting a musical genre, a film genre, as well as the cultural habitus and lifestyle of those who enjoyed them. Arabesk lovers now belonged to "arabesk culture"—banal, trashy, but most of all in-between, hence polluted and polluting, to invoke Mary Douglas (1966). Arabesk songs, singers, and films not only failed to conform to artistically established, pure categories of classification but also contaminated them. Similarly, those who belong to arabesk culture—the low-income immigrant populations swirling on the fringes of Istanbul—have lost the innocence, purity, and authenticity of their traditional peasant-folk heritage (but remained ignorant), without acquiring the urbanity of cosmopolitan life (but embraced its crass commercialism), and hence belong in neither of the two worlds. Arabesk culture connotes a half-breed world of pseudo-urbanism, one that contradicts and defies cherished categories. Neither peasant nor urban, arabesk culture becomes a placeless phenomenon, both residual and marginal, but also dangerous, because its boundaries are ambiguous and margins confused. The defining essence of arabesk culture—its hybridity—simultaneously essentializes the purity of Istanbulite's culture and also endangers it. In the discourse of the 1980s, the "pure" Istanbulites are an endangered species.

For cartoonists of the 1980s, the multiple connotations of the label *arabesk* provide a rich source of play on meanings. Latif Demirci's cartoons, a young artist who made a name for himself in the satire press in the early 1980s and later moved on to the pages of more expensive, glossy magazines, capture the flavor of this new genre of humor. His cartoons are full of material objects, drawn in loving detail to poke fun at overassimilation to the world of capitalist commodities. He enters the arabesk world of Istanbul's lower classes, considered vulgar because it combines the material signs of modernity in imperfect ways, to conjure a whole range of situations in which individuals are totally oblivious to any contradictions, completely unfazed by the cacophony of seemingly unrelated objects, words, and images that are a part of everyday life.

In Demirci's humorous lines, the fat man sitting with his legs tucked under and counting his prayer beads is supremely comfortable in his California sweatshirt (Figure 6.3). The two women being served coffee by the young son/daughter of the household are unfazed by her outfit and casually drop the word *transvestite* (Figure 6.4). Through parodic reproductions of arabesk culture, Demirci mocks the reader's own categorical boundaries that defines transgression and labels it offensive. But the cutting edge of his humor resides in defining arabesk in a new sense, such that the category is no longer confinable to a single social sector or class. The businessman dressed in his power clothes, wearing Nike sports socks while sipping his whisky (Figure 6.5), or the intellectual sitting among a tacky ensemble of incongruous objects (Figure 6.6) become a part of what they denigrate: arabesk culture.

Fig 6.4
Boy (in sibilant tone): "Welcome to the house."
Woman with black scarf: "We are getting old; it is a good thing that my younger son turned transvestite and helps with the household."
Woman with white scarf: "God be praised, he has become very beautiful."

Fig 6.6
"Write my dear: I hate Arabesk . . . "

While Latif Demirci's graphic style and blend of humor is distinctive, the themes he plays with run through much of graphic humor of the 1980s. There is an abundance of cartoons that parody the epithet *arabesk*, both as a label that designates a special form of urban aesthetic, considered vulgar because it combines the material culture of modernity in imperfect and partial ways, and also as a derogatory category that targets that whole sector of Istanbul's population, who, having lost their moorings in indigenous peasant culture, have begun to indulge in mass consumption. But the novelty of this genre of humor rapidly wore off, partly because the meaning of the term itself changed. It is no longer a discriminatory term aimed at lower-class populations of the city but denotes a kind of kitschy aesthetic, or lack of aesthetic, symptomatic of upper classes as well.

As an idiom of distinction, or lack of distinction, the word *arabesk* originally derived its meaning from a kind of vulgarism associated with mass consumption, associated with lower classes or sectors. This is a new form of "tackified" overconsumption that imitates with no regard to the original, substituting Formica for wood, polyester for silk. Thus, the accelerated circulation of the term in daily language coincides with a particular historical moment in time, when Istanbul's opening to world economy and the buoyancy of its consumer market pose a kind of new threat to prevailing cultural hierarchies—the vulgarism of overconsumption in the lower classes, as distinct from tasteless overconsumption among the rich. The "new rich" (in the classic sense of the term) emulate refinements of taste and threaten to erode cultural hierarchies by attaching a monetary value to them. The vulgarism of arabesk, in contrast, is dangerous because it totally disregards hierarchies of taste. In this sense, the derogatory label *arabesk* is no longer confinable or reducible to a single social sector or class, because the total disregard of taste now becomes symptomatic of the wealthy as well. By the end of the 1980s, the new channels of accumulation and upward mobility associated with the era of neoliberalism had given birth to a new category of rich in Istanbul. This is a novel breed of "new rich," however, who couldn't care less about matters of taste. They just luxuriate in their newly found wealth and look on their own hybridity with delight, so to speak, totally devoid of the status anxieties commonly associated with the term *nouveau riche* in French. In the absence of a name, the label *arabesk* expanded to capture this new syndrome, used to refer not just to a new breed of rich but, for instance, to a new breed of politician, who disregards distinctions of taste without compunction or embarrassment.[5]

Today, in the mid-1990s, the word *arabesk* has become an all encompassing metaphor to describe and identify a general malaise that seems to plague every aspect of life in Turkish society—arabesk democracy, arabesk economy, arabesk politicians—all suffering from a neither-nor situation of indeterminacy and degeneration. In the term *arabesk*, suggests

Meral Özbek (1996, 212), "we have finally found a name to express the identity problem of Turkish society."

But a new derogatory label surfaced from the pages of satire magazines toward the latter half of the 1980s, the *maganda*, and subsequently began to circulate in everyday speech gaining progressively wider currency to name an absolute "other," an aesthetic anomaly, produced by Istanbul.

THE INVASION OF *MAGANDA*

The word *maganda* was invented by a group of young cartoonists whose irreverent graphic style and humor gained immediate success among the young following of weekly satirical magazines such as *Girgir, Limon, Hibir,* and *Leman.* Such magazines proliferate on the newsstands of Istanbul, their longevity subject to the vicissitudes of a readership below the age of twenty-five and the propensity of young graphic artists to split off and regroup under new titles. New magazines appear and disappear as young readers float from one title to the next, following shifting fashions and their favorite cartoonists. But the low rates of survival and short life span of most magazines in this highly competitive market can be misleading. For the total circulation of Istanbul's satirical press has been fairly stable over the past ten years, reaching roughly 1.5 million young readers per month, not a negligible figure in a country where total monthly magazine circulation is estimated to fluctuate between ten and eleven million.

The young graphic artists who work for and/or publish satirical magazines and their readership form a distinctive social and discursive milieu, one that constitutes a foreign land for the uninitiated. Words, expressions, and graphic styles are continuously "invented," lose their novelty, and are replaced by new ones. Thus, what is referred to as "slang" by the mainstream adult world and "restricted code" by social analysts is part of a process of capturing and naming what is experienced, yet it remains unformulated in the discursive realm of the adult, mainstream world. Maganda was such an invented name, used to describe both a particular typification, produced and reproduced in situations of infinite variety, and also a graphic genre associated with these cartoons.

As initially formulated through the nonverbal codes of satirical magazines, the maganda is a figure of brute strength, hairy body, and unbridled sexual appetites, who infects and pollutes the cultural atmosphere of the social settings he appears in. Rather than representing a sociocultural type in the conventional sense of the term, the maganda articulates, in the graphic language of his creators, a cultural phenomenon that is experienced in the fabric of social existence but remains unarticulated. Thus, when pressed to define in words who exactly a maganda is, the graphic artists who coined the term provided the following description for the mainstream readers of one of the major daily newspapers in the early 1990s:

> Maganda is an assault on emotions, an aesthetic aberration. He is an anomaly which corresponds to ignorance, to brute force, to social climbing, to all degenerate values. We created him. He is the animal in us. . . . We allowed him to flourish. He is a stain which cannot be removed. He is like a plastic bottle which never degrades, never disappears.
>
> The maganda can be of any sex, any class, any race, any occupation. He is contagious, he infects. . . . Maganda is universal unfortunately.[6] (Sunday supplement, *Hürriyet*, January 12, 1992)

In cartoons however, the maganda is invariably depicted as a male and, more often than not, in a state of sexual arousal. So while the maganda is an "aesthetic anomaly" who gives rise to an "allergic reaction" in all situations he is present, he is most offensive when sexually aroused (see Figure 6.7). This is when he intrudes, offends, molests, assaults the senses through his warped sexual imagination and the vulgarity of his sexual practices. These are depicted in explicit graphic detail, showing the maganda to be devoid of cultural codes that define human sensuality and sexual conduct. Hence, the maganda is "the animal within us," the absolute other, whose physical repulsiveness is the embodiment of vulgar sexual urges.

The explicit sexual content of the maganda cartoons and graphic style associated with them cannot be divorced from broader trends in publishing and broadcasting industry of the 1990s in Turkey. This is now an Istanbul where 90 percent of homes have acquired color television sets. With the opening of Istanbul's advertising sector to joint ventures with multinationals, television commercials have acquired a new patina. A whole new range of glossy magazines from *Cosmopolitan* to *Penthouse* and *Playboy*, not to mention fashion and home decoration magazines, compete with each other in newspaper stands. Satellite dishes adorn every other roof, enabling the new commercial channels to beam into living rooms, projecting onto the screen glittering images of a shiny, clean, orderly world inhabited by beautiful people. The maganda cartoons can be interpreted as the antithesis of this world or, as the graphic artist Mehmet Çagçag put it in retrospect during an interview with the author, "our answer to the shining, glittering images."

Equally important perhaps, is that in Istanbul of the 1990s, sexuality has been opened to the gaze. Visual images of sensuality that were confined to sleazy movie houses barely a decade ago are now beamed into living rooms by competing TV channels. Thus, for the majority of Istanbul's youth, sexuality is no longer only a part of the phenomenal world of existence, taken for granted but unspoken. It has entered the realm of visibility, recognizable in the realm of public objectivity and hence open to rene-

Fig 6.7
Title above reads: "The Birth of Mevlut." ("Mevlut" is a man's name in Turkish, but in Arabic it means "birth" and has religious connotations.)

gotiation. The solidity of cultural boundaries separating the experienced world of sexuality (in brothels, backseats of porno movie houses) and the "public" universe of gender relations governed by strict codes of untouchability were fractured through the abundance of display for the gaze. The maganda typification is thus the product of a new generation of youth culture in the process of discovering, through the gaze, the aesthetics of practice and the cultural codes of permissiveness.

In its travel from the graphic language of satire magazines to the discursivity of everyday language, the label *maganda* has lost some of its immediate association with unbridled sexuality. It connotes, first and foremost, an offensive being—simultaneously distasteful (not simply tasteless) and also aggressive (not simply vulgar). Thus, for instance, in the lyrics of a rap song that topped the best-seller charts in Istanbul's cassette market in 1991:

> If you don't spit, belch, or litter the ground,
> Sneeze or sniffle
> Never grow a moustache
> Wear a gold chain necklace
> Open your collar and torso, . . .
> If you don't drink or get loaded
> Beat your wife at home
> Make two kids a year
> Hang a gold watch on your wrist
> Harass women on the street
> Molest them on buses and minibuses
> How could you become a maganda?
> Would it be credible? (*Vitamin*, Istanbul 1991)

In these lyrics, *maganda* is a label that condenses multiple negative attributes into a single absolute other: belching, spitting, wife beating, alcohol abuse, verbal harassment, as well as molesting. Thus, the maganda, with his pseudo-racial attributes, is an intrusive presence encountered on sidewalks, in traffic, sitting in the next row, or at the next table. A second song from the same cassette explains how the maganda has now become impossible to avoid in Istanbul:

> In the countryside, in bars, deluxe hotels
> Now everywhere in Taxim or Maxim
> Jogging, aerobics, bodybuilding
> Meetings, clubs, toilets
> . . .
> His soul wooden, his body a tree trunk, his head of pressed straw
> Even if he wears a gold saddle, a maganda is a maganda.

Thus, Istanbulites of the 1990s, having become reconciled to the invasion of Arabesk culture, now seem to find themselves confronted by a phenomenon of a seemingly different order. For the references of the maganda are that of active intrusion, rather than passive impurity. One last example will serve to illustrate how these terms can lend themselves to multiple and often contradictory meanings in their meandering circulation.

The daily newspaper *Hurriyet* recently allocated one of its back pages to the emergent lifestyles of the 1990s in Istanbul. Illustrated with aerial photographs of a wealthy new suburb, the write-up informed readers about the exclusive circles of Istanbul, ranging from alumni clubs and conference circuits, to imported yuppidom and Islamic suburbs, replete with names of prominent figures. The journalists who wrote the piece, after quoting a series of authoritative sources, claimed that these were the "post-modern tribes" of Istanbul. In the last section, subtitled "And the Maganda. . . ," they added a conclusion of their own:

And the Maganda . . .
One of the necessary rules in the formation of post-modern tribes is substantial financial worth. The only tribe that constitutes an exception to this rule are the maganda.
These maganda are members of the arabesk culture that emerges when the traditional culture of immigrants in the fringes of megalopolitan Istanbul, is fused with urban culture. They do not have a lengthy history. They answer the social needs of the past twenty years.
The coming together of the maganda is also an identity. But unlike the other post-modern tribes, they have neither suburbs, intellectual circles, nor labels. The sense of belonging of this lumpen tribe is established in stadium benches, neighborhood coffee houses and evening strolls on the streets. (*Hurriyet*, December 13, 1995)

This passage is worth quoting, both because it offers one example of how the word *maganda* crops up in journalistic discourse and is redefined and recirculated in unanticipated contexts, but also because it seems to capture, in a nutshell, the whole cultural cosmology of Istanbul in the 1990s. This is now an Istanbul in which the experienced world has been transformed through the flow of globalized images and words, providing new scripts through which the familiar is reinterpreted. Thus, the words *post-modern* (used in English), combined with *tribe* (translated into Turkish), when assimilated into the field of experience of contemporary Istanbul, lend themselves to a novel combination, the maganda-tribe. But it is only the cosmopolitan academic expert who can identify the disparate sources and genealogies of the words used in the passage here. In everyday Turkish, the passage makes perfect common sense. So it also reminds us of Gramsci's adage—common sense is always "strangely composite," appropriating and incorporating into its closed circle what does not fit into the existing scheme of things.

DISCUSSION

I began this chapter with Barthian mythologies, using them as a conceptual handle to come to grips with the phenomenon of an Istanbulite. An *Istanbullu* is a myth, I suggested, in the sense of a discursive construct that transforms the formless void of everyday experience into meaningful reality, and informs practices of inclusion and exclusion. Its taken-for-grantedness, its "naturalness," makes it invisible and ideological. As such, it operates as part of what Gramsci termed "common sense" or the "spontaneous philosophy" that underpins lived experience.[7] Through humor, the absurdity of "normal common sense" becomes visible in one instant of recognition. Hence, I set out to decipher, through a reading of a set of cartoons that poke fun at stereotypes of "others," how the mythology of an Istanbulite is constructed and circulated.

The analytical centerpiece of my argument was that the meaning of Istanbulite is never sealed or finalized but is always in the process of making through political enunciations of "the immigrant," whose unjustified presence is condensed and mediated through the metaphors of invasion, siege, and assault. In each of the typifications I focused on, the *haciaga*, the *arabesk*, the *maganda*, the original (i.e., the Istanbulite) is recovered and recaptured.

Each of these stereotypes is bound up with the historical ethos of prevailing times, and their succession does not imply some sort of progressive, cumulative change over time. In the graphic scene of Istanbul, particular genres of humor capture the imagination of audiences, are repetitively produced and reproduced, then go out of fashion. This is not only because they are grounded in the texture of "lived" reality but also because whatever subversive content humor might have, it rapidly becomes absorbed into mainstream culture, mapped out as a different "style" or "genre." Thus, cartoons that are very funny at one moment in time, cease to amuse in the next, as the ambivalences they play on begin to sound "perfectly natural" and make common sense. Common sense, suggests Gramsci, is "strangely composite" because it is always mobile, appropriating alternative views and artifacts in such a way as to soften and neutralize their specificity and antagonistic content. Thus, in 1997, during the writing of this chapter, maganda cartoons already lost their cutting edge. And the word *maganda* has become absorbed into mainstream language, in such a way that the sentence quoted earlier, "These maganda are members of the arabesk culture which emerges when the traditional culture of immigrants to the fringes of megalopolitan Istanbul, is fused with urban culture," makes perfect common sense.

But what do these derogatory labels, and the stereotypes associated with them, tell us about their makers and users? It seems self-evident (to my mind, at least) that the continuous circulation of the word *Istanbullu* has little to do with "preserving a high culture" in the conventional sense of the term. Nor is it, I would argue, about guarding the boundary between two rival camps of economic and cultural elites in the sense of Bourdieu. Rather, it is part of an ongoing cultural battle on two fronts, against the tasteless overconsumption of the rich and the vulgarism of mass consumption in the lower classes. As such, it is part of the cultural struggle to negotiate the "middle ground," the parameters of which constitute a middle-class way of life.

So I should perhaps paraphrase my initial question. Do the cartoons I have dwelled on say anything specific about the cultural ethos of Istanbul's middle sectors or classes in the era of globalism? The transformation of "the immigrant" from an outsider reflective of Istanbulite's urbanity to an absolute other whose moral offensiveness is inscribed upon his body, with all its attendant racial overtones, is, I have suggested, a product of the past decade. In the label *maganda,* there are few, if any, connotations of marginality or poverty. He is a total and totalizing other, whose presence in Istanbul is morally offensive. One possible theoretical script, or scenario, is to interpret this by attributing a "crisis" to Istanbul's middle classes, a product of policies of liberalization that undermine the economic basis of a middle-class way of life, on the one hand, and of global cultural flows that threaten to erode the symbolic basis of its reproduction, on the other. In this context, a growing literature emphasizes the "shrinking" or "disappearing" of a middle-class way of life, as several recent book titles (and their contents) such as *Fear of Falling* (Ehrenreich 1989) and *Falling from Grace* (Newman 1988) suggest. And in the context of Istanbul, there is little doubt that "tasteless and vulgar overconsumerism" has obliterated many of the visible signs and markers that distinguish a middle-class way of life. So it is possible to see the maganda as the reaction of Istanbul's middle sectors to "fear of falling."

But perhaps matters are more complex than this. For a middle-class ethos is not simply about markers of distinction in the realm of consumption but also about morals. What is significant about the stereotypes and typifications I have elaborated is the way they associate ways of consuming with moral qualities; their potency derives from combining distinctions of taste with moral attributes such as duplicity, fakeness, impurity, perversion, and so forth. Thus, I would venture to suggest that in the era of hyperconsumerism, at a moment in time when the markers and distinctions of a middle-class way of life in Istanbul seem to have dissolved into numerous and fluctuating plurality of hierarchies, the mythology of an Istanbulite rearranges them on moral grounds. In the ethos and rhetoric of Istanbul's middle classes, the maganda are the reason as well as the manifestation of how moral values (*manevi değerler*) appear to have melted into thin air. In this sense, the continuous valorization of the myth of an Istanbulite can be interpreted not as a manifestation of decline and fall from grace but as part of an active process of renegotiating and reconstituting the link among commodities, morals, and consumption in the era of globalism.

NOTES

1. I have attempted this elsewhere; see Öncü (1997).

2. For an interpretation of Bakhtin's work in relation to that of Gramsci, see Brandist (1966).

3. Walter Armbrust (1996) describes very similar themes in the Egyptian satirical press of the 1930s. See, for instance, pp. 75–86.

4. According to Claudio Lomnitz (1966), terms such as *naco* in Mexico, *cholo* in Bolivia and Peru, and *mano* in Ecuador have similar connotations of impurity and hybridity and designate a special kind of kitsch. He says that these terms resonate with the imaginary of colonial castes and were originally used as a slur against Indians and more generally against peasants, but their original meanings of "uncouth" or "uncultured" began to change in the 1970s. In Turkish, *arabesk* is a new label that also gained currency in the 1970s. It has few resonances with the word for peasant, *köylü*, who is the eulogized core of the Turkish nation. In the graphic scene of Istanbul, the peasant was never a major figure of parody. In the abstract political humor of the 1960s and 1970s, the bare feet of the peasant symbolize his potential as the proletariat of the future, and a radical force.

5. Perhaps the best example of this syndrome was Turgut Özal himself, prime minister and the architect of Turkey's neoliberalism. He shocked the cultural establishment by holding conversations with the press corps on the beach, with his pictures in a bathing suit, his pot belly sticking out, making front-page news in all daily newspapers the next day. He never missed an opportunity to attend popular concerts, be they by American rock stars or arabesk singers, sitting in the front row hand in hand with his wife and enjoying himself. Needless to say, such disregard for "taste" and "decorum" was deplored as "arabesk" by some and hailed as democratization in the cultural realm by others.

6. In Turkish, the third-person pronoun for *he/she/it* is a single word. I have simply used the "he" in English. Much of the original wording in this quotation is street slang. My English translations convey the meaning but not the style of expression.

7. On Barthian mythologies and Gramsci's concept of hegemony, see Hebdige (1993).

REFERENCES

Armbrust, W. 1996. *Mass culture and modernism in Egypt*. Cambridge: Cambridge University Press.

Barthes, R. 1972. *Mythologies*. New York: Hill & Wang.

Brandist, C. 1996. The official and the popular in Gramsci and Bakhtin. *Theory, Culture and Society* 13, no. 2: 59–74.

Douglas, M. 1966. *Purity and danger*. London: Routledge and Kegan Paul.

Ehrenreich, B. 1989. *Fear of falling: the inner life of the middle class*. New York: Pantheon.

Hebdige, D. 1993. From culture to hegemony. In S. During (ed.), *The cultural studies reader*. London: Routledge.

Jenks, C., ed. 1995. *Visual culture*. London: Routledge.

Lomnitz, C. 1966. Fissures in contemporary Mexican nationalism. *Public Culture* 9, no. 1: 55–68.

Markoff, I. 1994. Popular culture, state ideology and national identity in Turkey: the arabesk polemic. Pages 225–235 in S. Mardin (ed.), *Cultural transitions in the Middle East*. Leiden: Brill.

Newman, K. 1988. *Falling from grace: the experience of downward mobility in the American middle class*. New York: Free Press.

Öncü, A. 1997. The myth of the "ideal home" travels across cultural borders to Istanbul. Pages 56–72 in A. Öncü and P. Weyland (eds.), *Space, culture, and power: new identities in globalizing cities*. London: Zed.

Özbek, M. 1991. *Popüler kültür ve Orhan Gencebay arabeski*. Istanbul: Iletisim.

———.1996. Arabesk culture: a case of modernization and popular identity. In S. Bozdogan and R. Kasaba (eds.), *Re-thinking the project of modernity in Turkey*. Chicago: Chicago University Press.

Palmer, J. 1994. *Taking humor seriously*. London: Routledge.

Stokes, M. 1992. *The arabesk debate, music and musicians in modern Turkey*. Oxford: Clarendon.

7

Sounding Out
The Culture Industries and the Globalization of Istanbul

Martin Stokes

When Gustav Mahler described his symphonies as "worlds," the applicability of this formulation outside the domain of fin-de-siècle Viennese symphonic music would probably have been far from his mind. The idea that any piece of music contains or discursively "constructs" a world, that it bears the traces of wide historical and geographic experience, is, however, immensely suggestive. Music provides a means of constructing trajectories between oneself and elsewhere, a means of exploring and expanding, of "sounding out" actual and ideal social relations, of placing oneself in relation to others. The cultural forces that channel and constrain the way we imagine our relations with others operate with peculiar force in music, a consequence, in Western Europe at least, of a pervasive ideology of autonomous art, of which the late-nineteenth-century symphony was the ultimate expression. The apparent "disinterest" of this music was the key mechanism connecting it to real political circumstances (Wolff 1987). Mahler's "worlds," varied and heterogeneous, but brought under the disciplinary control of his own musical imagination and the orchestral conductor, represent the outlook of the Austrian bourgeoisie at the turn of the century, surveying the world from a globally dominant industrial Europe and possessing an unshaken faith in the "universal" qualities of the progressive Viennese symphonic tradition.

Music can also provide the means of imagining a more fractured way of positioning oneself in time and space, a technique more characteristic of those diasporic, displaced populations whose experience of modernity is one of transience, hybridity, and placelessness. In these musical forms, paradigmatically the popular music of the New World (see Gilroy, 1993), the cracks show, and nothing, apart from a pulsing dance beat, holds the whole together. The integrative technique of "cut'n'mix" (Hebdige 1979) declares itself, drawing attention to the ruptures and inconsistencies at the heart of the productive process itself and a diversity that cannot be reconciled or subordinated through any "higher" ordering principle, such as that operating in late-nineteenth-century Viennese symphonic form. These productive ruptures and inconsistencies draw attention to experiences of dislocation, through slavery or more contemporary forms of labor migration, and in turn provide a focus for opposition to hegemonic concepts of race or culture that have positioned these often forcibly dislocated populations so disadvantageously.

Music provides means by which people position themselves, and can be positioned in temporal and spatial schemes. On the one hand, these schemes can be underlined by the monumental technology of the symphony orchestra; on the other, all they may require is a transistor radio or one or two human bodies. The technique of power associated with musical monumentalism is easily dispersed and dissipated through casual techniques of resistance that may (although not necessarily) be organized around the music's more mobile technologies. Technology thus intervenes in musical experience in crucial ways and consequently intervenes in the way people use music to position themselves and others in time and space.

This is particularly clear when one considers the globalization of the recording industry. Music experience is poised in a complex struggle between globalizing media cultures on the one hand and a creative "positioning" response to this globalization on the other, both sides of the equation being mutually constitutive. Globalization produces rather than erases the local, as many have pointed out (see Hall,1992, 308), in opposition to the stark "cultural gray-out" view promoted by the theorists of cultural imperialism. The local in question can often be an idiosyncratic conjuncture of subculture, interculture, and superculture (to use Slobin's [1993] useful terms), as in the Afro-Celtic sound systems currently fashionable in metropolitan northwestern Europe, or the extraordinary success of Loreena McEvitt—a Canadian Celtic/New Age ballad singer—at the Istanbul Jazz Festival in 1996. Those involved in global media marketing construct notions of locality to appeal to particular markets (notably the Western concept and practice of world music) and to facilitate particular marketing strategies. This global "production of locality" is thus particularly true of music (Guilbault 1993; Cohen 1994; Langlois 1996). These imposed notions of "the local" are, in turn, met, contested, or appropriated by actual local and regional musical worlds, themselves the product of other outside forces. Global forces may thus encourage or inhibit a local industry,[1] encourage or inhibit state intervention, and encourage or inhibit music making outside the domain of mass media. The complexity of this

situation can hardly be encapsulated by the kind of dichotomistic logic
(good vs. bad, pluralizing vs. homogenizing) that has accompanied earlier
discussions of globalization. If micro- and macroapproaches to globalization are seen together, in terms of a dialectical and historically mobile relationship, we avoid the danger of simplistic dichotomizing, rendering the
micro, as little more than either a reproduction of the latter, or as an anarchic rejection. This approach to music and globalization lies behind the remainder of this chapter.

EAST VERSUS WEST

The history of twentieth-century Turkish music might be read as one of
competing ideas about the way music has been considered to place Turkey
and the Turks in global terms. The idea that music may provide a space in
which the conflict between East and West may be played out is particularly well entrenched from the *alaturka/alafranga* debates of the Tanzimat
era on. It continues to be endlessly elaborated today. Claims for the Eastern, Western, or indeed global status of a particular musical genre accompany claims for state subvention or protection and often promote scarcely
concealed chauvinist political agendas. Western performance techniques
may master and discipline other musical materials, as in the influential experiments of Huseyin Sadettin Arel in the 1920s–1940s, aimed at reconciling Western (polyphonic) and Eastern (*makam*-based, monophonic) compositional techniques. Arel emphasized the universal status of Turkish
classical music at a time when it was under sustained ideological attack for
its hybrid internationalism. This music, according to Arel (1969), had a history of participation in Eastern musical internationalism and could just as
easily be turned toward that of the West, connecting Turkish culture (*hars*)
with universal (i.e., European) civilization (*medeniyet*) in precisely the
manner so ardently desired by the Kemalist intelligentsia.

Arabesk in the 1970s and 1980s famously demonstrated the reverse: the
absorption of a variety of Western popular and classical genres and performance styles into a makam-based monophonic and Eastern/Turkish
form. It was, as a consequence, excoriated by the Kemalist intelligentsia.
Those who have done most to promote the idea that Arabesk is at least as
Western as it is Eastern have invariably done so in defensive response to
this ideological attack and its practical consequences, notably the exclusion of Arabesk from the state airwaves that operated until the late 1980s.
Participating in a musical genre involves participation in a view of where
Turkey and the Turks stand in the world, with a claim attached.

But this participation is no simple matter. The semiotics of East and West
in relation to Turkish music are not cast in stone but emerge from complex

processes of negotiation. A detail that I observed late one night in 1996 in the recording of a recent popular/market cassette by Ibrahim Can (*Bir Avuc Turku*, Coskun Plak, 1996) illustrates the way in which the "micro-politics of the mixing desk"[2] produce complex positionings in terms of social and geographic space. Ibrahim had decided to use acoustic guitars (both fretted and fretless) to provide what is conventionally regarded as the *altyapi* (substructure) in folk and popular music cassette production, which posed mixing problems that the recording engineer, the singer, and the producer had not fully considered until that moment. If the guitar was turned up relative to the voice, the result was *Bati:* Western, intimate, polyphonic, the product of shared group sociomusical processes. If the reverse, *Doğu:* Eastern, dependent on the authoritative, monophonic, coercive presence of the solo voice. A second instance involved the reconciliation of the *bağlama* (the long-necked lute) and the guitar, whose similarity of sound produced moments at which the two different tonalities (the former microtonal and monophonic, the latter equal-tempered and tonal) came into rather obvious conflict. Is the guitar turned down, or is the baglama play modified to conform to the guitar's equal temperament? Once again, the choice was between the weightings to be given to Western and Eastern elements in the musical mix. This choice was at one level between two quite different domestic markets: the Black Sea diaspora, requiring authenticity, and a younger urban audience requiring what they, and Ibrahim, would identify as a modern sound. It was also a choice between two politically and morally loaded alternatives; no one could decide (a product of the late hour as much as anything) and I was called on to arbitrate.[3]

Sound thus provides a manipulatable but politically loaded fund of symbolic difference ("the West," "the East," "the Turkish," etc.). Popular musical culture provides a variety of strategies for dealing with these constructed differences: placing them in relationships of hierarchy, synthesis, absorption, and so on. The social manipulatability of sound lies in the semiotic evasiveness that haunts musical performance. In a genre of performance that demands constant repetition, authoritative interpretation is always hard to establish, and rival interpretations are hard to exclude.[4] Its political power lies in the fact that the movement of music in public space is so difficult to police and control, a fact intimately connected to the mobility of musical technology and predominantly collective means of musical production.[5]

"GLOBAL" ISTANBUL AND THE NATIONAL IMAGINARY

Although *East, West,* and *Turkey* are the significant terms ("places") in this kind of discussion, musical experience in Turkey involves another key locale: Istanbul. Musical life has been heavily influenced by Istanbul's large and wealthy minority populations, who have provided an entrepreneurial and talented personnel able and inclined to mediate Western European, American, and Middle Eastern popular genres to the wider Turkish audience. From the Tanzimat period onward, the growing empowerment of Istanbul's Muslim and non-Muslim bourgeoisie turned the Ottoman capital into the center of a culture of entertainment revolving around music, popular theater, dance, and drink. The presence of entrepreneurial non-Muslims able to act as cultural intermediaries ensured that Istanbul retained its significance as the center of urban popular culture despite the establishment of Ankara as the capital of the Turkish Republic in 1923. The Turkish popular press, cinema, and music industry have thus from the beginning been based in districts of Istanbul which are still synonymous with Turkish journalism, film and music: respectively, Cagaloglu, Yesilcam, and Unkapani.

Istanbul also remains the major center of population and wealth in Turkey. Istanbul's spectacular growth since the 1950s can be understood in terms of the more general political-economic conditions that have driven the history of the Turkish Republic. Western credit, from the Marshall Plan onward, did much to shape an overproductive and increasingly dependent economy, a concentration of population and heavy industry in areas that had easy access to Western markets and the mass movement of rural populations to these areas. The interests of an indigenous mercantile bourgeoisie tied to the movements of global capital have prevailed, despite the efforts of the Kemalist intelligentsia to create a viable national alternative.[6] Structural adjustment over the last decade (as elsewhere in the Middle East) has entrenched the process. The political victory of laissez-faire economics over the state's reformist tradition was marked by the 1980 military coup and the liberal governments that followed. These were years that saw the most dramatic increase in the city's population and the most spectacular polarization of wealth both in the city, and between the city and the rest of Turkey (a process remorselessly documented in Sonmez 1996).

During this period, Istanbul made a dramatic entry into the national imaginary. When the state tradition held at least some kind of grasp on the production of national imagery, Istanbul was often portrayed as a relic of an Ottoman past, an image evoked only to remind modern Turks of what they had to forget: a world that was closed, concealing, irrational, absolute, and "Islamic." Ankara was its antithesis; embodying a reinvented Anatolian tradition (referring to the pre-Islamic past), open, revealing, rational, and secular. Literary celebrants of Istanbul, such as Ahmet Hamdi Tanpinar and Yahya Kemal Beyatli retained highly significant positions in the nationalist canon of Turkish literature, but it was a somewhat anomalous position. Their veiled and allusive literary idioms contrasted with the idealized models of Anatolian literary realism promoted during the high tide of Republican reformism. An analogous process took place through music, but with the aid of the state's radio station at the disposal of ideologues from 1948 onward—a reformulated musical tradition based on Anatolian instruments and genres, modernized and rationalized (through performance by large orchestras and choirs, and sporadic efforts to introduce Western compositional techniques). A huge variety of musical genres, some confined to an intellectual elite, but others much more widely appropriated, was labeled variously "urban," cosmopolitan, Islamic, and Ottoman and rigorously (if somewhat unsystematically) excluded from public life.

From 1983 onward, the process was reversed. Istanbul became both the symbol and practice of a new kind of politics, liberal, populist, and "global." As an object of liberal fascination, the city has increasingly been presented by its managers as a cosmopolitan melting pot, a global meeting point in which the best of Eastern and Western culture can flourish. As an object of populist politics, the emphasis on the Ottoman/Islamic heritage has legitimated many of the liberal governments' policies, evoking a triumphal golden age in which Turks were major players on the world stage. As an image of the global status to which the city's managers aspire, Istanbul is presented as the bridge not only between European and Middle Eastern business communities but between Europe and the emerging Central Asian markets. These new ways of "selling Istanbul" (Keyder 1992) have been insistent and effective, both from PR and image management perspectives, and claims to host major international events (the Habitat conference in July 1996, and the Olympic campaign) continue. The vast project of remolding Istanbul as a nostalgic site of Islamic heritage, begun by ANAP's Bedrettin Dalan in the mid-1980s, has been taken over today by Refah's Recep Tayyib Erdogan.

The city's managers have made use of all available means to pursue these politics. Music has been a minor but noteworthy aspect of this. From the early 1980s onward, the cliques established by Özal in the TRT (state radio and television network) resulted in an increasing prioritization of the urban art music tradition in preference to the state's reinvented Anatolian tradition and the live performance of a number of Arabesk stars on state television. This is the music of Istanbul but performed in a staid, modernized and somewhat sanitized form—very different from the kind of performance that one would encounter in one of Istanbul's *gazino* clubs. The "cleanup" of Beyoglu carried out by Refah's administration in 1994 was marked by the reopening of Cicek Pasaji, an event that included a conspicuous concert of Turkish art music by Mehmet Barlas (Kozanoglu 1995, 107). The Beyoglu cleanup, as Kozanoglu illustrates, was promoted as a means of "internationalizing" the city, making it fit for tourists and visiting businesspeople, turning it into a place in which, according to police chief Necdet Menzir, *"kravatli beyefendiler"* ("gentlemen in ties"; Kozanoglu 1995, 107) could wander around to their hearts' content. Making the place "fit for tourists" has been a means in Turkey (as elsewhere) of imposing notions of cleanliness and decency whose object is primarily a matter of disciplining locals and not accommodating tourists. As a number of commentators have suggested, the cleanup of Beyoglu was part of Refah's larger design for the city, involving the prioritization of business interests through systematic zoning (Kozanoglu 1995; Robins and Aksoy 1995), as well as the attempt to create, albeit cosmetically, an "Islamic" city. In 1996 the city administration sponsored the release of a recording of "Istanbul Sarkilari" (songs) and "Istanbul Turkuleri" (folk songs) (Cemre), performed, in a modernized and somewhat sanitized performance style redolent of the TRT in the 1980s. The cover carries the title in English over an Orientalist vision of Istanbul's skyline. As with Beyoglu itself, the CD carries with it an internally directed claim that Refah represents an Istanbul that is clean, tidy, and appealing to tourists and the international community.

Celebrants of life after nation-state have looked with some approval at the new ways in which localities, cities, and regions are becoming the key operators in an emerging global economy of signs and commodities. Instead of celebrating the decline of the nation-state and the paradigmatic forms of modernity associated with it (although these undoubtedly have problematic histories), we should perhaps consider whose interests the celebration of the world, the city, and the region, embedded in various forms of self-consciously postmodern theory, serve (see especially Robins 1993). Who benefits from this globalization, and who loses out? And should we assume that the nation-state has simply disappeared in the process?

A discussion of Turkish popular music can provide a useful and critical angle on the consequences of globalization in a city such as Istanbul, which I will pursue in the remainder of this chapter with three points. The first concerns the impact of media liberalization and the movement of large multinationals into the Turkish media market. The result, I will argue, following Aksoy and Robins (in press), is a consolidation at the top within the media industries and the emergence of a stifling conformity. The second concerns the continuing significance of the nation-state in the domain of Turkish popular music. The third concerns the need to carefully record and historicize the various ways in which musicians and the music industry in Turkey have responded to globalization: there is no simple line of "progress" from local to global, and the consequences of globalization may have been to limit and foreclose opportunities for musical participation rather than the reverse.

DEREGULATION AND CONSOLIDATION

The systematic media deregulation that began in 1990 has done much to promote a new form of both regional and urban *campanillismo*, in particular through local FM radio stations (of which there may now be as many as four thousand throughout Turkey). The liberal and Islamist managers of the city from the mid 1980s on have done much to shape and intervene in this sense of local loyalty. At precisely the same time, efforts were being made to harmonize Turkish copyright law with those of Europe and America, to pave the way for the movements of Warner Bros. and Poly-Gram into the Turkish media market and to cooperate with performance rights organizations such as MESAM and POPSAV, established with the active encouragement of the major Turkish recording companies.

Beginning in 1987, the five major cassette companies (Raks, Nora, Plak-san, Foneks, and Uzelli) were able to lobby effectively for more effective copyright legislation targeted at cassette piracy, which duly emerged in 1989. This entrenched a process that had already begun to separate major and minor companies. The former concentrated on producing a smaller number of extremely high-selling cassettes (the major stars selling up to two million during this period, where sales of only forty thousand are required to begin making profits[7]), and the latter produced a wider range of cassettes with much lower capital input for more specialized markets (Black Sea, Alevi, Kurdish, etc., where sales of about forty thousand could be expected, rising to two hundred thousand in successful cases) largely on the backs of performing professional musicians who would generally not expect to get paid for their efforts at all. By the mid-1990s, Raks had cornered practically all of the major recording stars, was able to lobby increasingly effectively through MESAM for more powerful copyright legislation and enforcement, now directed against private radio stations, was in a position to mark their commercial presence by brand-named retail outlets (strategically placed Raksoteks stores across the city) and to effectively price its rivals out of business.[8]

In spite of the virtual monopoly that Raks enjoys (dominating some 75 percent of the Turkish market), this strategy is still precarious. The costs of marketing and promoting new acts spirals upward. Many of the top echelon of musical performers now record out of the country on state-of-the art facilities in Europe or the United States. Systematic exposure on the main music video channel (Kral TV) is an extremely expensive business but now virtually the only effective way of advertising a major new act, and companies need to have at their disposal a distribution system that can shift (as in the case of Mirkelam's *Her Gece* in 1995) up to four hundred thousand cassettes and CDs in the space of the first month. Partnership with a large multinational such as PolyGram is clearly an important strategy, but the successs of the Raks-PolyGram partnership depends on the harmonization of Turkish and European copyright law[9] and the emergence of an effective mechanism for collecting copyright dues from private radio stations.

Media deregulation and new production technology (focusing on CDs and music videos) brought an explosion of new sounds to people's ears in 1990, but this has been followed by a consolidation at the top. The operative strategy for a company like Raks-PolyGram is to produce a small number of extremely high-selling acts. This requires a large capital outlay, and risks cannot be countenanced. It is no surprise that people speak of the paradigmatic popular musicians of the mid-1990s as if they were aspects of a composite, corporate media personality. The result: a consensus that operates in favor of the major companies whose products are substantially more homogenous and normative than those of the arabesk industry a decade earlier. Evidence, once more, that free markets do not, of themselves, produce diversity (Cloonan 1996).

TRANSNATIONALISM AND THE STATE

Not so long ago it was fashionable to assume that the institutions of the nation-state are now completely unable to operate coherent protectionist media policies. However, it is clear that in a very large number of nation-states, Turkey among them, state institutions continue to intervene in global media networks in surprisingly effective ways. To assume that this intervention is a relic of old modernist étatism that will soon be swept away by the inexorable tide of globalization seems to be quite erroneous; if anything, it is the reverse. In those nation-states with strong state traditions (authoritarian or otherwise), satellite dishes, personal computers, cassette and video recorders have posed challenges that have elicited ingenious and effective responses.[10]

Less obviously, many European states continue to operate quota systems in regard to their musical policies (notably Sweden and France) that have been relatively successful in creating and protecting a local industry. Quota systems in Tanzania (which pursued a 100 percent quota on local music from the 1970s onward), Jamaica, and the Antilles have in each case created strong local industries successfully exporting their musical produce.[11] In many European situations, state broadcasting institutions have a vastly more important role to play in shaping public taste than international cable and satellite channels, Britain providing an important example (Cloonan 1996). Rather indirect forms of censorship still operate in Turkey, with important consequences. It is well known that MTV was prohibited from using Turkish terrestrial stations following the fear of Kurdish broadcasting, a gap that provided Kral TV with the opportunity to establish itself as an immensely successful alternative, geared almost entirely to the domestic music market.

We should also note that nationalism is far from being a spent force. As many observers have pointed out, nationalism is now a kind of protest on the part of those who have found themselves excluded from the contemporary global order, a movement of disaffected young men against (to use Michael Ignatieff's well-known formulation) an international "regime of civility." The warm reception of Cartel (a Turco-German group originating in Berlin) and its rap by the Turkish right provides an eloquent illustration of the ways in which the global flow of culture, in this case recorded, marketed, and distributed from Germany, has nourished virulently anti-internationalist sentiments in Turkey. These are, then, two good reasons why we should attempt to maintain some critical distance from the more optimistic theorists of globalization: it promotes the big at the expense of the small, and it would appear that it has done much to shape and motivate violent ethnonationalist sentiments. It may be that some reformulated and more liberal and less culturally exclusive notion of the state may be the only realistic political response to this situation, and indeed, many left-inclined intellectuals in Europe are, following Habermas, cautiously coming around to this opinion (see Geulen 1995).

FOUR POPULAR MUSICIANS

This chapter concludes with four brief case studies of figures who personify distinct stances on the part of professional musicians and the music industry in Turkey in relation to the process of globalization: Münir Nurettin Selçuk, Cem Karaca, Orhan Gencebay, and Mirkelam. These names do not correspond to four stages in a simple, unidirectional process—in fact, quite the reverse. If anything, they demonstrate the utter impossibility of considering Turkish popular music as an increasingly successful movement toward global integration or, indeed, anything else. I have chosen them as a means of attending, as Stuart Hall recommends, to the various "articulations" of global and local and also to elicit the specific and various ways of imagining Istanbul that these confluences of global and local have produced.

Münir Nurettin Selçuk (1900–1981)[12] dominated the Turkish popular music market from the time of his first recording with HMV in Turkey in 1926. His connection with the urban classical tradition did little to endear him to the apparatchiks of the Kemalist cultural and political tradition. In spite of being attached to the Istanbul Municipal Conservatory for most of his working life (from 1942 to 1976), his most significant impact on Turkish popular music making consisted of his involvement in live radio concerts (as leader of the Conservatory Icra Heyeti from 1954 to 1976), musical films for Turkey's nascent film industry, and the first mass circulation hits in Turkey for HMV (including some fifteen recordings from the urban art music repertory, and some two hundred of his own compositions).

The contemporary image of Münir Nurettin Selçuk rests heavily on his relatively unacknowledged role as a reformer, as the man who "put Turkish music in western dress" (Kulin 1996). Along with experimenting with harmony and extending a more familiar Middle Eastern popular urban vocal style with bel canto techniques, he also introduced a modern division of labor, in which the solo star performed on his or her feet in front of the backing musicians, rather than sitting with them.

Münir Nurettin nostalgia is in part inspired by the current availability of his work through Coskun Plak's digital remastering of some fifty-seven original recordings, and in part inspired by the current revisionist delight in resuscitating cultural figures marginalized by Kemalist reformism. This interpretation misses two key points: his heavy dependence on HMV, which did much to manufacture his reputation in Turkey, and it provided him with a scholarship to pursue his much publicized musical studies in France in 1926 (reputedly at the Paris Conservatoire). The second is the way in which, quite the reverse of westernizing Turkish music, he "domesticated" a wide range of current global styles, through Turkish versions of European music theater, Egyptian musicals, and Argentinean Tango. Instead of obliterating local difference, the early recording industry, whose recording and distribution costs were relatively low, was happy to operate within local markets. Rather than introducing radically new concepts, the popular market operated through "versioning" imported genres, subordinating them to what was in effect a performance genre widespread around the eastern Mediterranean throughout the first decades of the twentieth century. The genre dominates Odeon, Pathe, HMV, and Columbia's lists up to the mid-1960s, when the first rock, chacha, and English language numbers began to appear.

It is perhaps striking that the first composer of Turkish Tangos (Necip Celal) composed many of his Tangos to words that celebrated Istanbul's beauty spots.[13] Istanbul and its beauty spots, as a recurrent topos in the popular repertory of the first half of the twentieth century, had a particularly important role in localizing transnational trends throughout this period. As Murat Belge has illustrated, Kanto emerged at a time in which Istanbul's social and architectural fabric had been radically transformed by a modern, planned transport system, initiating an elaborate popular culture of excursions and trips amongst Istanbul's bourgeoisie. It became possible to experience and simply to see Istanbul in ways that had not been imagined before. The Istanbul of popular song texts in the first half of the twentieth century was one of palpable excitement at the mere possibility of observing and moving around the city, together with the opportunities for flirtation and illicit affairs that public transport made possible (Belge 1983).

The modern, as theorists of modernity have stressed, is a melancholic affair, disorientating and transitory. The very forces that turned Istanbul into a symbol of the modern generated a simultaneous nostalgia for what was necessarily lost in the process. By the late 1940s, Istanbul was already a "lieu de mémoire," to use Pierre Nora's influential formulation; and as a topoi in popular music lyrics (notably, e.g., Münir Nurettin Selçuk and Yahya Kemal Beyatli's famous *Aziz Istanbul* recorded in 1948), Istanbul is already an Istanbul of the memory, distant and evasive. Bülent Ersoy's controversial reworking of *Aziz Istanbul* in 1996 undoubtedly draws on this implicit nostalgia in Münir Nurettin's songs of the city, a nostalgia that remains a potent cultural and political force. In this particular articulation of global and local, the city was a central point of reference.

Cem Karaca (b. 1945) is credited by most contemporary observers as the creator of Turkish rock. In this particular genre, Istanbul has been conspicuous by its absence. His first bands in the early 1960s performed versions of American rock and roll numbers largely in English. The impact of Elvis and Bill Haley in the late 1950s was mediated primarily through films, sparking off a wave of Turkish imitators, mostly sons and daughters of Istanbul's petite-bourgeoisie, many resident in Kadikoy, and many, like Cem Karaca himself, members of Istanbul's non-Muslim minorities and graduates of the prestigious foreign language schools.[14] Despite relatively privileged positions in Turkish society, they had to devote highly inventive efforts toward finding recordings, record players, guitars, and amplifiers (often only possible through trips to Europe, and even here currency control and import regulations meant that enormous guile was required). Although Münir Nurettin Selçuk could find the basic technological resources he required in Istanbul, the first generation of rock and pop performers were obliged to travel to Europe to find instruments, concert venues, and adequate recording facilities. The most rudimentary stereo recording facilities, which rock, unlike early arabesk, requires, were not introduced in Turkey until the mid-1970s.

For many, including Cem Karaca, Europe was an uncomfortable and alienating experience. His last trip, following the emerging political radicalization of Turkish rock, amounted to a period of exile that only ended in the late 1980s with a highly public endorsement of Özal's politics that dismayed many of his former fans. A small number of stars were selected by the music industry as the favored mediators of translated American rock and pop (notably Erol Büyükburç and Ajda Pekkan), and Cem Karaca and Apaşlar were initially among them. His Western pop–style *Resimdeki Gözyaşlari*, recorded with Apaşlar, sold some six hundred thousand recordings—a huge media success.

However, the combination of foreign language education in Istanbul and opportunities for travel and study abroad available to these musicians brought the political radicalization of middle-class youth in the 1960s to bear on Turkish cultural experience. Their identification with the European and American counterculture produced a strong desire to create a distinctive Turkish contribution to those movements and to establish a dynamic and radical musical counterculture in Turkey itself. What gave their efforts a particular edge was opposition to (what they considered to be) the slavish "versioning" of Erol Büyükburç and their dissatisfaction with the kinds of Turkish music being promoted by the state. The refusal of the TRT to permit the radio or television appearances of any but the most anodyne of these groups added to their sense of mission.[15]

For Cem Karaca, and many of his contemporaries, this initiated an experimental process of reconciling urban and rural Turkish instruments and techniques with those of Western rock. Cem Karaca's work with a number of these bands, including Kardaşlar (1969–1972), Mogollar (1971–1974), and, finally, Dervişan (1974–1978), marked various stages in this process. Each group found ways of bringing electric keyboards, guitars, and drum kits together with the *yayli tanbur*, the *bağlama*, the *kabak kemençe*, and a variety of Turkish rhythm instruments in performance that was predominantly organized around the rhythms and textures of rock. The lyrics associated with the Anatolian *aşik* (folk poets) tradition (in particular the urban and politically radicalized such as Ali Ihsan and Mahzuni Şerif) provided a major source of inspiration. Ironically, their antistate nationalism and identification with the international counterculture of the late 1960s were in some ways highly dependent on national institutions. Many associated with Anatolian rock were trained in the state conservatories. For Cem Karaca, as for many others, military service provided a wider experience of Turkey and its provincial musical cultures, and national competitions organized by newspapers proved indispensable for creating names for themselves in the country through Anatolian tours.

Given the fascination that Anatolia held for these musicians and their collective experience of European cities, it is perhaps not surprising that Istanbul does not figure heavily in Anadolu rock's lyrics or musical references, despite the fact that practically all of the Anadolu rockers were Istanbul born and bred. Places in Istanbul figure in only Cem Karaca's versions of texts by radical poets such as Nazim Hikmet (*Ben Bir Ceviz Agaci Gülhane Parkinda*) and Orhan Veli (*Istanbul'u Dinliyorum*), otherwise not at all. Globalization, in the form of connecting with the European and American counter-culture, thus produced a distinctive vision of the nation, not the city.

The city reappears in arabesk in an interesting way. Musicians associated with the genre, which was condemned throughout the 1970s and 1980s for its subversive "Easternness," are in fact decidedly cosmopolitan in outlook. Perhaps the most celebrated of these is Orhan Gencebay (b. 1944).[16] Gencebay cites Bach and Elvis as the formative influences in his life, rejects the label of arabesk (precisely because his music, if it is to be categorized as arabesk at all, does not derive its sole inspiration from Arab music), and is at pains to point out that his first music teacher, a Crimean refugee and friend of his father in his native Samsun, had been educated in the Soviet music system and provided him with a thorough grounding in the techniques of Western classical music. Gencebay had more in common with the popular music of the 1940s and 1950s; and in contrast to the popular music of the 1960s, this was a music whose producers were able to make do with the materials that came to hand and were attuned to turning a wide range of materials (Western rock, Anatolian rural genres promoted by the radio, the music of Egyptian and Lebanese radio stations) into music that could be played on that most domestic and transportable instrument, the baglama. Instead of internationalizing a local music, as the proponents of Anadolu rock attempted to do, arabesk localized a wide range of "exotic" music. Arabesk is a music that readily incorporates and is believed to be at least potentially capable of containing "everything."

But more than anything, arabesk was the creation of a nascent Turkish-based cassette industry, from the mid 1970s on.[17] Cassette technology was, in comparison to 45 rpm and LP production, relatively cheap and mobile—able to respond to demand quickly. Demand in the late 1960s was increasingly being shaped by rural-urban migration. Orhan Gencebay's first single, *Bir Teselli Ver*, recorded with Columbia, sold approximately six hundred thousand on its release in 1969. Its appeal as a music that spoke directly to the urbanizing aspirations of a migrant proletariat are clear and in complete contrast to the democratic, pro-rural aspirations of Anadolu rock. Cassette production made possible a locally based industry, characterized by a small number of large firms but also a huge number of smaller operations, in many cases (as with Gencebay's Kervan, established in 1973) owned by the music stars themselves. While the music was rigorously excluded from the state airwaves, its commercial presence was tolerated by the state (lacking any clear mechanisms for excluding it and quite likely considering its politically quietistic lyrics to be unthreatening) and thrived through live performance in clubs and cheap cassettes, in tacit opposition to the arid style cultivated by the TRT. Under these conditions, the chief commercial function of the smaller firms was to provide a form of advertisement for the solo artists and occasional and quite poorly paid wages for backing musicians, all of whom made their living primarily through live appearances and other small business ventures, and not from recording royalties.

This was, then, a genre that occupied a distinct space between a local recording industry based in Istanbul and a local culture of entertainment based on the discretionary income of a class of aspiring rural-urban migrants in Istanbul. As a musical genre, arabesk was also very much a music of and about the city, embracing a wide variety of styles from outside Turkey (including, but not being limited to, Egyptian film music), subordinated to performance conventions that were familiar from nonrecorded performance contexts (in particular the music of the baglama and solo voice) and the music promoted by the official Turkish media. The imagery of Gencebay's lyrics is diffuse, portraying intense but quite abstract emotional states of alienation, separation, failure, and humiliation at the hands of a remote and manipulative lover. The big city, implicitly but sometimes explicitly Istanbul, provides a dramatic framework in arabesk films and also acts as a metaphor of dangerous desire, like the "modern" female temptresses who have a stock part to play in the arabesk drama in luring the (usually male) protagonist toward his final humiliation.

Despite Gencebay's more recent reinvention of himself as a rock musician, his music has a quite separate history from that of Anadolu rock. Whereas Cem Karaca openly identified with the labor movement in Turkey (and his recording of Nazim Hikmet's *1 Mayis* was the principal cause of his departure from Turkey in 1979), arabesk stars such as Gencebay have tended to support, actively or passively, the populist liberal right. Gencebay's approval of Özal is well known and echoed by a large number of arabesk stars in the late 1980s, all of whom benefited from the gradual disintegration of the TRT's stranglehold of the radio and television airwaves. While Cem Karaca sought a version of Turkish music that would connect with the sounds and values of the international counterculture, Orhan Gencebay has been driven by precisely the reverse concern: the domestication of an international soundscape and presentation for a Turkish audience. As with Münir Nurettin Selçuk, but for a predominantly proletarian rather than bourgeois audience, Istanbul once again becomes an important symbol of an ambiguous, problematic modernity.

The continuities between arabesk and the most recent genre of Turkish pop have been discussed by a number of Turkish intellectuals. Mirkelam and Orhan Gencebay have much in common. Both enjoy the support of the currently dominant rightist political elites and return that support (but at the same time claiming that they have no interest in politics). Both have had early formative musical experiences, being introduced through their families to a wide variety of non-Turkish music, and both have evidently been inclined to apply rapidly changing music technologies to more familiar musical experiences: rhythmic patterns referring to the conventions of rave and techno, but underpinned by the conventional rhythms of urban Turkish social dancing, solo voice–oriented genres patterned around the melodic conventions associated with Turkish art music. Both are inclined toward a certain eclecticism. Whereas Gencebay protests at his categorization as an "Eastern" musician by stressing his rock roots and his knowledge of Bach, Mirkelam protests his admiration for Ibrahim Tatlises.[18] This is also a music that addresses the cultural aspirations of a wealthy bourgeoisie that has been created by the structural adjustment process and those that aspire to the wealth and leisure that this bourgeoisie so conspicuously enjoys. As with arabesk, Istanbul—or, more precisely, an anonymous suburb of Istanbul—provides the framework for his video of *Her Gece*, while the words elaborate an abstract lexicon of loneliness and desire.

What has changed is the technological and industrial basis of this music. Gencebay remains an entrepreneurial individualist, the hard-working rural-urban migrant who has created his own world and his own wealth, whereas Mirkelam, hardly a "person" and more, in his own words, "a project," is the product of a sophisticated industrial machine.[19] Even if Gencebay is no less the product of a commercial project (see Karakayali 1995), his music is very much a product of the small business ethos so enthusiastically promoted by Özal. It is not difficult to see in Gencebay's films and lyrics, bound up in a language of love and individual struggle, the promotion of Özal's ideological message: "work hard and you can do it." Mirkelam, on the other hand, appeals to and shapes a very different attitude: Mirkelam as a self-conscious "project" is product rather than producer, and the appeal is to a national-lottery mentality: the industry could choose anyone, put them through the machine and onto the nation's popular cultural stage. Why not me?

Although the huge majority could not aspire to Gencebay's fame and prosperity, they can at least play his music (and self-styled Orhancis—followers of Orhan—were a feature of every local music club I visited throughout the 1980s). The participative potential that has always characterized arabesk as a form of music making and that made it so popular to laissez-faire individualists such as Özal has been swept away by current media conditions. Although Gencebay's music could be played by anybody with the wherewithal to purchase a baglama, now baglamas have become relatively expensive, and guitars, though increasingly available in mass-produced, acoustic forms in Beyoglu, are still not cheap, and electric guitars are prohibitively expensive. To participate in this domain one needs either to reinvent the ethos of the early Anadolu rockers and comb flea markets for cheap and obsolete instruments that can be reinvented in an experimental context (an approach adopted by experimental band Zen) or to find the $500 to $600 required to buy the most rudimentary imported electric guitar. The participatory opportunities offered by Arabesk have disappeared, dividing Istanbul into a world of musical haves (who can participate in the vibrant life of Istanbul's rock bars) and have-nots, for whom even the purchase of a single baglama is now a serious undertaking.

The multiple worlds that globalization promises are in many ways only available for the few; many more are left with a sense of worlds beyond their reach, which they can observe only as spectators. Music connects with this fact in a complex way. It has, over the past few decades, provided ne's place in relation to the world, the city, ographies illustrate. And one does not have o buy a cassette of Münir Nurettin Selçuk, y, or Mirkelam. Indeed, more music, both in e terms, is undoubtedly available on the CD market, radio, and television than ten years ago, despite the consolidation of the mainstream mentioned earlier. But for many, the spaces in which one can participate in these musical genres, except by sitting in front of a television, may be diminishing. Theorists of globalization need to consider carefully the gap that is emerging between those for whom the world is expanding and those for whom it is, if anything, contracting.

NOTES

1. See in particular Manuel's (1990) analysis of the northern Indian recording industry after the introduction of cassette technology in the mid-1970s, where cassettes made possible a vibrant local industry. Manuel's somewhat optimistic approach may be set against Malm and Wallis's (1992) well-known discussion of the music industry in a number of small countries, where cassette piracy has inhibited the emergence of strong local industries.

2. I borrow Chris Waterman's useful formulation, in a paper delivered at the 1991 International Association for the Study of Popular Music (IASPM) conference, Berlin.

3. As I remember, it was desperately late, and my main concern was to get to bed. I could tell that everyone seemed to prefer a guitar-centered sound but were somewhat reluctant to mark such a decisive break with Ibrahim's earlier recordings, so I believe that I merely articulated the conclusion that would have emerged anyway. The conflict between guitar and baglama was deliberately left unresolved: I have always enjoyed the clash of tempered and untempered intervals. The producer wanted the baglama and the guitars to be in absolute conformity, which meant that the baglama would have to modify its line. Ibrahim clearly felt that this would violate the melody as he knew it. I argued with him, against the producer. For the sound engineer, revealingly, this provided a Turkish *lezzet* (taste) to a fundamentally Western musical structure, and this was the way it stayed.

4. A point that has been persuasively argued in the poststructuralist musicology of the early 1990s. See in particular the contributions of Susan McClarey, Lawrence Kramer, and Carolyn Abbate in Solie (1993).

5. This approach draws on the work of Walter Benjamin, in opposition to the mechanistic and deterministic (but still highly influential) critique of the culture industries in the writing of Theodore Adorno. See Middleton (1990, 64–99).

6. Keyder's analysis of twentieth-century Turkish history notes the continuities that have underpinned the apparent and dramatic eruptions of the Kemalist military forces in national political life. This brief account draws heavily on his *State and Class in Turkey* (1987).

7. These figures, drawn from my discussions with small producers in Unka-pani in 1989, largely conform to those of Nazife Gungor (1990, 31).

8. Interview with Sacit Suhabey, managing director of Raks's S-Muzik, July 23, 1996. S-Muzik is Raks's elite arabesk division, recording and distributing Ibrahim Tatlises (whose recent "Klasikleri" alone is believed to have sold six million copies), Zeki Muren, Bulent Ersoy, Kayahan, and many more.

9. This is, however, far from being harmonized internally. See Laing (1992).

10. Iran's efforts to control satellite broadcasting are well known, and Ger-many's efforts to censor Internet pornography are providing an important test case for state control of that supposedly anarchic transnational communications space.

11. For a discussion of quotas and the creation of musical export industries in the third world, see Malm and Wallis (1992) and Guilbault (1992).

12. My sources of information are Kulin (1996), Rona (1970), and the sleeve notes to Coskun Plak's recent CD series by Orhan Telmen. Secondary sources on this crucial figure are few and far between. John Morgan O'Connell's forthcoming biography will fill an important gap. I am grateful to him for confirming a number of facts in this very brief survey.

13. Note in particular his first, *Bogazda Renkler Her Gece,* recorded in 1928. See Akgun (1993).

14. Cem Karaca's father was a Shia Muslim from Azerbaijan and his mother an Armenian from Bakirkoy. He attended Istanbul's prestigious Robert College. I have drawn on my own and Anne Ellingsen's interviews with Cem Karaca (July 23, 1996) and a long interview with Akin Ok published in Ok (1996).

15. Mazhar, Fuat, Ozkan, Baris Manco, and Uc Hureller were the exceptions; Erkin Koray, Mogollar, and Cem Karaca were, as far as the TRT was concerned, well beyond the pale.

16. Interview with Orhan Gencebay, August 4, 1995. I also draw on Meral Ozbek's (1991) excellent study and a number of other published interviews (in par-ticular Boom 1992; Cumhuriyet 1996).

17. Ozbek (1991, 123–24, n. 38) provides the following brief history of the Turk-ish cassette industry. The first Turkish firm, Sencalar, began to operate alongside the main multinationals (HMV, Odeon, Pathe, Columbia) in 1962, producing 45 rpm singles. Cassette production resulted in the first production and distribution of Turkish cassettes by Plaksan in 1976. As reproduction technology improved and found its way into Turkey, a number of other firms followed. Sabra was established in 1978 (later becoming Raks), and, after 1980, Teletrans, Uzelli, Nora, and Bantsan.

18. This and other details concerning Mirkelam are drawn from Hulusi Tunca's (1995) journalistic account, "Mirkelam Nereye Kosuyor?"

19. In the words of his record company's style consultant, Serra D'Autry, "be-cause American culture is to be found all over the world, we created an image which is a little reminiscent of Ayhan Isik, a little of gipsy, a little of Che Guevarra, and a little of Freddie Mercury" (Tunca 1995, 50).

REFERENCES

Aksoy, A., and K. Robins. 1996. *Peripheral vision: cultural industries and cultural iden-tities in Turkey* (in press).

Keyder, C. 1987. *State and class in Turkey: a study in capitalist development*. London: Verso.
———. 1992. Istanbul'u Nasil Satmali? *Istanbul* 3, pp. 80–85.
Kozanoglu, C. 1995. *Pop cagi atesi*. Istanbul: Iletisim.
Kulin, A. 1996. *Bir tatli huzur: fotograflarla Münir Nureddin Selçuk*. Istanbul: Sel.
Laing, D. 1992. "Sadness," scorpions and single markets: national and transnational trends in European popular music. *Popular Music* 11, no. 2: 127–40.
Langlois, T. 1996. The global and the local in Algerian rai. *Popular Music* 15, no. 3 (special issue on the Middle East, ed. R. Davis and M. Stokes): 259–73.
Malm, K., and R. Wallis. 1992. *Media policy and music activity*. London: Routledge.
Manuel, P. 1990. *Cassette culture: popular music and technology in North India*. Chicago: University of Chicago Press.
Middleton, R. 1990. *Studying popular music*. Milton Keynes: Open University Press.
Nora, P. 1989. Between memory and history: les lieux de memoire. In N. Davis and R. Starn (eds.), *Representations: Special Issue on Memory and Countermemory* 26: 7–25.
Ok, A. 1994. *68 Cigliklari*. Istanbul: Broy.
Ozbek, M. 1991. *Populer kultur ve Orhan Gencebay arabeski*. Istanbul: Iletisim.
Robins, K. 1993. Prisoners of the city: whatever could a postmodern city be? Pages 303–29 in E. Carter, J. Donald and J. Squires (eds.), *Space and place: theories of identity and location*. London: Lawrence & Wishart.
Robins, K., and A. Aksoy. 1995. Istanbul rising: returning the repressed to urban culture. *European and Regional Studies* 2, no. 3, 223–35.
Rona, M. 1970. *Yirminci yuzyil Turk musikisi*. Istanbul: Turkiye Yayinevi.
Slobin, M. 1993. *Subcultural sounds: micromusics of the West*. Hanover: Wesleyan.
Solie, R., ed. 1993. *Musicology and difference: gender and sexuality in music scholarship*. Berkeley: University of California Press.
Sonmez, M. 1996. *Istanbul'un iki yuzu: 1980'den 2000'e degisim*. Ankara: Arkadas.
Tunca, H. 1995. *Mirkelam nereye kosuyor?* Istanbul: Aci.
Wolff, J. 1987. The ideology of autonomous art. Pages 1–12 in R. Leppert and S. McClarey (eds.), *Music and society: the politics of composition, performance and reception*. Cambridge: Cambridge University Press.

This chapter is about the changing forms of housing and creation of space in Istanbul. I will consider three periods in the postwar evolution of the city: the early stage, when rural migration circumscribed the old urban core with peripheral development of shantytowns; the middle period, when national development led to a differentiation of residential space for middle-class housing; and the current situation, when globalization engenders a variety of fragmenting dynamics. Although there is a temporal succession to these three components, the first does not end when the second starts, and both peripheral shantytown development and middle-class differentiation continue during the final phase. Hence, it is their contrapuntal evolution that determines the resultant picture.

THE HISTORICAL BACKGROUND AND THE POLITICAL ECONOMY OF URBANIZATION

Istanbul regularly scores at the top of lists of third world metropolises in terms of the proportion of "illegal" housing. Exact figures vary depending on the count but usually exceed 50 percent. The definition of *illegal* in this context is not always clear: it refers to not being properly regulated by the prevailing legislation, but the range of illegality is wide. In some cases the dwellings have been constructed on public land or on land belonging to private owners, and de facto squatting is the result; in others construction has violated zoning regulations, building on farmland or what has been reserved as park space (green area); or construction has been carried out without regard to municipal ordinances, without the proper inspection and permits, and disregarding the engineering, sanitary, aesthetic, or habitation norms set by the authorities. What is clear is that Istanbul's growth from one million to ten million during the second half of the twentieth century has been possible primarily because of the expansion of illegal housing. I will first discuss the legal and political context within which such development occurred and then the implications of this particular kind of urban growth on social ecology.

An important dimension of urbanization is the necessary appropriation of land for purposes of residential construction. Land, of course, is a special (fictitious) commodity, signifying the difficulty of its acceptance as an item that can be the simple object of commerce (see Polanyi 1957). But, before capitalist accumulation proper may begin, it should be possible to appropriate land privately: private real property with relatively few and acceptable restrictions is a precondition of fully achieved capitalism. Legal systems prevailing in precapitalist societies generally accommodated the perception of the public with respect to the use of land. In the Ottoman Empire, all land, unless it was explicitly recognized as private or belonging to a foundation, was considered to belong to the state. The land under cultivation, as long as taxes were paid on it, was held in possession (usufruct rights) by the cultivators. Land that was under state ownership could be reclaimed by peasants; and, if taxes were paid properly, it would be considered land with a usufructuary claim on it—but not private property. In urban areas houses and gardens were generally registered as private property. Nonetheless, history and folklore were filled with ample warnings about too much accumulation that would incur the jealousy and the wrath of the authorities and culminate in confiscation. In reality, no claim on land was secure. Hence, the categories of ownership in the Ottoman Empire belonged to a quite different universe of meaning than the capitalist case to which they were forced to adapt.[1] This was especially true for the rubric *state land* that, in practice, operated as a residual but, as legal fiction, legitimated the continuing presence of the state in the social world. From the point of view of the subjects, real property was something that had to be carved out of the realm possessed by the state, that had to be defended from the state, and that could at any time be lost back to the state. Its security depended on the balance of power and on the ingenuity of the usurper. But, as long as the claim on the property accorded with the broader notion of moral right, problems were minimal.

Transition from customary conceptions of property based on the supremacy of the state to inalienable rights of individual ownership and private accumulation was never easy. Most often in the periphery, this transition was the result of colonial conquest and imposition. In a few other cases such as the Ottoman, modernization imposed from outside meant the promulgation by local rulers of new laws recognizing private property closer to the Western norm. It was however, difficult for the state elite, and for the communities, to abandon notions of a moral economy based on the peasantry's access to land. Nineteenth-century Ottoman modernization brought about new laws that reflected this ambivalence, affirming land as a commodity on the one hand—registrable to individual ownership—while imposing numerous restrictions on its accumulation and commerce on the other. The social forces supporting modernizing legislation were puny and more often than not prone to be isolated as foreign, colonial, or comprador. Hence, the very idea of private property on land was identified with the imposition of alien cultural norms.

Land that was not under actual cultivation was considered public domain. Given the prevalence of land that was not privately appropriated, steps toward the modernization of the property regime resulted in a situation in which the state became the proprietor of most of the realm. Even today some two-thirds of the surface area of Turkey is under state ownership.

After independence, with the nationalization of real estate abandoned by Armenians and Greeks, the category of land owned by the state expanded. Between 1915 and 1925, a total of more than two million Armenians and Greeks were killed, expelled, exchanged, or departed of their own will. This Christian population had constituted a disproportionate portion of the wealthier urban dwellers of the late empire. With their disappearance, not only houses but also land near the inhabited part of the cities were left vacant. Most of this land was nationalized, but some remained under titular ownership of former Ottoman nationals who were no longer there. Complicated arrangements were made to safeguard such ownership, which generally amounted to individuals who had lost their citizenship being unable to sell their land. These arrangements meant, for example, that the estate of a departed Greek was de facto assimilated into the same category as public land.[2]

BEGINNINGS OF URBAN IMMIGRATION

Before the 1950s, there was no pressure to acquire the state land surrounding the inhabited urban area. Urban population between the 1920s and 1945 remained stable and, in most cities, below the pre–World War I totals. It was quite common in Istanbul during that period to find large areas of garden plots or dairy farms interspersed within the urban fabric. Most of this urban agriculture was located on abandoned plots, land belonging to departed Christians, or now defunct waqfs[3] where property had reverted to public ownership and nobody could make any claims. In fact, compared to the within-the-walls density of premodern European cities, Istanbul always presented a picture of noncompactness, a sparseness—a fact on which many a traveler remarked.

Istanbul's population explosion dates from the 1950s: from over one million in 1950 to three million in 1970, four million in 1975, six million in 1985, and nine million in 1995. Most of this growth, averaging 4 to 5 percent annually over the half century following 1945, was due to new immigration and the higher birthrate of immigrants. It was empty spaces within the inhabited city that were first filled with illegal squatter (*gecekondu*[4]) housing. The potential supply of this inner-city land, however, was far too little to satisfy the needs of the vast wave of migrants that began to arrive in the city after the end of the war. Besides, being too much in the public eye was not always desirable for squatters. Hence, the natural space for expansion became the immediate perimeter of the settled area—land that was primarily public (i.e., de facto ownerless).

The picture that emerged when immigrants started settling in the city was an urban planner's nightmare: the jigsaw pattern of established private property, abandoned non-Muslim holdings, waqf land without claimants, former agricultural holdings, and above all various kinds of publicly owned land, translated to a similarly unpredictable intertwining of zoned and gecekondu settlements, resulting in a surprising juxtaposition of villas and expensive blocs of flats with shacks, even in the wealthiest neighborhoods of the city. "Illegal" settlement occurred in places where least resistance was encountered. Accordingly, the pattern of settlements has resulted in one of the most dispersed and low-density habitations in the world. Istanbul metropolitan area extends almost a hundred kilometers on an east-west axis paralleling the shores of the Marmara Sea, in a band whose width varies between ten and twenty kilometers.

The principal factor permitting this development was the state's inability or unwillingness to institute a capitalist regime of property relations. As "owner" of most of the peripheral land in the city that was potentially available for settlement, the state could adopt several options as policy. These options were debated and defended by various interest groups and political movements at various times. In the end, public authorities simply yielded to inertia and did not proactively adopt a policy. There were, of course, advantages to this strategy, but it also contributed to the chaotic development of the city and to the emergence of the legal-illegal division. At one extreme, the state could have actually protected publicly owned land, effectively prohibiting settlement on it. This strategy would probably create a density of settlement in the legal city and would lead to a process of slummification; it would also require coercive measures to keep the immigrants out, which could only be sustained in an authoritarian regime. At the other extreme, public land could simply have been auctioned off, leaving the capitalist market to take care of the housing problem. Neither of these two extreme strategies was ever debated as a possibility. In between were several other options containing various degrees of social engineering. One would have been the subsidized

individuals or for cooperative development; another, a
building public housing to be rented out. Both of these op-
ittently on the agenda, defended in social democratic and
but were brought to life in a few small projects, realized only
d, the vast inertia of populist clientelism prevailed.
lated to keeping public lands out of the realm of the mar-
ds, populist practice coincided with the view that saw pri-
land as an alien imposition. Since nationalism and inde-
be legitimated, at least to some extent as the upholding of
inst the civilization of Europe, the state elite of the Turkish
eir counterparts in other developing countries, and even in
—see Leontidou 1990) were never comfortable defending
capitalist market with any vigilance. Besides, in a situation
uals considered public land as potentially awaiting private
ie state did not have a legitimate status as proprietor.
s themselves were torn between accepting the tenets of cap-
tion and providing for the moral economy that would re-
eration of a market based on private property. Because post-
lation involved at least lip service toward an antiliberal
(antimarket) stand, the selling off of public property in order for the market to work untrammeled was thought to be unjustifiable. Besides, the formation of the new Turkish state had involved nationalization (more correctly "statization") of a large portion of the land that was held as private
property by the very social groups who had benefited most from the adoption of legislation making land a commodity. The ousting of the Christian
population was, after all, one of the implicit goals of independence. Popular appropriation of public land simply confirmed the nationalist rhetoric.
Thus, the formation and sovereignty of a nation-state and the expulsion of
the supporters of the liberal model could be interpreted to imply (among
other things) victory for the popular notion that land, in fact, should remain
extra commercium. Under these circumstances an attempt to openly com-
modify land would lead to the erosion of the legitimacy of the new state.

Clientelism provided a baser motive, appealing to the political logic of
those in decision-making positions. If patronage were to remain an effective mechanism, the rules of allocation of public land, and the dispensa-
tion of public services to new settlements, had to be deliberately left vague.
A simple distribution or allocation on the basis of an advertised rule would
preclude the striking of particularist deals through which a politician
could emerge as the patron of a newly urbanized group. In other words,
politicians generally preferred to retain the privilege of arbitrary allocation
to create and maintain popular support and thus strengthen their own positions. The existence of such clientelistic relations was predicated on informal appropriation of land.

DIVISION OF THE CITY INTO LEGAL AND ILLEGAL

The entire process of land occupation and allocation, indeed of construction, was imbued with uncertainty, which continued after a house was
built—as long as it was not legally recognized with proper title. The high
proportion of "illegal" housing shows that official recognition was not extended easily. In fact, even in the more advanced stages of the process, the
uncertainty in zoning regulations was such that except in the old city or
"modern" neighborhoods where blocks of flats predominate, whether a
construction has actually finished is always open to question. Expansion,
or putting up of another floor, is indexed to official attitude. On the eve of
an election, a populist mayor may give a covert signal that zoning regulations will not be enforced, and a frenzy of construction activity may add
new floors to existing buildings. Politically, it is much less likely that a
house with people in it (even if only half-finished) will be torn down by
the police, with cameras capturing heart-rending scenes.

Land occupation was usually a collective affair—an informal partnership organized by entrepreneurs who received the entrepreneurial returns
(monetary reward, political allegiance) that was due to them. Since the
land that came under occupation was often in public ownership of the central, regional, or local government, there was no question of a market price
to be paid to the owner; there were, however, bribes that had to be paid to
the relevant officials who then, hopefully, ignored the infraction. More often than not such bribes insured that conflict with the authorities was post-
poned to a time when the squatters established themselves both physically
and politically, so that an ousting would lead to costly and unpopular confrontation.

Collective action continued after settlement. One form that took the center stage during the process of formalization was the campaign for collective goods (see chap. 9 in this volume). In fact, municipal services often arrived soon after a neighborhood evolved. When new municipalities were
established in the periphery of Istanbul, with higher autonomy and a need
to establish popularity with their local constituencies, the eventual provision of services became even more dependable. There were very few cases
of ongoing official vigilance against illegal construction: all sides were
aware that when a neighborhood or even a single house was inhabited, the
likelihood of the authorities to tear it down decreased drastically. With the
addition of new floors as circumstances permitted, the life cycle of a squatter neighborhood was such that after a few elections it could become an
area of multiple-story apartment buildings. The first gecekondu area
that was extensively studied in the 1960s is a case in point (Karpat 1976).
Hisarustu now boasts four- or five-story buildings facing streets barely
wide enough for a single car to pass through. In this particular example

proximity to the urban center was the principal factor behind rapid development. In other gecekondu areas, neighborhoods have evolved as quasi-autonomous towns where they provide most of the middle-range functions and services expected of second- or third-order settlement nodes in an urban hierarchy, including employment. In fact, it would not be too inaccurate to think of Istanbul as a conglomerate of such gecekondu districts with limited organic unity. As new gecekondu areas are added—inevitably to the outlying perimeters—more nodes are strung on the web in a serial manner.[5]

The legal-illegal division corresponded to the social and cultural divide that came to characterize Istanbul's ecology. The housing experience was the initial and defining element of life in the big city. In addition to suffering cultural isolation and the resentment of native Istanbulites, immigrants also had to confront the state because of their illegality. Inhabitants of shantytowns were defined as existing outside the law from the moment they acquired land and started the protracted building process. For many there actually were legal proceedings that, however, mostly remained inconclusive. Local city planners and architects' associations and most of the media in the city told them that they lived illegally. The legal order represented by the state, emerging concretely in the law and regulations affecting real property, criminalized the immigrants; this official imposition naturally came to be seen as a burden that had to be avoided, circumvented, battled, or bribed aside. The state's reluctance to commit itself fully to instituting a property regime, the ambivalence of the attitude toward a full implementation of the market logic, the uneasy coexistence of commodification with a moral economy, shaped identities and generated life spaces where avoiding the state was a primary concern. This criminalization became the defining element of existence and affected all other interaction with the authorities: immigrants were forced to evolve a confrontational ideology. The urban came to be seen by the immigrants to represent an alien legal system where property was regulated on the basis of an imported law. Hence, all the vectors that divide the conceptual universes along axes of Western and native, alien and authentic, imposed and home-grown, were overlaid with the dimension of space, where the urban proper was counterposed to the illegally occupied, not really urban, the shantytown.[6]

The "urbanization" process of the immigrants paralleled the legalization of the space they inhabited. The state did not simply represent an intractable legal impediment; it was also the principal modernizing force, seeking to transform the population in ways that the masses found alien, resented, and resisted. This imposition and the inaccessible dimension of the city were easily identified with each other. Hence, the fact that obstacles in the legalization process derived from state policy served to exacerbate the already existing tension between state-pursued modernization from above and the evolution taking place through its own dynamics in the experience of the everyday.

At first immigrants were tolerated because they were peasants in the city: they either could be made to know their place or pulled out of what was considered their cultural abyss—if and when they adopted urban ways. The pace of social and geographic mobility, however, far exceeded the manageable transformation envisaged in the earlier period.[7] As immigrants evolved their own politics, their own life worlds, their own public spaces, the incompatibility between these new creations and what the native Istanbulites identified as modern was widely remarked: the perception was that a divided city had emerged whose contours paralleled the legal-illegal division of the physical space. Gradually, this perception yielded to an alarmed sense of besiegement, because the modern of the elite was increasingly marginalized in the face of politics and culture characterized by the dominance of the gecekondu.

CHANGES IN MIDDLE-CLASS HABITATION

Along with population increase, economic transformation brought about by national development, and greater exposure to postwar consumption norms, the "legal," zoned, urban area also expanded responding to middle-class demand. This was a differentiation trend where the movement was from socially heterogeneous neighborhoods in the old city to newly created, more homogeneous neighborhoods reflecting a spatial division consonant with an economy growing more complex. As Istanbul quickly became the growth pole of a relatively successful process of national development based on import-substituting industrialization, incomes increased, consumption patterns changed, and consumer durables were purchased widely by the growing middle class. All this led to a new pattern of demand for housing. Larger kitchens and bathrooms, constructed with the products of a booming construction materials industry churning out ceramic goods and tiles and chromed fixtures, began to set the standard, requiring newly built blocs of flats, preferably in newly emerging middle-class neighborhoods (Öncü 1988).

Such middle-class demand was primarily met through new construction on land that was (or was made) undisputably private property. Ottoman summer houses were common on the Asian side and, although fewer, on the European side, along the banlieu rail routes paralleling the coast of the Marmara Sea. These all boasted large gardens. During the 1960s, much pressure was applied to regulate zoning restrictions to allow the subdivision of these properties with the eventual result that several five- to ten-story apartment buildings were constructed on each lot that had been the garden of one wooden summer house. A crucial factor was a new law permitting independent ownership of apartments (condominiums) in a residential building. Until then, ownership of flats was on a cooperative basis with individuals holding shares in the land on which the building was constructed. With the new legal situation, the growing middle classes became full owners of their homes. During the 1960s, ownership of a newly built flat (rather than a house in the suburbs) became *the* middle-class aspiration.

The usual mode in which development was carried out was through "contractors" (*muteahhit*) who were entrepreneurs mostly from the provinces (predominantly from the Black Sea region where a tradition of seasonal migration to Istanbul for construction work had existed since the previous century) who had sufficient capital and, more important, the connections to mobilize a construction crew, often from their own district of origin. Muteahhits were generally small-scale contractors: land availability, on the one hand, and the nature of the demand, on the other, were not of a dimension to warrant the involvement of large developers. Old Ottoman houses were demolished; the owners of the land, generally the heirs of an old Istanbul family, contracted to receive half of the apartments in the new buildings against their ownership of the grounds. The contractor sought to sell the flats before construction was finished (preferably when the ground was broken) to raise working capital. In fact, in a situation in which no organized credit market existed for the purchase of residential real estate, this method where prospective middle-class buyers paid for the flats over two or three years constituted the only mechanism of payment in installments.

Of a smaller impact were various "building cooperatives" formed usually by professionals with privileged access to some level of the political authority. These associations generally were tipped off by an insider in central or local government that a particular piece of public land could be finagled for the cooperative's use. Members paid an initial sum toward the acquisition of the land and subsequently monthly dues during the construction process. Military officers, judges, journalists, and doctors were some of the more prominent corporate professional groups that availed themselves of this opportunity. The granting of corporate privileges, along with clientelism, is often a feature of political orders that try to avoid the liberal precepts of self-regulating markets.[8] The granting of permits to such cooperatives was a continuation of the populist-clientelist mode described earlier. The well-connected professionals shared in the great amounts of urban rent that accrued to any construction during the boom period; in fact, residential housing became the major vehicle of middle-class accumulation during this period.

The evolution of middle-class neighborhoods was specific in terms of urban geography. Parcelization of privately owned gardens occurred mostly along the Marmara shore, and dominantly on the Asian side, while

cooperatives developing public land operated predominantly in the highlands of the European side (Levent, Etiler). These two centers of gravity of
middle-class habitation emerged as the counterposition to gecekondu development within the urban ecology of Istanbul. Compared to their combined weight, gentrification of old Istanbul neighborhoods was of negligible importance in providing the residential units deemed to conform to
modern standards. Hence, the old-city neighborhoods that were left behind
when those who could afford flats in the new developments moved out
(e.g., Fatih, Laleli, Beşiktaş), remained as less expensive, less desirable areas,
providing housing to a population that was beginning to suffer a slow but
irreversible downward mobility. Even the highest-rent areas near Beyoglu
(Şişli, Nisantaş) eventually succumbed to this process of déclassement.

In the zones where the described process of middle-class development
operated fully, gecekondus were excluded. In other words, if the pre-1950
ownership patterns in an area were such that all the land belonged to private owners, with no public or nationalized land in the cracks, the appearance of the same area by the end of the 1970s was one of exclusive middle-class development of modern apartment buildings. Or, if prospective
middle-class residents acted early enough to establish "cooperative" development, land that would otherwise be occupied by shantytown developers remained immune from illegal housing. Together with the old
neighborhoods of the city, some of which remained relatively poor but
never became slummified, and other developments of modern apartment
buildings (this time interspersed with gecekondus), these new concentra-
tions, in contrast to the illegal peripheral developments, constituted the
"legal" city (zoned or imarli, in city planner parlance).

This era of middle-class residential differentiation coincides with national development: the architectural idiom was a refracted version of the
postwar European apartment building, but the architectural and technical
standards were lower. Often, the contractors worked from a previously
tried blueprint and the services of an architect were deemed unnecessary.
Construction was labor-intensive and used low-wage, unskilled, new immigrants into the city. Materials were locally manufactured by a construction industry where demand was growing so rapidly that quality had
never become a concern. A protectionist trade regime dictated that imported materials were simply not available.

The middle-class neighborhoods thus created were relatively comfortable compared to the residential standards of the old city. Aesthetically,
however, they were seriously lacking. The poor quality of the materials,
combined with a general failure to recognize the importance of landscaping and indifference to public areas such as entrances into the buildings
and the lobby (which often remained unfinished), made these buildings
seem like failed imitations of an ill-understood ideal.

THE IMPACT OF GLOBALIZATION

During the 1980s, new spatial developments in Istanbul reflected the impact of globalization—the intensification of transnational flows of capital, commodities, people, information, and signs that came to shape the city's transformation. Liberalization in the economy and the grudging and incomplete repudiation of populist intervention by the state elite were necessary preconditions for the imposition of a self-regulating market. Without the market, the flows that constitute globalization may not be fully realized. In the realm of creation of space, this condition translated to land being made available for legal development, which, in turn, made possible the increasing impact of capitalist enterprise in housing and, interdependently, the emergence of large construction firms.

Access to land was facilitated through increasing venality of the officials and the relaxation of some laws pertaining to land use. Thus, the government was persuaded to clarify the zoning status of large tracts of land in the immediate perimeter of the city, which were subsequently sold or transferred to large developers and banks. Waqf lands and lands belonging to departed Greeks received expeditious legal clearance; a law was passed easing the ban on construction in the Bosphorus area. In a few cases developers were able to consolidate their holdings by purchasing the "titles" in the hands of informal owners of gecekondu plots.

The developers in the post-1980 era, compared to the small-scale competitive market of muteahhits in the previous period, were a different caliber altogether. About a dozen large firms had gained experience contracting in the Middle East and Libya during the oil boom (ENKA, Maya, and Dogus are the examples) and through this rapid accumulation had come to rival the giant holding companies of the import substitution period in business volume. Those holding companies, as well, responded to opportunities in the market and (like Koc and Alarko) branched out into the high-profit contracting sector. Because financial liberalization quickly incorporated the banking sector into world markets, profit opportunity in Istanbul's construction sector attracted a bubble of investment funds; foreign contracting firms put together joint venture packages in which they would guarantee dollar loans in exchange for a piece of the action. In the inflationary environment of the 1980s, real estate became the highest-profit sector in Istanbul, where political corruption, capitalist development, and international finance intersected.

A portion of the new land, new funds, and the entrepreneurial energy went into the construction of business spaces in the form of office towers, shopping malls, five-star hotels, and exhibition grounds, appropriate for an internationalizing economy. At the same time, however, these construction companies embarked on large projects of residential development responding to the globalizing aspirations of a middle class, emerging through the increasing opening of the economy to the world. Under the impact of a globalizing economy, Istanbul generated a cohort of rapidly enriched yuppie businessmen and professionals. Unlike the relatively staid, national-oriented middle class of the previous era, these new groups were much wealthier and "footloose" (Lash and Urry 1994), traveling in other global cities of the world, acquiring international taste. The now open economy allowed them to indulge in consumption habits that would have been impossible a decade earlier. In addition to globalization of commodities and their own mobility, the free flow of signs, and the global distribution of images and information beamed through screens induced them to aspire to qualitatively different standards of residential space.

Advertising contributed significantly to the construction of exalted images (Öncü 1997; Aksoy and Robins 1995). The international idiom of clean spaces in landscaped nature sites, with swimming pools, playgrounds, and nearby golf courses, were selling points. Large villas or luxury flats in the style of the globally rich and famous, constructed with imported materials to international quality standards, were advertised as providing contemporary lifestyles. The main selling point was that lifestyles promised by these material amenities could be conducted in segregated spaces. These compounds were self-contained, with their own shopping centers, country clubs, and even schools; furthermore, they could be isolated from the dirt, confusion, and noise of the city and secured behind guarded walls. According to overly optimistic advertising copy, they could be accessed by a short drive on rapid roads.[9] Television coverage and glossy magazines dedicated to writing up the interior decoration and furnishing of these new homes contributed to the advertising effort, operating in that new mode where the line between sales and reportage is often unclear.

The phenomenon of gated compounds is, of course, not unique to Istanbul: the worsening of income distribution and the demand for first-world luxuries and lifestyles to be enjoyed in isolation seem to have created a universal blueprint. This ubiquity explains the attention gated compounds have attracted as manifestations in space of postpopulist social polarization. In Istanbul, too, the emergence of ostentatious luxury consumption identified with the spatial segregation of the rich has constituted the most visible and controversial aspect of the new order. The encroachment of compounds on what a mere decade ago was considered to be empty land or the territory of the shanty has been rapid.

Postpopulist development is not, however, confined to one end of the spectrum. Despite its prominence in the public and scholarly eye, the incidence of luxury compounds at the high end is dwarfed by the increasing share of residential high-rise complexes at lower income levels. Concomitant with the relaxation of the tight control over the land market, a demand for mass housing created a pressure on the government to allocate some of the public land to private or semipublic developers, or to grant new zoning permits, for the construction of blocks of flats. This process gained speed as greater autonomy was given to peripheral municipalities that sought to normalize the status of illegally occupied land in their jurisdiction. In some cases the public agency, Mass Housing Administration, created in the 1980s, undertook the development directly; in others it allocated land where individual cooperatives could build and obtain government-subsidized credit for their members if they followed the master plan drafted by the municipal office. But, because the potential market is vast, private contracting companies have also joined the fray. The product is often a cluster of ten- to twenty-story buildings, four or five apartments to a floor, with minimal landscaping in the public area and shoddy infrastructure; the interiors are relatively large (one hundred square meters is the norm) and crudely finished. If it were not for the evident pride the inhabitants take in graduating to apartment living, visible in the continuous attempts to upgrade (one of the rapidly increasing sectors of the retail market has been do-it-yourself supermarkets, attracting much foreign capital in the form of international chains—Götzen, Bauhaus, Mr Bricolage) and the care taken to keep the interiors clean, the buildings would look very much like "projects."

The volume of new development is enormous: there is a ring of such projects circumscribing the city, all about an hour's distance from the center but with the prospect of becoming centers in their own right. Unlike for the top range of professionals, lower middle-class employment is much more decentralized, and some large companies relocating to the edges of the city have participated in building flats for their personnel in nearby residential areas. There are usually several such contiguous projects in each area, typically consisting of a minimum of several hundred flats. In one such area, called Beylikduzu, about forty kilometers southwest of the city center, fifty thousand units are said to be under construction. A similar development is taking place in the opposite end of the compass, in Yakacik. Prices are rockbottom: flats advertise (in the summer of 1997) for between $10,000 and $15,000. Term-payment plans are available, and cooperative membership allows for cheap credit organized by the Mass Housing Administration.

The principal factor allowing this transformation has been the willingness of the state to relax the legal restrictions that heretofore had rendered all development informal. Through allowing public property to be appropriated by municipalities in some cases, rezoning of land in others, and simply clarifying status, new territories have been opened to residential construction. Coinciding with the emergence of a demand from within the gecekondu population, the replacement of gecekondu neighborhoods in the perimeter of the city with inexpensive high-rise flats is now the principal dynamic of Istanbul's development. Rather than the division between the illegal and the legal, the current line accordingly seems to be drawn between those who remain in the gecekondu and those who are able to make the move to the high-rises. New immigrants naturally come into gecekondu areas and become illegal, whereas an older cohort, perhaps second-generation and more likely employed rather than petty entrepreneur, join the ranks of the legal city, fulfilling the expectations of an earlier theory with a lag. The effects of this new legality on the political and cultural disposition of the erstwhile immigrants will be interesting to observe. This, plus the impact on social life of leaving a physical environment much like the village for one representing vertical modernity, will be of significant consequence on the global/local dialectic.

Two more developments characteristic of the current era must be mentioned. One is gentrification, expressing similar concerns of distinction and lifestyle and appealing to the same stratum as its counterparts in global cities of the core. The process of individualization, however, has not been as rapid in the Turkish context. There are not large numbers of unmarried professionals; nor is there a significant development of personal services, ethnic restaurants, art galleries, or bars. Gated compounds are prevalent because they target families, preferably with children, who constitute the vast majority of the service workers at the top of the hierarchy. Thus, gentrification exists; but its incidence so far is confined to a few villages along the Bosphorus (see chap. 10 in this volume) and to a small section of Beyoglu (see chap. 2).

At the other end of the spectrum is a quantitatively much more important development. It was already mentioned that illegal occupation of land and the construction of dwellings eventually receive some recognition owing to political expediency. When recognition extended to a succession of amnesties, especially in the earlier-developed shantytowns, houses were gradually replaced by three- to four-story buildings divided into flats. Informal entrepreneurs became landlords, and gecekondus became urban dwellings, in a simulacrum of the middle-class style. Yet, there are still no titles and not much change in the nature of the interior or the exterior (public) space. Density increases without great impact on social relations. There is no cachet to living in such a building rather than an independent house. In fact, growing density is reflected in the increasing incidence of rental units in gecekondu neighborhoods, indicating the settlement of a poorer cohort of immigrants. In contrast to the immigrants of the 1960s and 1970s who had been attracted by what the city had to offer, those of the 1980s and 1990s were driven out of their Anatolian habitats by economic and political crises. These new immigrants arrived in Istanbul destitute and with hardly any connections to their villages from which they could expect starting assistance. The accommodation they could procure was accordingly modest; they did not have the chance to occupy and build on public land independently. Accordingly, the current transformation in shantytowns, as population density increases, is in the nature of a peripheral slummification.

CONCLUSION

Istanbul's urban ecology has been taking shape in new directions where the creation of residential space and the building of environment are conditioned by a complex interweaving of its own history and global determinations. While development was national, class polarization remained modest; corporatist and populist practices allowed a containment of inequality providing the middle class with a share of the urban rent and the new immigrants with land to occupy and to build on. The principal division then was between the zoned and the shantytown districts that constituted the material basis of the cultural segregation between moderns and the others, or Istanbulites and Anatolians (see chap. 6). With the end of national development, inequality in incomes and consumption patterns becomes much more pronounced, leading to sharply distinct residential spaces where the "corporate international bourgeoisie" build for themselves villas based on the global blueprint. At the same time, the clear delineation that characterized the Istanbulite-immigrant duality is no longer valid because the distinctive appropriation of Western modes of behavior that Istanbul's middle class had made its cultural capital has ceased to enjoy high yields. The project of constructing a national culture along the westernized conceptions of the urban elite no longer carries much credibility. On their part, immigrants have long become a numerical majority and have put their stamp on the politics and culture of the city; but, more important, they are differentiated as well—on the basis of years in the city, accumulation, employment, and cultural and political orientation. This reflects in the new forms of housing that emerge: high-rise mass housing, gecekondus turned into apartment buildings, slummified shantytowns, and so forth, where former inhabitants of the shantytown now find differentiated accommodation. The material and cultural impact of globalization has been toward the emergence of patterns of differentiation in the capitalist mode.

NOTES

1. For the classical Ottoman land system, see Inalcik (1973).
2. This was also the provision of the Exchange of Populations agreement of 1923. See Pentzopoulos (1962) and Alexandris (1983).

3. Waqf is a foundation set up under Islamic law where the revenue is designated for a special purpose or for income, but the entrusted property cannot be sold. In the Ottoman Empire, it often served to keep the authorities away. If a property was set up as a waqf (rather than private, inheritable estate), it could not be confiscated.

4. *Gecekondu* literally means "set up overnight," implying that the habitation it refers to had to be constructed before the authorities woke up. It is the Turkish equivalent of *favela, bidonville, barrio,* and other similar terms. It refers both to the form of housing and to neighborhoods formed by such housing.

5. This phenomenon is equivalent to the edge-city development in the United States where suburban centers become self-contained business environments for many functions.

6. Yael Navaro-Yasin's discussion of the construction of the native is relevant here; see chapter 4 in this volume.

7. The material reasons for the inability to absorb the immigrants into the project of modernization-from-above were obvious: economic transformation as laid out in the statist development project did not occur rapidly enough. The expectation of a smooth modernization had been predicated on the motor force of the economy. It was through their integration into the modern economy that the immigrants were supposed to become part of the modern social order, transform their politics, and be open to the homogenizing culture of national capitalism. The evolving modern economy, however, failed to create the absorption capacity expected of it. Immigrants generally found employment but not as workers in factories; instead, they became part of a sprawling informal sector, testifying to the failure of the development model and inviting disillusionment. Hence, the "illegal" status of dwellings often corresponded to an "illegal" employment status reinforcing the alienation from the ideal of the modern sector.

8. There is an extensive literature on corporatism in southern Europe. See, for example, Wiarda (1973).

9. In a cinema when a short clip advertised such a compound and the voice-over claimed that the drive to the business district was only fifteen minutes, the audience burst into laughter. In the daily worsening traffic of Istanbul, the attraction of living far from the city runs into a snag when the commute time is considered.

REFERENCES

Aksoy, A., and Robins, K. 1995. Istanbul between civilization and discontent. *New Perspectives on Turkey* 10, 57–74.

Alexandris, A. 1983. *The Greek minority of Istanbul and Greek-Turkish relations, 1918–1974.* Athens: Center of Asia Minor Studies.

Inalcik, H. 1973. *The Ottoman Empire: the classical age.* New York: Praeger.

Karpat, K. 1976. *The gecekondu: rural migration and urbanization.* Cambridge: Cambridge University Press.

Lash, S., and J. Urry. 1994. *Economies of signs and space.* London: Sage.

Leontidou, L. 1990. *The Mediterranean city in transition: social change and urban development*. Cambridge: Cambridge University Press.

Öncü, A. 1988. The politics of the land market in Turkey. *International Journal of Urban and Regional Research* 12, no. 1: 38–64.

———.1997. The myth of the "ideal home" travels across cultural borders to Istanbul. Pages 56–72 in A. Öncü and P. Weyland (eds.), *Space culture and power: new identities in globalizing cities*. London: Zed.

Pentzopoulos, D. 1962. *The Balkan exchange of minorities and its impact upon Greece*. Paris: Mouton.

Polanyi, K. 1957. *The great transformation*. New York: Rinehart.

Wiarda, H. J. 1973. Toward a framework for the study of political change in the Iberic-Latin tradition: the corporative model. *World Politics* 25 (January): 206–35.

9

Where Do You Hail From?
Localism and Networks in Istanbul

Sema Erder

FROM THE "OLD ISTANBUL" TO THE "NEW ISTANBUL"

Istanbul has always been a destination for migrant populations, changing and cosmopolitan in its composition. Nonetheless, until the 1950s, the heterogeneity of its population was contained under a perceptual umbrella formulated as "urbanity," and the principal dimension of difference among its inhabitants was thought to derive from their confessional diversity. Until the 1950s, ethnicity referred to the delineation of difference among the non-Muslim population—a difference articulated at legal and institutional levels. Armenian, Greek, and Jewish populations were, however, seen as integral components of the city: constituting the very diversity that made Istanbul cosmopolitan.

After the 1950s, when Istanbul began to rapidly gain population, the composition and diversity of its population started to change radically. On the one hand, forced and voluntary emigration of the non-Muslim population and, on the other, a vast wave of immigration from Anatolia rendered Istanbul's population profile qualitatively different. Although the city became much more homogeneous from the point of view of religion, its cultural heterogeneity was maintained. Its new diversity, however, proved to be more difficult to accommodate and led to substantial social tension and conflict.

The first change apparent to the old urbanites of Istanbul was that the new arrivals from Anatolia were "peasants." In the early 1950s there had been a wave of immigration from the Balkans, but this group had arrived in Istanbul in a rather orderly manner in a process overseen by government officials and supervised through international agreements. The immigration of the Anatolians, however, was a different matter. Their mode of arrival, occupation of land, construction of housing, search for employment, and style of life they led were seen as alien by the old urbanites and were scrutinized in cultured discourse. From then on "peasants in the city" remained as the principal item on the agenda of urban problems. The urbanite-peasant duality, and the cultural difference this duality was supposed to indicate, became the focus of an argument within which peasantization of the city was the key formula explicating the nature of the urban problem. Until the 1980s, the media as well as academe were involved in discussing the problems of the integration of the peasants (still perceived as undifferentiated) into the city. Integration was defined as changing the lifestyles of the new arrivals so as to assimilate them into the social fabric dominated by the old urbanites. Urban problems were seen through a perspective in which the immigrant peasants who refused to become properly integrated and urbanized were blamed.

Initially, those peasants who settled in village lands and other empty lands around the city, relying on their own initiative, lived in complementary harmony with the urbanites. Despite unavoidable frictions, the men proved to be cheap and docile workers, and the women mostly served as domestic labor, albeit "in need of education" in the ways of the civilized world. For politicians they were a potential store of votes to be tapped, and for government officials they were "people" less demanding than citizens and ever so grateful for populist policies. Only in the 1980s did this harmony start to come apart. In the self-consciously ironic phrase of the urbanites, "the people began to crowd out the citizens." This change was first noticed in the composition of the local political class, then became apparent in the formation of interest groups and urban movements. Hence, social differentiation in Istanbul could no longer be reduced to an urban-peasant divide in which the latter were clearly subordinate.

The politicians who came to power after the 1983 elections, both from the point of view of their social background and in the way they formulated urban problems, served to awaken the old urbanites. These new politicians were, themselves, of rural origin, but they were not burdened by any complex of provinciality. On the contrary, they seemed to boast of their non-Istanbul background. In fact, they defined their mission not as "solving the peasant problem" but as solving the problems of the newly urbanized peasants (Koksal and Kara 1990). These new governors focused precisely on employing public means to ease the plight of the newly urbanized.

A parallel development within the population was the evolution of a new type of social organization based on localism. These new associations explicitly rivaled groupings that were class based, and they aimed at a membership that cut across the heterogeneous social background of their members. Relying on a loyalty and solidarity allegedly reflecting a shared sense of provincial origin, these new organizations became the building blocks of neighborhood clubs, professional associations, and even political parties. An immediate consequence was the changing nature of rivalry, conflict, political competition, and alliance in the city.

The initial conflict between the new urbanites and the established order had been occasioned during the immigrants' attempts at securing land for shelter. The occupation of land by the newcomers was considered an illegal act fit for the police to handle, but confrontations along the same lines quickly became daily events where the immigrants aimed to gain recognition and to secure minimal municipal services. This mode of struggle continued to be the principal means of articulating the demands of the new population, an established tactic with its own rules of conduct and expected outcomes. They involved all the heterogeneous strata sharing the same inhabited space. Their popularity and success depended on an organization that allowed participants, especially the low-income dwellers of new neighborhoods, to voice common demands arising from the desire to rectify urban inequalities.

In the recent period, however, the nature of such movements has changed somewhat. While the departure of the non-Muslim population had signaled a degree of homogenization and the official discourse began to talk about a Turkish and Islamic city, the recent urban social movements (since the 1980s) seem to be organized along the lines of new ethnic and confessional solidarities, such as Laz, Kurdish, and Alevi. Some of these movements are more directly concerned with identity politics—demands for cultural recognition and group identity, although ethnicity is usually instrumental in the sense that it serves the immediate organizational needs of the movements. Most, however, have been concerned with problems of public space. Heterogeneous in terms of class background, participants in these movements target locations of social reproduction and objects of collective consumption; hence, they are constituents of "urban social movements" (Castells 1977; Eckstein 1989; Lowe 1986; Mingione 1981; Fuentes and Frank 1989). Their mobilization reflects both the frustration and the demands of the newly urbanized, whose integration into the city is achieved through their own initiative and through informal networks and who, consequently, suffer various kinds of inequality, especially at the level of access to municipal services.

FROM SOLIDARITY TO INFORMAL NETWORKS

The existence of networks among the newcomers, based on kinship and local origins, has been widely noted since the initial wave of urbanization. At the time, these affiliations were thought to characterize a "peasant" mentality, representing a continuity with traditional village cultures and therefore transitional. In fact, the solidaristic nature of these networks was regarded as lightening the burden on public authorities in responding to various problems associated with the absorption of the peasantry into urban life. Certain practices contributed to the development of this attitude. For instance, the cultural attitudes of urbanites who considered the periphery as rural and peripheral inhabitants as peasants were paralleled in public administration: the legal boundaries of the city did not expand, and the urban periphery was classified as belonging to the domain of rural government—within the jurisdiction of the gendarmerie rather than the urban police. Obversely, urban institutions and formal government were considered adequate only for the urban centers. This separation led to the constitution of local public spaces with their own rules and institutions (Smith 1987; Williams 1987; Leeds 1994).

Two important factors contributed to the success and spread of informal networks among the immigrants. The first relates to the fact that migration to the cities occurred entirely outside existing formal institutions. It was the informal market that regulated the transformation of the countryside circumscribing Istanbul into residential property for the immigrants. The new settlements that today account for at least half of the urban area were realized neither through public planning nor through the workings of the formal market. Rather, it was the hidden rules of the informal economy, where unofficial institutions and networks dominate, that created these new urban spaces. It is necessary to uncover the complex links and relationships that generate informal networks to understand the dimensions, dynamics, and the patterns of the constitution of "the local" in Istanbul's periphery (Pahl 1970; Saunders 1981).

The second factor relates to the specificity of the agrarian structure in Turkey and the nature of the migration to urban areas. Turkish agrarian structure is characterized by the dominance of small peasantry, and the rural population is stratified on the basis of income levels, size of holdings, and nature of production (Keyder 1987; Boratav 1995). It is also the case that Turkey is a population mosaic in terms of ethnic background—a diversity due to its being the destination of various waves of migration (Andrews 1992). For these reasons, migration to the cities also reflects a full diversity of ethnic and social background. Migrants are far from constituting a homogeneous group, especially since there have been mass migrations from certain regions of their entire population, including the urban and the rich as well as the villager and the poor, the politically powerful as well as the peon.

In the case of chain migration, would-be migrants were able to acquire information about their destination and, upon arrival, material support from their kin who preceded them. This type of migration led to clustering in the city of those migrants who share a local affiliation and implied that relations with the place of origin will continue. For this reason, chain migration is relatively more sensitive to economic conditions and may even result in returns to the village if urban opportunities do not prove promising. This is especially true if the migrants still possess some claim to land in the village of origin and because the survival of the nonactive family members is much more easily assured in the countryside (Francis and Hoddinot 1993; Grieco 1995).

Chain migration increases the level of interaction and interdependence between the city and the country. Unlike mass migration, it also leads to a greater density of relations among those sharing a similar position in social stratification. This concentration of relationships creates conditions for the construction of reciprocal exchange relations and networks based on mutual confidence. Informal links in the community prove especially important since the urban formal structure fails to provide the minimum conditions and necessities of survival. Such links based on local origin are not confined to the new immigrants; the same kinship and place-of-origin networks extend to include earlier arrivals from the same locality—more educated and middle-class urbanites who may become patrons of the newcomers. In fact, business associations, political organizations, and social activities usually involve both ends of the social scale, thus showing that informal networks serve other purposes than solidarity among the poor shantytown dwellers.

What follows derives from my fieldwork in a new neighborhood in the periphery of Istanbul (Umraniye) and seeks to demonstrate the importance of informal networks in such basic processes as looking for housing, finding work, and daily life.

"WHERE DO YOU HAIL FROM?"

The last forty years have witnessed a mass movement to Istanbul of migrants from diverse regions who have brought with them a similar diversity of cultures. In 1990, 40 percent of Istanbulites were born in the city, but only 20 percent of the heads of household were (Gokcay and Shorter 1993). In the neighborhood where I conducted the aforementioned research, only 11 percent of the heads of household were born in Istanbul. In most cities that experience mass immigration, there is a certain resistance and isolation of the newcomers, which become a factor in increasing solidarity among the migrants. It appears that Istanbul's experience was quite different, perhaps because of demographic balances where Istanbulites no longer enjoyed an overwhelming majority but also because of the large absolute numbers of the newcomers and their diversity. In addition, the fact that the non-Muslims among the city's elite had emigrated, and that the remaining Muslim elite felt powerless vis-à-vis the political class in Ankara, was a contributing factor. As a consequence, each of the groups that arrived in the city could settle without experiencing much resistance or a sense of alienation and could comfortably establish their own networks. The competition within the city occurred not so much between the newcomers and the old elite but rather among the rival networks established by diverse newcomers.

It seems that place of origin provided the most effective marker in determining the composition of such networks. In the research mentioned earlier, the interviewees had been living in Istanbul for two decades, yet they would not define themselves as Istanbulites, nor, however, did they feel "alien." This attitude is due to the fact that when they arrived in the city, they immediately found patrons who had previously migrated from the same region and never had to confront or experience the opposition of native Istanbulites.

The most important assets that immigrants bring with them are their family and kinship relations. Kinship constitutes an institution whose rules and workings are well established and predictable—although variable across region, ethnicity, and social strata. This is one reason that varying kinds of kinship relations may be encountered. Another is that chain migration is by nature selective, and, therefore, kinship relations cannot be transferred intact from the village to the city. Consequently kinship relations in Istanbul exhibit different forms, densities, and hierarchies as compared to place of origin.

Relations of localism (sharing a place of origin) are totally constituted anew, responding to needs in the city. Hence, there are no prior rules or expectations attached to this category. Among the people we interviewed almost all said that they had co-locals in the city, but only some engaged in relations with them. It is not sufficient that co-locals exist; there has to be a felt need for the networks provided by this group and the means to access the network. Chain migration usually constitutes an environment where localism becomes an accessible and useful relation. This elective character of localism implies that a varying meaning is attached to it among different groups: for some it is a small, identifiable, and compact network (usually in the same neighborhood), providing useful contacts; for others it is a more abstract notion referring to the large group in the city. Hence, localism in practice exhibits variations in the quality of the relationship, ranging from an abstract identity through networks of communication to face-to-face reciprocity. These relationships are established via concrete experiences and may serve different functions, carry different meanings, and vary in intensity for each household. Their spatial extent also changes accordingly.

THE TRANSFORMATION OF RELATIONS OF LOCALISM

The most widespread and intense relations of localism are those that develop out of residential neighborhoods in shantytowns. They are generally instigated through the search for a place to settle where information is provided by co-locals and an appropriate land or house found within the same neighborhood. These groups form on the basis of real kinship or sharing the same village of origin, or even sheer coincidence. Relationships evolve during a risk-ridden process of land occupation, illegal construction, and settlement, often requiring confrontation with the authorities. This is why the mutual confidence they engender renders them one of the most important of relations in the urban context.

These relationships continue after land occupation and involve all members of the household; hence, they permeate the daily lives of the inhabitants, providing reciprocity, security, and solidarity. In fact, although different than traditional kinship in terms of extent and because of the absence of hierarchy, they may be interpreted as fictive kinship constituted and redefined in the urban context (see Eisenstadt and Roniger 1984). Because they are based on face-to-face interaction and involve the entire household population, their extent remains limited. In fact, other co-locals in the same area may be totally excluded from such proximate neighborhood groups.

Sharing a place of origin implies different types of relations with different functions, purview, and intensity, if household populations are not involved. These are relations that continue between men, involving larger numbers of participants, but with lower intensity and different patterns of interaction. The privileged locales for such relations are coffeehouses. In shantytown neighborhoods where the population of co-locals reaches a certain magnitude, it is possible to find different coffeehouses serving groups of different local origin. Men will attend such coffeehouses regularly to discuss matters relating to the neighborhood but also to convey and receive relevant information, especially about opportunities of employment. The leaders and patrons of groups of co-locals, as well as the political entrepreneurs relying on such groups, also frequent these coffeehouses.

A second type of coffeehouse resembles guild halls in its function. Chain migration usually results in co-locals concentrating in similar professional groups, and a form of guild solidarity becomes the reason that coffeehouses serving a professional need (e.g., exchange of information about employment opportunity) become prevalent, usually in more central location of the city. Networks resulting from such informal professional organization, but initially based on co-localism, are also constituted by men and do not involve the household.

A third locale for the perpetuation of networks that rely on place of origin is "associations." These are formal organizations bringing together migrants from the same town or district, with formally declared goals of solidarity and action, showing that co-localism has transcended the limits of fictive kinship and has become a form of organization oriented to more abstract and less particularistic goals. The proliferation of such associations shows that co-localism, independent of its traditionalist connotations, has become an accepted form of organization in the urban context (Kurdoglu 1989). Some of these associations are of narrow scope, confining themselves to a particular neighborhood and usually initiated by the leaders of land occupation and settlement, or the "notables" of the place of origin. In activity and purpose and in the constituency they address, these are hardly distinguishable from the neighborhood coffeehouses already mentioned. Nonetheless, because these are formal organizations, they have an advantage in appealing to local authorities in matters concerning the neighborhood and the community.

Other associations target larger constituencies based on a more abstract notion of co-localism. Both the founders and the members of such associations tend to be the elites of the group, distinguished by longer years in Istanbul, education, and business success either in the place of origin or in the city. These associations organize nights of entertainment (where the construct of a local culture takes center stage), picnics, and sports through which an "imagined community" is sustained. Publications inform co-locals of success stories in the city and news "from the country."

But perhaps the most important function their founders expect of these associations is political: to mobilize the co-locals. Among the founders are usually found political aspirants belonging to various parties, hoping to convert a rather abstract notion of localism to political support. Interviews with the founders revealed that they had a highly exaggerated estimation of the number of their potential clients. Interviews in neighborhoods showed that a very small proportion of the heads of household were actually aware of the existence of such citywide associations, and an even smaller proportion had participated in any of the activities sponsored by them. These latter tended to be the political elite of the neighborhood. We may conclude that despite their expected appeal to the entirety of the co-local population, participation in the activities of such associations is self-selected, with low intensity and an express purpose—based on their anticipated effectiveness in urban politics.

FROM SOLIDARITY TO RELATIONS OF POWER

Four decades of migration into Istanbul has resulted in urban clustering of migrants deriving from different cultural environments, ethnicities, and social structures. Their experiences during the settlement process and later have led to the formation of localist relationships specific to the group and its circumstances. The processes especially of acquiring residence and finding employment have shaped the range of mutually dependent, solidaristic ties that constitute the basis of social networks. These ties are rather kaleidoscopic in the sense that they may relate to different strata, with varying range and intensity, establishing alternative patterns according to need. They are flexible and informal or nonbureaucratized (Leeds 1994, 214–18), but they may be appealed to in the solution of everyday problems or activated at a moment's notice in case of a crisis. Some of these localist networks operate with greater intensity akin to kinship relations, as in proximate neighborhood relationships. Despite, or because of, the loose and flexible structure of these networks, they may also constitute bases of mass mobilization when needed. This, in fact, has been the way in which shantytown demands regarding municipal services or legal recognition of ownership have been brought to the attention of the authorities.

Precisely the success of such mobilizations and the fact that co-localism has emerged as the dominant form of association in shantytowns have led to the further entrenchment of informal networks based on localism in the city—to the degree that the public space is occupied entirely by the competition of such groups. Thus, all the informal leadership of groups of co-locals, the entrepreneurs in land occupation and settlement, the local political leaders, conduct their relationships with official authorities and institutions through clientelistic networks. Such conditions have helped clientelism become the dominant form of interest mediation in the public sphere (Eisenstadt and Roniger 203–19).

When ties based on mutuality formed in the private sphere begin to extend into the public sphere, solidaristic and reciprocal relationships are easily converted into those of inequality and power. The research mentioned earlier has revealed various instances of such conversion in which those that helped or led their co-locals during the initial process of settlement had attained positions of power vis-à-vis those who became clients. Hence, a solidarity with kin or co-villagers was transformed into a relation of power under conditions of urban life. On the other hand, there are payoffs to such patronage if the relationship fulfills its promises in terms of a more advantageous articulation with the urban social and political structure. In the urban structure that has evolved, access to established positions of power by individuals is difficult and unlikely. Besides, the political space is already occupied by patronage groups, and politics is conducted through their competition (Leeds 1994, 222–24). The presence of such groups is reflected in membership in political parties or representation within the factions of political parties as well.

It is also true, however, that some solidaristic groups and networks have been excluded from successful representation in this competition. Those who have not been in harmony with the prevailing ideological and cultural preferences of the generally authoritarian state have been left out, and the patronage attempts of their leaders have been frustrated. The Sunni groups, for example, have been generally successful in obtaining funds for religious schools and the like, whereas Alevis have not had the same privilege of access to the central government, even if they held local power. We may surmise that for these groups the solidaristic associations, because they will not be able to deliver, will be of passing importance. Because they will not be successful players in the political scene, their leaders will attempt to find other modes of organization and articulation of their demands. In fact (and to end on a hopeful note), their failure may paradoxically create the conditions for transcending the existing form of urban politics and a potential for new Istanbulites to establish themselves in the public sphere.

NOTE

Translated by Çağlar Keyder.

REFERENCES

Andrews, P. A. 1992. *Turkiye'de etnik gruplar*. Istanbul: Ant.

Boratav, K. 1995. *Istanbul ve Anadolu'dan sinif profilleri*. Istanbul: Tarih Vakfi.

Castells, M. 1977. *The urban question*, London: Arnold.

————. 1983. *The city and the grassroots*. London: Arnold.

Eckstein, S., ed. 1989. *Power and popular protest: Latin American social movements*. Berkeley: University of California Press.

Eisenstadt, S. E., and Roniger, L. 1984. *Patrons, clients and friends*. Cambridge, Cambridge University Press.

Erder, S. 1996. *Istanbul'a bir kent kondu: Ümraniye*. Istanbul: Iletisim Yayinlari.

Francis, E., and J. Hoddinot. 1993. Migration and differentiation in western Kenya. *Journal of Development Studies* 30, no. 1: 115–45.

Fuentes, M., and A. G. Frank. 1989. Ten theses on social movements. *World Development* 17, no. 2: 179–91.

Gokcay, G., and F. Shorter. 1993. Who lives with whom in Istanbul? *New Perspectives on Turkey* 9: 47–73.

Grieco, M. 1995. Transported lives: urban social networks and labour circulation. Pages 189–212 in A. Rogers and S. Vervolee (eds.), *The urban context*. Oxford: Berg.

Koksal (Erder), S., and N. Kara. 1990. 1980 sonrasi yerel siyasetin orgutlenmesi. *Toplum ve Bilim* 48–49.

Keyder, C. 1987. *State and class in Turkey: a study in capitalist development*. London: Verso.

Kurdoglu, A. 1989. *Kentlesme surecinde hemsehrilik dernekleri: Istanbul Örnegi*. M.A. thesis, Marmara University.

Leeds, A. 1994. Locality power in relation to supralocal power institutions. Pages 209–31 in R. Sanjek (ed.), *Cities, classes and the social order*. Ithaca, N.Y.: Cornell University Press.

Lowe, S. 1986. *Urban social movements*. London: Macmillan.

Mingione, E. 1981. *Social conflict and the city*. Oxford: Blackwell.

Pahl, R. 1970. *Whose city?* London: Penguin.

Saunders, P. 1981. *Social theory and urban question*. London: Hutchinson.

Smith, D. 1987. Knowing your place: class, politics and ethnicity in Chicago and Birmingham, 1890–1983. Pages 226–305 in N. Thrift and P. Williams (eds.), *Class and space: the making of urban society*. New York: Routledge & Kegan Paul.

Williams, P. 1987. Constituting class and gender: a social history of home, 1700–1901. Pages 154–204 in N. Thrift and P. Williams (eds.), *Class and space: the making of urban society*. New York: Routledge & Kegan Paul.

10

A Tale of Two Neighborhoods

Çağlar Keyder

LALELI

I spent the greater part of my childhood in Laleli, a neighborhood roughly in the shape of a rectangle, about two hundred by five hundred meters. It is located on the Byzantine Mese, the main street leading from the palace to the city gate opening toward Thrace and Europe, and less than a mile from the palace—well within the radius of the "walking city." Close to the main road, the markets, the seashore, the Ottoman Porte, and the Istanbul University of Republican vintage, it is a neighborhood that has been under constant habitation through the Byzantine, Ottoman, and Turkish periods. It was served, after the 1910s, by a major route of electric streetcar traversing the length of the old peninsula.[1]

Laleli had always been a residential neighborhood favored by bureaucrats whose offices were only a short distance away, university teachers and personnel, and modest tradesmen. As with most of Istanbul, the area was often ravaged by fires that razed many neighborhoods to the ground with some regularity. It was also one of the first districts in the old city to shift to less combustible construction materials. Especially after the great fire of 1911, brick-and-mortar townhouses rather than wooden houses had become common. During the interwar period, some of the larger wooden houses with their gardens were torn down to build multiunit apartment buildings. By 1950, very few houses or empty lots were left.

A typical building had five stories, with two apartments on each floor. Facing the street would be the entrance, an unassuming lobby, a stairwell in the middle to the upper floors. Apartments were designed around a central hall where the stove would be located (unlike the new part of the city, these buildings had no central heating): toward the street side would be the living room and a "good" guest-receiving room, and toward the back, with a balcony overlooking the garden, the bedrooms. The kitchen and the bathroom were rudimentary; in the mode of prewar Europe before American plumbing set the standard.

There was no space between the buildings; there usually was a garden in the back, however, retaining trees from its earlier incarnation, for the joint use of the tenants, to which opened a hovel of two rooms where the concierge (*kapici*) lived. The kapici was, in fact, a family of early immigrants who cleaned the building, did a good deal of the daily shopping for the tenants, and, most important, carried wood and coal from the sheds in the garden (one for each family) to the flats. The wife or the daughters may also be engaged for daily cleaning of the apartments. In fact, during this pre–mass immigration period, a significant proportion of rural immigrants (mostly from the nearer Black Sea coast—traditionally the source area for migrants in the Ottoman period) were in domestic service, and it is somewhat surprising in retrospect that many of the families of modest means inhabiting Laleli, despite the rather restricted availability of space, engaged live-in servants.

This was a profoundly local world in the immediate post-1945 era. The general tenor of the neighborhood was given by limited incomes and respectable lifestyles where men walked to public transport and offices in the morning and returned at a not too late hour. Many women also worked: in the ten flats of my building, I recall five of the families in which women worked, in government offices or as schoolteachers. There was much visiting, among women during the day but also at night when men were present. This was accomplished through the embassy of a child knocking on a neighbor's door and delivering the message that his or her parents would be over for coffee. "If you are available" was attached to the message, but refusal was hardly an option.

In the early 1950s streets were asphalted, but there were very few cars on the road. Residents and shopkeepers knew each other; on each street there was a small grocery store, a butcher, and perhaps a haberdashery. Of the many bakeries within a few blocks of each other, every household had a different favorite. There was also a nearby permanent market in the neighborhood immediately to the west—Aksaray Pazari—where fresh produce, fish, and dry goods were purchased in a daily activity; refrigerators were a rarity, as was bulk buying. Children played outside all day and walked to a primary school ten minutes away and a secondary school that was slightly farther. As a child I remember excursions outside the neighborhood as rare events. One would take the streetcar to Beyoglu or Taksim Square (the center of the new city) on a special occasion, a distance of no more than five kilometers. Shopping trips to the old bazaar and the textile district below it (both less than two miles away) were more common but still occurred no more than twice a month.

Change intruded abruptly in the shape of Menderes, a populist politician, prime minister between 1950 and 1960, who was executed by the military following a coup. He is an object of lasting adulation by the masses (see Keyder 1987, chap. 6). Of course, immigration into Istanbul, beginnings of import-substituting industrialization, and changing parameters of social stratification had already started disturbing the fleeting balances, but Menderes was the chosen expediter who played his role to Mosaic perfection in his penchant for urban engineering. He was particularly fond of cars and large boulevards and did not much like public transport. Accordingly between 1955 and 1958 he imposed his personal stamp on Istanbul, tearing down large swathes of old neighborhoods to build six-lane roads, redesigning squares for swift flow of traffic, and, most drastically, getting rid of the old streetcars that had been the symbol of neighborhood and manageable scale, sustaining an image of convivial urbanity. In quick succession, both the Aksaray and Bayezit Squares, framing Laleli from the west and the east, were converted into traffic circles without character; the main axis identified with the streetcar was taken over by cars and buses; the permanent marketplace of Aksaray was demolished along with the Greek neighborhood south of it with its narrow streets and nineteenth-century single-family houses. A shore road similarly cut through settlements to the south of Laleli.

In September 1955, concurrent with the start of Menderes's reconstruction of Istanbul, a government-instigated crowd—in reaction to the bombing in Salonica of "Atatürk's house," according to the official story—had destroyed and pillaged Greek property, demolishing shops and burning churches. (Sparks from one church two blocks to the south reached the back balcony of our apartment.) It turned out that the events of September 5–6, as they came to be known, had adumbrated a more determined assault in the name of urban planning, with roads cutting through densely packed Christian areas of the city. For the old city, the second half of the 1950s spelled the end of multiethnic coexistence. The number of Greeks (those declaring their mother tongue as Greek in the census) declined from sixty-five to thirty-five thousand between 1955 and 1965, or from 5.2 percent to 2.0 percent of Istanbul's population (Devlet Istatistik Enstitusu 1958, 1968). By 1965, non-Muslims living in the old city were a rarity.

Istanbul's population increased from 1.3 million in 1955 to 1.5 million in 1960, but its car population doubled, from seventeen to thirty-five thousand (Devlet Istatistik Enstitusu 1966). As traffic increased, secondary and tertiary streets opened to cars, eroding the ease and intimacy of street life. New shops were added to the familiar suppliers of groceries, bread, and meat, reflecting rapid commercial development. Laleli was an obvious district for a change in function: it was easily accessible, and its real estate a bargain. The owners of the apartment buildings were stuck with tenants from a more stable time whose salaries did not keep up with inflation: hence, they were willing to sell. All these developments meant that long-time residents also wanted to get out. Introduced to consumer durables and the promise of better plumbing and central heating, those whose incomes kept pace with the general growth of the economy wanted to escape the old, to buy a flat in the newly developing middle class areas of the city. Berman's (1983) imperative for the Bronx began to operate in Laleli.[2] Families who could not get out were the vanguard of the great wave of déclassement that functionaries and stable-income earners endured after 1960.

Within this déclassement that it suffered, the role Laleli played in the urban ecology shifted, reflecting the transformation of the urban political economy. At first it was that great industry of post–World War II fordism that defined Laleli's commercialization: cars. Within the development project that was adopted, the Turkish elite were convinced to give up on statist models and opt for creating the circumstances of private initiative and infinite individual needs. Lifestyles and consumption packages patterned by American hegemony came to dominate. The destruction and neglect of public transport in favor of trucks and passenger cars were aspects of this model. Cars were not produced locally until the 1970s; they were imported exclusively from the United States in the 1950s but increasingly from Europe in the 1960s. Nonetheless, the automotive sector still played a crucial if not leading role. Roads were built, gas stations opened; most important, there was a huge development of spare parts and car repair shops. Many a fortune was made through the importing and retail of spare parts. Laleli was the beneficiary of this blight on the urban fabric: for some years from the mid-1960s on, it accommodated a concentration of automobile "galleries" (showrooms for used cars) and small shops catering to the spare-part needs of the myriad brands on the streets. As could be expected, owners and customers in this new trade changed the human composition in the area. Traffic associated with this new trade clogged the streets and effectively put an end to the closed and intimate lifestyle that had characterized the neighborhood earlier.

The exigency of urban rent asserted itself in the next stage. As mentioned, Laleli was walking distance from all the tourist attractions of the old city— the palace, the principal mosques, and the old covered bazaar. It was close to the university and a number of decent, inexpensive restaurants. As Istanbul was gradually inserted into global circuits of tourism, the opportunities inherent in Laleli's location were not ignored by prospective entrepreneurs in the hotel sector. This was a dense fabric, however, and large hotels built for the purpose were excluded. Instead, older apartment buildings were rebuilt and converted to modest hotels of up to fifty rooms, incorporating the erstwhile gardens in the process. The clientele attracted to this particular niche was a particular segment of culture—tourists on limited budgets, with a copy of Frommer's guide in a duffel bag. The neighborhood transformed itself to cater to the needs of these tourists: gift shops, restaurants, rudimentary nightclubs, and discos opened. Then, unexpectedly, arrived a big opportunity in the form of a new source of tourism and revenue.

The oil crisis was both boon and bane for Laleli. At about the same time that five-star hotels in London were said to be invaded by rich Arab patrons, Istanbul became a magnet for the less wealthy and more budget-conscious tourists from the newly oil-rich countries of the Middle East. At the time Turkey's relations with its neighbors in the Middle East were at an all-time high. There was an increasing volume of investment by Arab capital (mostly in real estate and the financial sector), especially because of the civil war in Lebanon, which made Beirut unavailable. Trade relations grew; Turkish contracting firms undertook dozens of large projects in the Gulf and in Libya. All this activity familiarized a sector of the Arab middle classes with Turkey and Istanbul, leading to the opening of new hotels and shops oriented exclusively to an Arab clientele. Laleli was the center of this tourism during the late 1970s and the early 1980s.

Although tourism was the dominant interest, there was significant trade as well, especially in gold jewelry and silk. Merchants learned Arabic and contracted jewelers and textile manufacturers to produce according to Middle Eastern tastes. All signs on shops and hotels were now in Arabic. Restaurants and pastry shops expanded and began to employ migrants from southeastern Anatolia, whose food culture intersected with Arab tastes. Nightclubs multiplied featuring entertainment that was unavailable in Arab countries. Newspaper accounts of drunken brawls, fights between locals and tourists, suggested an inland version of a tawdry entertainment district, complete with prostitution and drugs.

A peak was reached in the early 1980s, by which time the transformation of Laleli was complete. The neighborhood was now entirely commercial; its population, dominated by migrants from the Southeast, acquired a reputation of toughness; its name connoted an atmosphere of cheap and nasty goods and services—in short, a corner of urban reality that one may find in any self-respecting world city. In the end, the decisive factor that terminated this particular incarnation of Laleli's fortunes was the end of the oil boom. However, as Arab tourists dwindled and the neighborhood was about to revert to its earlier, less specialized position as a district of small and inexpensive hotels, world events prepared a new opportunity for Istanbul and Laleli.

It is not often that a district may reinvent itself so effectively as Laleli did within the years following the passing of the Arab tourist wave. By the mid-1990s Laleli, with its less than two dozen small city blocks, was said to account for between $5 and $10 billion dollars worth of "informal" exports. The neighborhood accommodated several thousand small shops with street windows, as well as entire buildings housing retail space on each floor. All available buildings, except for the hotels, were subdivided and turned into shops. This time the signs were in Russian, and shopkeepers and hotel receptionists were fluent in Russian, Romanian, Polish, and Bulgarian—for the new tourists, the *shop-turisty* in Russian and those engaging in suitcase trading (*valiz ticareti*) in Turkish, were East Europeans, Russians, Moldovans, Ukrainians, and others of ex-Soviet origin.[3]

The collapse of communism in Eastern Europe and the Soviet Union was greeted with much enthusiasm in Turkey. Already in 1990 a Black Sea Cooperation Agreement was signed with the distant aim of a trade bloc among the littoral countries of the Euxine. The Turkish government dreamed of Istanbul emerging as a natural command center of the region, providing financial and other high-value-added services. For a few years there appeared to be some justification to this aspiration despite Russian opposition, but, mired by instability, the government never garnered sufficient political will to carry the project through. Instead, events prepared Istanbul to attain its age-old position as the center of transit trade, organized at the market level and on small scale, successful in spite of the political structure rather than because of it.

The trade started around the time of glasnost, on an informal, small scale, with tourists arriving in buses, filling their plastic sacks and suitcases with textiles to sell at a retail market back home. In a few years, however, volume increased and there was considerable concentration: big traders who regularly made the trip (some every two weeks) spent large amounts, traveled in planes chartered for the purpose, and had their purchases airfreighted. Transactions were in cash. When these merchants returned to Moscow, they sold their wares wholesale in a special market organized for this purpose. This trade was informal in name only; its magnitude probably reached a third of Turkey's formal exports, but the authorities on both sides found it expedient to treat it as "suitcase trading." In other words, the goods were registered as wares bought by tourists during a visit and thus were exempt from customs declaration and taxes.

Laleli continued to provide the hotels and the restaurants and the nightclubs; especially during the early years of opening, there was a prostitution trade as well. In time, hotels became adjunct to suitcase trade. Merchants made their deals as a package: they stayed in the same hotels that they also used as temporary warehouses. Contacts were usually sustained; Turkish shopkeepers were allied with manufacturers who were very flexible indeed and could supply whatever was desired within a few days. Each merchant in Laleli was connected to workshops in other parts of Istanbul where dozens of workers produced apparel in designs specified by the mostly women purchasers. Almost the entire trade was in textiles (some cloth, but mostly apparel) and, to a smaller extent, leather goods. Many buildings were converted to malls where dozens of shops exhibited what was on offer; only the relatively less accessible upper floors remained residential, often as housing for single men who worked in the district. Mainly Kurdish *hammals*, waiting to haul large bundles of textiles to nearby *kargo* shops, waited in the corners; there were dozens of small stalls selling packing material with which to make the bundles.

In its new guise, Laleli came to resemble a much aggrandized reincarnation of a premodern bazaar, of which there were many in imperial Istanbul. It specialized in a few goods, its principal trade was wholesale, its contacts and customers were stable, and they could be counted on to return. There were also *hans* and *caravanserais* in the area to provide associated services. The silk road analogy applied in more ways than one. In a world where states were losing their ability to restrict and regulate cross-border commerce, there was a return to "informal" arrangements whose main virtue was the avoidance of paperwork and official controls. Laleli had been reinvented as a very successful terminus of a new route in market-dominated global commerce. It was no longer a neighborhood; it became a regional mart.

ARNAVUTKÖY

Since the early 1980s, I have lived in Arnavutköy, "the Albanian village," so named apparently because of Albanians who were settled there by the Ottoman sultan in the fifteenth century. As with many of the settlements on the Bosphorus, Arnavutköy was centered around a small creek reaching from the highlands down to the water; steep hills on either side of the valley ranging toward a harbor. The hills are sustained by ancient stone walls making for streets that follow the contours of the elevation. The creek has long been paved over by a road that links the village to the highlands. Arnavutköy was in continuous habitation during the Byzantine and Ottoman times. Its hills were given to vegetable and fruit gardens: there is even a variety of strawberry named after it. It is only in the last few years that cows have disappeared; they used to roam the grassy sides of the valley. Down below were fishermen, and more recently taverns and tea houses that attracted idlers from the central parts of the city, about four miles to the south. During the nineteenth century when carriages became more common, Arnavutköy began to serve as a residential district for commuters. At the end of the century a steamboat line was instituted, and before the war an electric tram line was built connecting the villages along Bosphorus to the business districts. It was again before the war that an

American College for Girls was built on a large estate on the hill bought from an Armenian landowner.

For all its beauty, location, and proximity to the city, Arnavutköy remained a neighborhood of modest dwellings. There were some Ottoman bureaucrats' mansions on the water and a few large wooden houses surrounded by ample gardens on the hills, but during the latter part of the nineteenth century, the prevalent tenor of the place was a relatively dense fabric of two- or three-story family houses belonging to a rising middle class of Greeks. A handsome Greek Orthodox church (one of the largest in Istanbul), rather in the tradition of merchant-maritime churches of the Mediterranean, stands in testimony to a growing middle class during that period. Most of the houses were rebuilt in wood after fires in 1887 and 1908. There were also a few stone houses (a sign of wealth in Istanbul, where wooden houses were the rule) that belonged to the merchant notability of the small neighborhood. The now-standing, modest mosque was built in the 1910s, some two decades after the Greek church. It was an ethnically mixed neighborhood with Greeks in the majority; a Greek school still stands across the square from the church. Where the Armenian school was there is now a Turkish state school. The neighborhood association and the sports club were dominated by the Greek community and located in buildings owned by the church (Artan 1993; see also Johnson et al. 1922).

With its population of a few thousand around the turn of the century, Arnavutköy reproduced some of the social dynamics of coastal towns in the empire.[4] In most coastal towns (and more so in the great port cities), the nineteenth century had witnessed growing commercialization and the evolution of a Greek middle class. Along with cosmopolitanism and coexistence, this ethnic differentiation could also lead to resentment and at times to communal strife, culminating in organized violence.

There was no active repression against the Greek population of Istanbul during World War I, although many Christians departed between 1914 and 1924. The compulsory exchange of populations with Greece in 1923–1924 did not apply to the "established" residents of Istanbul (Alexandris 1983; Ari 1995). Hence, by the time of the consolidation of the Turkish Republic in the 1920s, the population of Arnavutköy had not been seriously depleted or changed much in ethnic composition. The port-city atmosphere of a bye-gone era survived in the tranquil life of the village during the interwar period: population did not increase, and its composition remained stable. Even the notorious wealth levy of 1942, ostensibly an extraordinary tax of war profits but in reality a thinly disguised penalty imposed on non-Muslims, did not harm Arnavutköy much—its inhabitants were not rich enough to merit the wrath of the tax collectors (see Keyder 1987, chap. 5).

As in the rest of Istanbul, ethnic tolerance and coexistence gave way to distrust and coercion after the 1950s. In the 1960s the government expelled long-term inhabitants of Istanbul who were also citizens of Greece (Demir and Akar 1994). After Turkey occupied northern Cyprus in 1974, many more Christian Greeks left. In 1998 there were fewer than a dozen Greek households.

The wave of departures coincided with the arrival into the neighborhood of immigrants from the Black Sea area. Some properties did not have proper titles; others had been abandoned or entrusted to friends and relatives who could not defend them; yet others belonged to foundations and could not be sold. Restrictions were imposed on property transfers by expelled Greek citizens. During the 1960s and the 1970s, there were illegal occupations of land and building of gecekondus on the empty hills; there were also cases of thuggery where houses changed hands because their ownership could not be defended. In a history impossible to research but intimated by the elders, a massive transfer of ownership occurred from Greeks to newly arrived Black Sea immigrants.

Arnavutköy experienced the illegal housing boom of the rest of Istanbul in a different form. Here gecekondu construction remained limited; instead, there was a taking over of old housing stock: mainly wooden, small single-family houses. This is also the reason that its distinctive urban fabric could be preserved. The new immigrants who took over were too poor to tear down these turn-of-the-century, vaguely art nouveau houses to build concrete buildings of flats; besides, each house stood on a small plot, and there was not much profit to be made from the conversion. When most of the neighborhood was left standing in its old and rather poor form, would-be renovators also shied away. Arnavutköy acquired a reputation as a poor neighborhood where rents were low, where new immigrants looking for work could find rudimentary, single-room accommodation. Thus, in the great wave of reinforced concrete and brick construction that characterized Istanbul during the 1960s and 1970s, the physical look of Arnavutköy remained almost unscathed.

After 1980, a new legislation made it illegal to change the outside appearance of old houses. According to this law, the entire Bosphorus basin was declared a historical site, meaning that old wooden houses could be renovated only after a difficult bureaucratic process of obtaining a permit, and the exterior had to be preserved as in the original. In other words, old houses would be torn down, rebuilt in concrete and brick with the wood exterior nailed on. As it turned out, this approach proved an appropriate recipe for gentrification.

The social background of gentrifiers seems to be remarkably constant across geographies.[5] It is the new professional middle classes who create for themselves a new stock of symbolic capital that serves to distinguish them from the old middle class. For them the city is a cultural heritage to be cultivated, its diversity and social heterogeneity something to be cherished.

They find middle-class areas with their standard-issue habitats (suburban houses, or flats as in Istanbul) boring. The nostalgic image of the neighborhood where one may walk to the shops and the cafés, where there is a chance of getting to know the merchants, is attractive. Arnavutköy was the perfect counterpart to such as yet unarticulated aspirations: it was one of the only neighborhoods with a concentration of still-standing "Ottoman" houses; its quaint cobblestone streets were full with street life; it was a place where residents greeted each other on the street. Furthermore, it was on the Bosphorus, traditionally a desirable location; and, most important, the modest size and appointment of the houses made it affordable.

Professionals in Istanbul were yuppified during the 1980s, rewarded through the opening of the economy to greater integration with the world. Foreign trade and foreign investment increased, and financial liberalization led to a banking boom. New service activities developed, some oriented to the world market. For the first time relatively young employees in banking, media, advertising, and education could afford, with the money they themselves were making, to design for themselves a residential style as a statement of their chosen, self-constructed identity.[6]

The new style became possible as the heavy yoke of populist nationalism was lifted off the shoulders of the educated elite following the military coup of 1980 and the global disarray of the left. Those who ten years previously would champion rural populism now started hanging engravings in Orientalist style on their walls, depicting scenes from Ottoman Istanbul. Several glossy magazines were launched with drawings and old photographs of Ottoman architecture and style; a fortnightly called *Konstantiniyye* (an old Ottoman name for Istanbul that had been eschewed during most of the Republican period because it alluded to the Byzantine past) hit the newsstands. It became fashionable to wax nostalgic about the multicultural past and to declare oneself a patriot of the city. One aspect of the distinction sought by the gentrifiers was the partiality for neighborhoods that still contained an atmosphere of the Ottoman past, preferably with visible signs such as still-functioning churches and synagogues. Along with Arnavutköy, other Bosphorus village neighborhoods which satisfied these requirements were "discovered" around the same time, notably Ortaköy and Kuzguncuk. The gentrifiers' preference was for houses, rather than the standard middle-class habitat of an apartment. Living in a renovated house in Arnavutköy was a modest gesture compared to the more grandiloquent manifestations of the same current among the wealthy who restored huge Ottoman mansions on the Bosphorus, but it certainly appeared more authentic.

Gentrification acquired new momentum as the empty areas around Arnavutköy were gradually reclaimed by real capitalist development projects. The restrictions on new construction increased prices of properties with a Bosphorus view, and success at consolidating smaller holdings to obtain a construction permit became highly lucrative. The promise of high profits attracted developers, and the last decade witnessed an unprecedented land development in the hills above Arnavutköy, with several small scale *sites* (gated compounds), one of which contains two dozen villas with tennis courts and a swimming pool, each costing about $2 million. Other *sites* are more modest: they contain less ostentatious flats that cost about $500,000. These were built by established contractors on land that was legitimately acquired. The developers had to painstakingly trace the ownership of the individual plots and purchase them (often from Greek owners who had long left the country) in a process that in all likelihood required much bureaucratic lubrication. The new residents are the products of the same wave of global economic integration that created the gentrifiers below the hill, but they are obviously wealthier and higher up in the corporate hierarchy. It is the bank vice presidents above and advertising agency copywriters below.

Although all this development implied an increase in the average level of income and wealth of Arnavutköy residents, there was not much mixing between the village center and the hills above. Gentrification continued in a different vein in the old village, with a younger, more diverse, and even a somewhat bohemian crowd, content to live in the smaller, wooden townhouses, without landscaping and groundkeepers or concierges. This gentrification has been slow: the neighborhood is still mixed and diverse, with extreme discrepancies in income and lifestyle. The old coffeehouses have sufficient clientele, although the especially ramshackle one that doubled as an exchange for day labor seems to be on the wane. Street life continues, and small merchants still dominate the community. Some old grocers have gone upscale; there are new supermarkets that sell kiwi fruit and avocados and other global luxuries. An old coffee store, run by an Armenian denizen of the neighborhood, is studiedly a remnant of the prenationalist days. The owner obliges with stories of peaceful coexistence between Muslims and Christians when he is inevitably interviewed by nostalgia merchants. There is the obligatory "antique" shop, along with new cafés offering international menus and tasteful classical music from brunch till late night, and a number of successful night spots. One features Ethiopian dishes and African rock music; another specializes in new syntheses, fusion music of a global sound such as Laz-jazz; a third is the "in" venue for serious Turkish rock. There is even a wine bar.

Against these new-style establishments, the older fish restaurants that catered to a clientele coming from the city, simply to eat on the Bosphorus, seem to embody a bygone era. They are in decline as evidenced in a rapid turnover of ownership. Unlike the more conventional crowd patronizing these older restaurants, the customers of the new-style establishments are younger and more hip: the local gentrifiers or those who come here to be in Arnavutköy, which itself has become a commodity to be consumed, much like the renovated old quarters of other old world cities. An integral part of this consumption is the re-creation of an imagined cosmopolitanism of yore. In fact, there has evolved a new cosmopolitanism with many foreigners living in the neighborhood: some working in the nearby American College or at the university, which is in the next village north; students staying at a research institute; stray poets and artists visiting; drifters who are sampling the scene.

This is the contemporary equivalent of the role Arnavutköy played in the nineteenth century: then, too, it accommodated a population that derived from, but was not integral to Istanbul's role as a world city. The formation of the nation-state after World War I, which forced the city to relinquish its extrovert character, steadily changed Arnavutköy's population and social orientation until it had become indistinguishable from other, relatively peripheral neighborhoods in the city. It was inhabited by new immigrants who were poor and conservative and inward looking. After the 1980s, however, the opening of Istanbul, the new economic and cultural currents creating a new professional middle class associated with the information service sector, led to the rehabilitation of the neighborhood through a gentrification process. It seems that the current episode has sufficient momentum to carry this transformation to its natural end—albeit slowly.

REINVENTING NEIGHBORHOODS IN A GLOBALIZING CITY

Functions of cities are transformed in relation to their location in the world economy. In an ever changing context, this is a process of continuous reconstruction that concurrently configures urban ecology. Neighborhoods are shaped and reshaped to fulfill functions framed by the city's overall situation. Until the 1980s, Istanbul was a third-world metropolis whose earlier incarnations in a global and intercivilizational role had been eclipsed by the exigencies of national development. Even before it implied a transforming economy, national development was understood as eliminating the vestiges of cosmopolitanism from the fabric of the old imperial capital. Thus, population shifts preceded ecological change in a deliberate attempt to privilege ideology. In the case of Laleli "nationalization" did not have a sufficient impact to govern the direction of ecological change, although the decision to build new roads in Istanbul and their placement might have been influenced by a desire to destroy Greek neighborhoods. In Arnavutköy, the departure of the non-Muslim inhabitants due to policies of the nation-state had a preserving effect, permitting the neighborhood's conservation as a relatively unspoiled Ottoman corner of an otherwise rapidly changing city. Evolving class balances through national development changed the composition of both districts: Arnavutköy became an area where a certain segment of the new immigrants were accommodated; while Laleli, losing its old middle class associated with a stagnant, state-centered order, was drawn into the expanding commercial center of the city.

More rapid transformation started with the greater opening of Turkey to world flows during the 1980s. Istanbul was naturally the focal point where intensification of flows of people, money, goods, and symbols was felt most intensely. Different neighborhoods came under the impact of these flows in different ways. In Laleli's case, the increasing flow of people in the form of tourism, combined with small volumes of trade, provided the main thrust of transformation. This was followed by a distinctive version of an accelerated flow of goods conducted in a newly created space of the global economy. Laleli became an informal market area that owed its existence to the dismantlement of national controls over the cross-border flow of goods. This transnational informal trade brought along with it a significant flow of people, mostly women traders from the ex-Soviet area, leading to the construction of a hybrid commercial culture, a new lingua franca, and mixed marriages. Globalization implied the consolidation of the commercial role that Laleli had assumed, but now on a regional scale.

As Arnavutköy remained a residential area, its transformation after the 1980s was more gradual. Here the impact of global flows was transmitted through assumption of new cultural strategies by newly forming middle-class groups. These representatives of the rapidly transforming economic life of the city, employed in the most information-intense service sectors, behaved very much like their counterparts in other globalizing cities in constituting themselves as a culturally distinct group. It was not artists who blazed the trail and embarked on the gentrification of Arnavutköy, but those that did were self-conscious in seizing, or reinventing, a pre-Republican cultural tradition of Ottomanism with the appropriate cosmopolitan stance. Once again, a neighborhood previously understood through its location in the urban ecology of a third world metropolis undergoing national development may now be read only with appropriate attention to flows that define the cultural strategies of similar social groups across globalizing cities of the post-1980s world.

NOTES

1. See Kuban (1994) for a compact account of Laleli's history.
2. Berman (1983) describes how he came to understand that even without Robert Moses's Cross Bronx Expressway, the traditional neighborhood of the Bronx would have been destroyed because its residents really wanted to "get out" when they made it.

3. Deniz Yenal is conducting doctoral research on this trade in the Department of Sociology, State University of New York–Binghamton. Also see Blacher (1997).
4. A discussion of nineteenth-century port cities appears in Keyder, Ozveren, and Quataert (1993).
5. For New York, see Zukin (1989).
6. Glossy weeklies are full of pseudo-sociological analysis of this phenomenon. An insightful early account is Kozanoglu (1990).

REFERENCES

Alexandris, A. 1983. *The Greek minority of Istanbul and Greek-Turkish relations, 1918–1974*. Athens: Center of Asia Minor Studies.

Ari, K. 1995. *Buyuk mubadele*. Istanbul: Tarih Vakfi Yurt Yayinlari.

Artan, T. 1993. Arnavutköy. Pages 313–16 in *Dunden bugune Istanbul ansiklopedisi*. Vol. 1. Istanbul: Tarih Vakfi Yayinlari.

Berman, M. 1982. *All that is solid melts into air*. New York: Simon & Schuster.

Blacher, P. S. 1996. Les "shop-touristy" de Tsargrad ou les nouveaux russophones d'Istanbul. *Turcica* 28: 11–52.

Demir, H., and Akar, R. 1994. *Istanbul'un son surgunleri, 1964'te Rumlarin sinirdisi edilmesi*. Istanbul: Iletiş im Yayinlari.

Devlet Istatistik Enstitusu. 1958. *1955 nufus sayimi*. Ankara: Basbakanlik Matbaasi.

———. 1966. *1965 istatistik yilligi*. Ankara, Basbakanlik Matbaasi.

———. 1968. *1965 nufus sayimi*. Ankara: Basbakanlik Matbaasi.

Johnson, C. R., et al. 1922. *Constantinople today: the pathfinder survey of Constantinople*. New York: Macmillan.

Keyder, C. 1987. *State and class in Turkey: a study in capitalist development*. London: Verso.

Keyder, C., Ozveren, E., and D. Quataert, eds. 1993. *Port-cities in the eastern Mediterranean*. Special Issue of *Review* (Winter).

Kozanoglu, C. 1992. *Cilali imaj devri*. Istanbul: Iletisim.

Kuban, D. 1994. Laleli. Pages 187–89 in *Dunden bugune Istanbul ansiklopedisi*. Vol. 5. Istanbul: Tarih Vakfi Yayinlari.

Zukin, S. 1989. *Loft living: culture and capital in urban change*. 2nd ed. New Brunswick, N.J.: Rutgers University Press.

Synopsis

Çağlar Keyder

Globalization has replaced modernization as the paradigm of social change in what used to be called the third world. One reason for this shift is the apparent failure of the nation-state in securing the modernization it had promised; another reason is the undeniable acceleration of all the international flows that nation-states were subject to. These flows now seem to dominate the field of social transformations heretofore accepted as delimited by national territory and belonging to the interaction between the state (carrying the mantle of modernization) and the society (implicitly presented as the inertia-ridden terrain of tradition). The metropolitan population of the developing world constitute most willing receptors of transnational flows. Not only is this population wealthier and more educated and attuned to a shared global culture (more *evolués*, to use the vocabulary of nineteenth-century globalization), but they also have access to the technological and infrastructural nexuses that permit the transmission and reception of the flows. The principal tension in the globalization of these metropolises arises from the double determination of the context they find themselves in: they are part of a network of global flows of money, goods, people, information, and signs; as such, they have to be seen and analyzed within the transnational field of a global system. At the same time, though, they are part of the territorial rule and sovereign jurisdiction of their own states. While this is not necessarily an impediment to globalization, especially because the powers of the state are visibly on the decline, it does mean that unique negotiations occur that affect the way global flows are accommodated in different contexts.

At the urban level, the declining powers of the state translate to an end to the populist policies of the previous era, leading to political and ideological instability. Combined with the privileged reception of global flows, third world metropolises begin to reflect all the conflicts of the global era in a magnifying mirror. From the point of view of system integration, these are the conflicts of governance between the more autonomous workings of the global system and the normatively expressed choices of nation-states.

187

At the level of social integration, what gains prominence is the increasing polarization between the globalized classes and those who remain excluded—who thereby feel condemned to marginalized locality. This polarization finds expression within the political and ideological contests between globalization and localism, between liberalism and communitarianism, that increasingly define the politics of the nation-state.

Global cities directly reflect the economic restructuring, employment patterns, and the ensuing changes in population and class formation that take place globally because people and business units who perform the crucial control roles over global flows are located in such cities. These cities provide services such as control over information, taste, the dissemination of symbolic markers of status, and the flow of financial resources, to global players—producers and consumers alike. The global cities acquire a particular employment structure consonant with the prominence of sectors engaged in providing producers' services. This employment structure is shaped not only by the existence of sophisticated and well-paid positions in producers' services but also by the second-order effects of such primary employment: high-income earners in a postfordist world tend toward labor-intensive consumption patterns that involve a differentiated range of productive and service activities. Highly diversified clothing and food, sold in boutiques, specialty restaurants, and gourmet shops; gentrified housing requiring specialized construction and care; custom-built furniture; personal services ranging from nannies to trainers to bodyguards; leisure and entertainment activities—all this employment is created because of the existence of a new social stratum whose consumption habits are sharply differentiated from the old middle class of the fordist and developmentalist era. The complicated social commerce between the new global class and those who cater to their luxury needs, on the one hand, and between these and the "old" middle and working classes, on the other, makes for political and ideological conflict and negotiation that constitute the basic framework for analyzing global cities. Thus, the global-city construct is not simply one that revolves around political-economic change in the world system; it also has implications for the analysis of social structure, accommodation, and conflict in the new metropolises.

It is not possible, however, to argue that Istanbul's evolution and conflicts in the new era can be understood primarily through the global-city perspective. Although, because of its history and geography, Istanbul had the potential of emerging as a global city in the sense of constituting an important node in the global economy, to a great extent this potential has remained unfulfilled. As recounted in the introductory chapter to this volume, the reasons that the opportunity has not been seized have to do primarily with the lack of political accommodation of the legal and infrastructural requirements that make possible a global-city position. Turkey's political transformation remained incomplete after the initial euphoria of liberalism; stability in domestic and international politics alike could not be achieved, and foreign capital was reluctant to come in. As a result, Istanbul's global position has evolved in ways where political obstacles have successfully been bypassed through informal arrangements: "underground" flows of money, "criminal" activities such as in drug trade, and "informal" international trade. These activities are fueled precisely by the incomplete transformation of the legal and policy environment from a statist-nationalist to a liberal-internationalist one, creating an environment where corruption flourishes and favors the extension of short-term, high-risk activities that operate in the slippery gray area between the legal and the illegal. While ingenious in exploiting the geographic advantages of Istanbul, these activities do not compensate for the absence of an infrastructure, a calculable business environment, and a labor supply that may provide those unique goods in the form of producers' services in finance, law, and information that global cities specialize in. They also create a type of global player whose lifestyle, consumption habits, political leanings, and ideal and material interests diverge radically from the global-city norm based on formal activities undertaken mostly by a corporate sector.

On the other hand, it would be difficult to understand the processes of change in the city without reference to the global-city concept. This concept, with its promise of glory and material rewards, has become a reference point requiring politicians and vision makers to take position for or against it. It has changed their conceptual universe so that they feel the need to subordinate the developmentalist and populist terminology of the previous era to a rhetoric that displays an awareness of global options and dilemmas in determining urban fortunes and city futures. Even conservative politicians embrace the global-city construct while adopting a defensive and localist position toward cultural change associated with globalization. Their attempt to divorce the material from the cultural is similar to the torn stance of the nationalists several generations earlier who wanted to reject westernization while embracing a technology-dominated modernization.

The global-city awareness figures in the quotidian sensibility of the denizens of the city as well. There is a newfound consciousness that Istanbul is one of the great cities of the world, deserving to host significant global events such as the Habitat conference or the Olympics. Debates on cultural perspectives and clashes over the signification of public space, despite their irreconcilable acrimony, nevertheless share the basic assumption that the city is destined to play an important role beyond national boundaries. Not only does the business community adopt the international style of the global corporate bourgeoisie, but also the commoners share in the glorified image.

The achievement of global-city status has eluded the city, but the cultural and economic impact of intensifying flows on social and spatial change have continued unabated. Istanbul has become an obvious laboratory for observing the multiple effects of globalization, because of both the magnitude of the impact and also the intensity of the conflict it has led to. The conflict is not framed as for or against the continuation of global influence; rather, globalization transforms the nature of the conflict and provides a context and a vocabulary for political struggles. It becomes the medium within which positions are defined. As with "modernization," as it was understood during the period of national development, it both provides an irresistible material momentum and dominates the discourse.

The globalization perspective argues that localist and defensive positions themselves are shaped by and owe their contemporary expression to the impact of globalization. Ayfer Bartu's chapter demonstrates how cultural heritage has become a battling point under the exigency of presenting a particular image of the city to the global audience. What is to be preserved and highlighted from a multilayered past when every choice implies the valuation of different political and cultural positions? How will the city be packaged for purposes of different negotiations with the sweeping impact of globalization? These questions are continuously on the agenda, shaped by the everyday struggles of various actors but also punctuated by the more consequential outcome of choices such as expressed in municipal elections. The evolving shape of the city results from the strategies of social groups as they negotiate an identity for themselves, and for the city, within the parameters defined by the forces of globalization.

Yael Navaro-Yasin focuses on the nature of this identity politics, especially the dominant polarity that Istanbulites have inherited from the high modernist days of the Turkish Republic: secularism versus Islam. The Republic averred an irreconcilable conflict between modernization and traditionalism, and the latter was identified with the Islamic religion. This was an inherently defeatist position because the local and the authentic were assigned to Islam, thus relegating secularism to the status of an alien imposition. This is, of course, an identification that the Islamic political movement would like to perpetuate, which leads the secularists to have to argue the case for their own locality and authenticity. Navaro-Yasin's target is the facile acceptance of Islam as the true "native" culture in a context where modernization previously, and globalization currently, have grown substantial local roots and have created a constituency for secularism. Thus, under the dissolution of national identities that globalization has effected, the defenders of a secular, liberal, and "global" lifestyle—the westernized Istanbulites, in short—find it necessary to wage their struggle in the civil arena, without a facile recourse to the powers of the state.

Islamic currents resisted the modernist ideals of the Republic, but they were neither alone in this opposition nor unitary. Tanil Bora discusses the complex heritage of imperial and Islamic historiography that depicts Istanbul as deserving of global status—either because of its pure essence, as a promised city to the believers, or because of its Ottoman cosmopolitanism. Islamic writers have regarded the city with ambivalence, as a holy capital that at the same time displays too much "Westernness." When the religious party won the municipal elections in 1994, it embraced a rhetoric of Istanbul as global city and sought to mobilize the Ottoman past to this end. The positions taken by the elite of the Islamic movement with respect to Istanbul's global role clash, however, with the populist rhetoric that makes the Islamic party attractive to its constituency of recent immigrants. As the Islamic movement found expression in Istanbul's politics, it was itself fragmented under the influence of the very forces it sought to oppose. Some Islamic thinkers appealed to their own version of globalism and sought to promote Istanbul as *the* city of that project, while others remained within the confines of a localist populism. Jenny White's chapter takes Istanbul to be emblematic of the "multifaceted and multilayered" city that simple oppositions between Islam and secularism or between the global and the local cannot capture. She demonstrates the fragmentation of the constituency that the secularists are content to label as Islamic. Behind the Islamic garb, and especially the head scarf worn by women, that seems to unite the group are differences of social affiliation, economic means, and ideological stance. The aggressive consumerism that characterizes the era of liberalization and the availability of all the world's consumables are reflected within the desire to distinction, the chic, that pervades the Islamic constituency. At the same time, globalization signals the autonomization of a civil society with its own evolutionary dynamics, which can no longer be captured in the categories provided by old dichotomies. For Istanbul, the global has ushered in a social and ideological fragmentation that the modernist equations of the nation-state could not possibly contain.

Globalization subjects populations to cultural flows of many kinds that shape the nature of the conflict, the lines of defense, and the potential for compromise or hardening. Social groups who are in a position to ride the wave of economic transformation are the advocates of Istanbul's globalization. They feel themselves to be the privileged recipients of the global message and the chosen manipulators/consumers of the "dizzying array" of cultural signs that are available in the flows of media and signs. Ayşe Öncü traces the way in which these signs were and are employed to define the true Istanbulite in contradistinction to the other citizens—the uncultured immigrants to the city. The nature of the attributes of the authentic inhabitant changes in tandem with the assigned unculturedness of the othered. Humor, and specifically cartoons, both display the assumed difference and subvert the facile self-confidence of the Istanbulite. Öncü traces the nature of the exclusion in its historical stages (from lack of urbanity to moral offensiveness), as reflected in popular humor—cartoons in mass magazines. At a time when globalization has upset established hierarchies and provides the new rich with access to the most rarefied cultural goods because everything has been commodified, Istanbul's established middle class takes refuge in a defense of culture and taste against vulgarity and overconsumption. They castigate the uncultured who are not morally deserving yet avail themselves of the vast potential of new commodities and signs made accessible by globalization.

Martin Stokes analyzes the music industry in Istanbul, which reflects similar tensions of adaptation to tastes that are increasingly shaped by global flows. Popular music also comes to provide the means to position one's self in the context of a fractured life world, where the global continuously produces and re-produces the "local." Against the background of stark polarity between Eastern and Western music as defined by the modernizing discourse, the postnational period has witnessed the birth of genres and categories that challenge the clear division. Stokes argues, however, that the more optimistic anticipations that globalization will create a wide spectrum of diversity have to be tempered with the realization that transnationalism leads to media multinationals controlling local production of music. Global corporations promote music that can potentially address big markets while excluding variety. Thus, global flows of popular culture expand the spectrum of consumption, of spectacle, but most are excluded from participating in the shaping of these flows.

Istanbul lost some of its ethnic diversity after the departure of its Christian populations, but it gained a much less advertised heterogeneity through the arrival of immigrants from the rest of the country, itself an ethnic mosaic. This is, of course, why the city could hardly be characterized by urbane gentility, but it does exude a rude vigor. The new immigrants were initially expected to assimilate and become part of a notional urban homogeneity; more recently, however, the fragmentation of the façade of cultural unity has made the organization and construction of networks on a self-consciously subcultural basis—mobilizing along the lines of confession, ethnicity, and localism—more likely. Sema Erder shows how the weakening of the hold of the nation-state has led to movements of identity politics that, at the same time, establish the context for operating in the urban economy and municipal politics. Immigrants bring with them their networking capital, in the form of family, kinship, and localist relations. These relations are then mobilized to pressure for public services, to find or build housing, to secure funds and employment—in short, to be able to use the city. As in other global cities, immigration is never final, so relations based on place of origin are reinforced and reproduced through the easy contact between Istanbul and the region of emigration, and with the diaspora in Europe.

I describe the residential built environment of the city as it was transformed during the era of immigration. Istanbul expanded through the construction of squatter shantytown neighborhoods, but legalization was relatively easy owing to the peculiar legal history of property relations on land. In addition to these peripheral neighborhoods, middle-class housing in the city also underwent an upgrading and relocation during the heyday of modernization. The consequence was a radical change in the spatial differentiation of the city. Now, under the impact of global models of luxury housing, new residential forms come on the agenda, especially the ideal globalized middle-class habitation of a villa in a gated compound and, for a different status group, the gentrified "Ottoman house." I look further at the history of two Istanbul neighborhoods through the Republican and national periods to show how globalization has affected their social and economic function and character. This exercise seeks to demonstrate changes in urban ecology in relation to the principal stages of the city's history: Republican stasis, nation-state modernization, and globalization.

One common theme in these chapters is the importance of the spatial dimension in shaping social identity and conflict. Social processes create urban space and unfold within (and are in turn shaped by) the spaces thus created. Identities are not simply the product of social structure; individuals and social groups are unmediatedly connected with the physical space they inhabit. They struggle to ascribe it with meaning and the transformation it undergoes also shapes them. There is inevitably conflict over the meanings that will be attached to public space. "Public space" here is both concrete and abstract: it refers to city squares and airwaves, to ceremonies and the print media, to billboards and memorials and festivals. The battle is waged over all the space that cannot be privately appropriated but is, at the same time, used by all. This, of course, is what is distinctive about a city: the presence of diverse and conflicting interests in a space that has to be shared by all.

What has attracted the greatest attention in the case of Istanbul has been the struggle over Islamic and secular representations of public space. These representations derive from and directly relate to the larger questions of modern and traditional, global and local. At the apparent level, the positions are basic and elemental and incompatible. In fact, Istanbul's symbolic position in the imaginary of Europe, occupying a permanent battleground between the East and the West, exacerbates the image of irreconcilability. The essays in this volume argue that the global defines the local as the modern has shaped the traditional. It may be that civilizational concerns fuel the acrimony of the debate, and in some sense global ideological concerns are played out on Istanbul's stage, thus raising the stakes and forcing sides to appear more intransigent than they are warranted to be. In fact, the sides are too intertwined and fragmented to frame a neat conflict of global and local, or East and West.

In its combative use, "the local" represents local ways of doing things, a physical environment that is considered uncontaminated, a specific culture. The material articulations of the global-local dialectic are evident in physical space—in the constitution of the urban, in the ways inhabitants use and relate to and ascribe meaning to their built environment. Of course, it is the case that all conceptions of the local are new and re-created. Neither the physical space nor the everyday life now found in the urban shanty-town or in the city's center existed previously. The urge to claim authenticity derives from real needs of the participants in the contest—needs that evolve during the confrontation with the culture of globalization, as new identities are shaped. In Istanbul, as in all cities of any size that exhibit a similar social dividedness and reflect a diversity in terms of images sustained about the entity as a whole, the question of who will define the city is crucial. Claims are constantly being made, expressed, and reexpressed in different ways (dress, humor, music), in different walks of everyday life. Urban entrepreneurs and boosters promote the image of a vibrant metropolis, straddling continents, able to reach and dominate its presumed hinterland, where all the amenities required by producers and consumers are available. For informal and/or illegal entrepreneurs, its globalization is the very source of profit but not to be broadcast. For old style politicians Istanbul is a third world megacity that provides maximal opportunity for patronage, for the accumulation and the appropriation of rent. The residents, however, especially those in the areas remaining outside the purview of global business and globalized consumption, are on the receiving end of these projects and practices. They are engaged in the defense and conservation of a precarious decency, articulated in yearnings for communitarian solidarity and social justice, but finding expression in a cultural traditionalism that conserves age-old patterns of domination and oppression.

***

Does globalization create an ordered duality where there is a constant stream of defections to the globalized sector and what remains behind diminishes in scope? Or, is it the case that the material transformation engendered by globalization is necessarily limited and self-enclosed, leading to a permanent dividedness between a globalized enclave and its excluded and oppositional hinterland? The duality implied in these questions ignores the way in which globalization changes the nature of the division. The line between the included and the excluded is continuously redrawn. Thus, Istanbul's urban politics has acquired a dimension of civilizational conflict precisely because the issues of social integration of immigrants into the city have been magnified in the mirror of globalization. Problems of social integration have existed since the 1950s when large-scale immigration into the city started. During the period of national development, however, conflict was channeled to party politics mobilizing rival patronage mechanisms. The ideological divide was circumscribed within a unified developmentalist paradigm where the debate basically revolved around the pace of elite disfranchisement. The concepts and platforms associated with the terms of globalization make ideological positions more intransigent and their mutual accommodation more difficult; the increasing rigidity of the positions makes participants forget the more hopeful social processes of diffusion and accommodation. Even the reaching of material compromise in terms of policy (as in the case of tavern tables on sidewalks that an Islamic mayor initially wanted to ban) is no guarantee for the softening of cultural and symbolic acrimony.

This is not to say that compromises are not reached: the city functions at some practical level where platforms are porous, malleable, open to mutual accommodation—as evident in the performance of the Islamic municipality of Istanbul. Nonetheless, the polarization caused by globalization is all too real: income levels, lifestyles, consumption patterns, and, increasingly space have become divided. In some neighborhoods residents wait in line to buy bread that is a few pennies cheaper; in others all the glitzy displays of wealth can be found. Luxury sedans proliferate, while homeless children become more visible on the streets. There are sections of the city where a photographer could frame a crowd scene and pretend it to be from Kabul; others could stand in for any modern neighborhood from a European city. In a city such as Istanbul, where in living memory residential space reflected an interpenetration and coexistence of different levels of status and class, the separation of space and the exclusionary habitation that has become the pattern are novel and upsetting.

When polarization is seen as a fundamental feature of globalization, it becomes easier to understand how Islam has become a metaphor. The famous title suggesting that the clash is between Islam and the homogenization of world culture (Barber 1995), if not accurately reflective of the cultural complexity that derives from globalization, still correctly identifies the metaphoric character of Islam as the principal opposition. This is not simply because of Islam's ready availability or ingrainedness or the fact that "traditional" culture could be represented through the sole mediation of religion. All these assertions can be disputed: there were other available ideologies, and the new form of Islam is a major departure from the folk religion that was prevalent in the relatively closed communities of the prenationalist era. It is also because Islam itself has achieved a global reach; in a context where the terms of the debate have to take cognizance of globalization, it offers a platform that credibly ranges over the same territory as a homogenized global culture. Islam has been successful precisely because it provides an overarching framework within which local resentment gains meaning. The success of Islam as a mobilizing mode of thought depends not on its civilizational prospects but on its efficacy in providing a vocabulary of resentment presumed to express the need for the defense of the local, and Istanbul has emerged as a privileged lieu of this metaphoric mobilization.

The concepts of the globalization paradigm tend to substitute analyses based on cultural contestation and exclusion for those of conflict based on class formation and political economy. However, not only does the struggle over globalization overlap with the cleavages in the transformation of the social structure, but it is also overtly political. Istanbul commands between a third and a half of the national wealth and income, and one-sixth of Turkey's population live here; hence, urban and national politics tend to merge. National political platforms directly or indirectly imply images and designs for the city, while urban politics, and especially the campaign for the global city, imply a national platform. As all the familiar conflicts of the earlier period are rephrased in new vocabulary and globalization replaces modernization, Istanbul gains a new centrality, because it is the repository of all the flows that make up globalization. The struggle of the international bourgeoisie and the new professional and managerial classes of Turkey for the city's soul is in fact a struggle for the future orientation of the country as well.

Unlike modernizers, the party of globalization is not necessarily committed to national solutions. They have affiliations and interests that are flexible; they form virtual communities with kindred groups globally. Their very lifestyle based on minimizing the need for public amenities is an admission of nonengagement: office buildings with electronic sensors, phalanxes of bodyguards, drivers and doorkeepers, private life behind the tall gates of housing compounds represent a withdrawal, a reluctance to engage in the struggle. But all this also adds up to an undeniable economic force, perhaps with determining weight on the destiny of the city. As Mike Davis (1990) has argued, the logical implication of such privatization may be militarization; this, however, has not happened yet, except in the far reaches of the informally globalized sector.

But this vision of a permanently divided city may be overly pessimistic. Metropolises are condemned to restructure themselves; they are the immediate receivers and processors of changing material forces and conditions. During the last two decades, globalization has come to dominate this process of restructuring. As the lives of all the inhabitants of Istanbul are inexorably transformed, the immediate impact has indeed been a hardening of the battle lines and a militant creation of the local. But this is surely a transitional phenomenon in which the sides do not seem to inhabit the same world. If and when the momentum of globalization prevails, the conflict may well assume a more familiar visage, of a struggle over distribution, unfolding within a shared universe of conceptual and physical space.

If globalization is taken to signify the new avatar of modernity, the conflict between the optimism of the modernist outlook and the pessimism of social and spatial differentiation is once again on the agenda. As we know from the history of the cities of the West, there is no single answer to this dilemma. Great historical currents cause upheavals both in social and spatial differentiation, and the promises of modernity change shape. All we can do now is to diagnose the moment.

REFERENCES

Barber, B. R. 1995. *Jihad vs McWorld: how the planet is both falling apart and coming together*. New York: Times Books.
Davis, M. 1990. *City of quartz*. London: Verso.

Index

About the Editor and Contributors

Ayfer Bartu teaches anthropology at Koc University in Istanbul. She is currently working on an ethnography of Catalhoyuk, investigating the politics of heritage.

Tanil Bora is the editor of *Toplum ve Bilim*. He is the author of numerous articles and monographs on nationalist and religious movements in Turkey.

Sema Erder teaches at Marmara University in Istanbul. She is the author of several articles on Istanbul's immigrants and of *Umraniye: A Shanty City in Istanbul*.

Çağlar Keyder teaches sociology at Bogazici University in Istanbul and the State University of New York at Binghamton. He is an editor of *New Perspectives on Turkey*.

Yael Navaro-Yasin teaches in Social Anthropology at Cambridge University, U.K. She is currently preparing a monograph on politics of identity and cultures of the state in Turkey.

Ayşe Öncü teaches at the Sociology Department, Bogazici University, Istanbul. She edited *Space, Culture and Power: New Identities in Globalizing Cities*. She is an editor of *New Perspectives on Turkey*.

Martin Stokes teaches in the music department at the University of Chicago. He is the author of *The Arabesk Debate: Music and Musicians in Modern Turkey*.

Jenny White teaches anthropology at Boston University. She is the author of several articles and a book on Turkey, *Money Makes Us Relatives: Women's Labor in Urban Turkey*.